Fun with the Family™ in Virginia

Help Us Keep This Guide Up to Date

Every effort has been made by the author and editors to make this guide as accurate and useful as possible. However, many changes can occur after a guide is published—establishments close, phone numbers change, hiking trails are rerouted, facilities come under new management, and so on.

We would love to hear from you concerning your experiences with this guide and how you feel it could be improved and kept up to date. While we may not be able to respond to all comments and suggestions, we'll take them to heart and make certain to share them with the author. Please send your comments and suggestions to the following address:

The Globe Pequot Press
Reader Response/Editorial Department
P.O. Box 480
Guilford, CT 06437

Or you may e-mail us at: editorial@globe-pequot.com

Thanks for your input, and happy travels!

FUN WITH THE FAMILY™

in VIRGINIA

Fourth Edition

HUNDREDS OF IDEAS
FOR DAY TRIPS WITH THE KIDS

CANDYCE H. STAPEN

The Globe Pequot Press

Guilford, Connecticut

Fun with the Family is a trademark of The Globe Pequot Press

Text design by Nancy Freeborn
Maps by M.A. Dubé

ISBN 0-7627-2234-7

Manufactured in the United States of America
Fourth Edition/First Printing

To my favorite traveling companions,
Alissa, Matt, and David

Contents

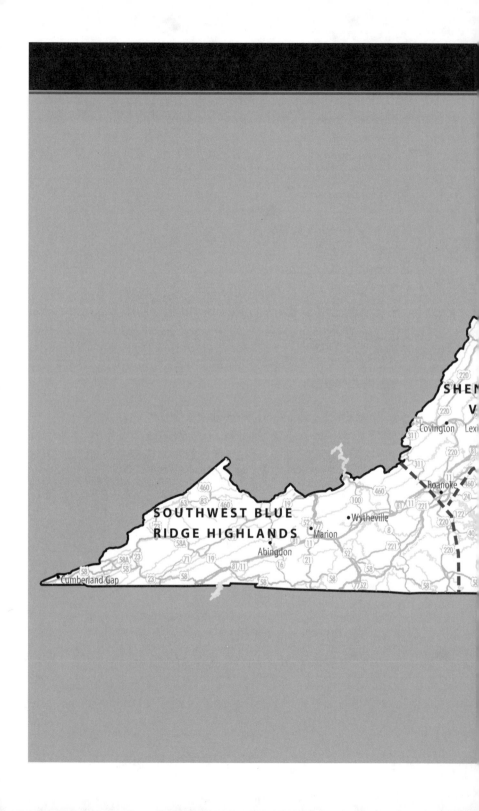

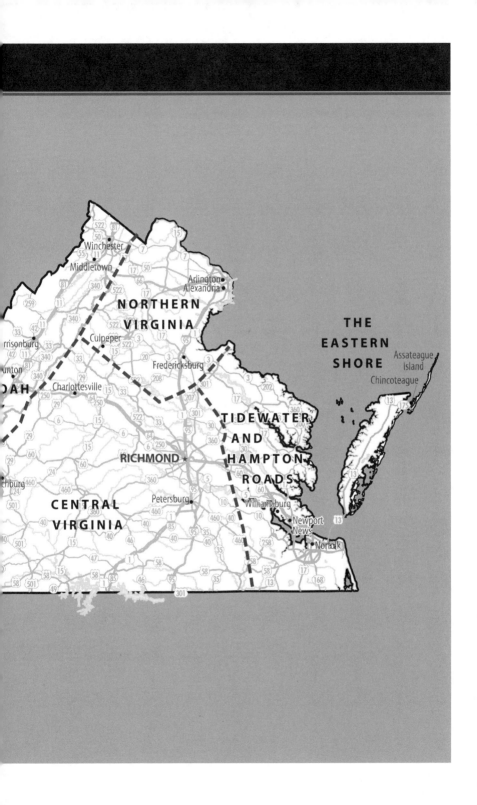

Acknowledgments

I want to thank Diane Ney for her valuable assistance.

Introduction

Virginia has much to offer families. Historic towns, plantations, battlefields, scenic drives through softly curving mountains, bustling beaches, quiet wildlife sanctuaries, luxurious resorts, and wild roller coasters are just some of Virginia's charms.

To get the most out of this book, use it to help plan explorations for your family. First, select a region of the state that appeals to you. Then thumb through the corresponding section of the book to find attractions that match your interests. Next chart your itinerary, including only the stops you choose. You can splurge on an upscale resort that features children's programs and golf or travel on a more conservative budget by lodging at family-friendly bed-and-breakfast inns and moderately priced motels. Be sure to underplan to allow time for serendipitous discoveries and to take advantage of Virginia's numerous parks and open spaces. Plan to revisit a region you enjoy to follow different fancies and explore new sites.

Each region of the state has its own allure. The Shenandoah Valley stretches for some 200 miles between the Blue Ridge and Allegheny mountain ranges and offers some of the state's most spectacular countryside made of craggy mountain peaks and rolling farmland. The underground wonderland known as Luray Caverns offers the chance to see fantastical formations of stalactites and stalagmites.

The Shenandoah region is rich in history. At Washington and Lee University, in Lexington, you can see Robert E. Lee's office just as it was on the day he died. At Staunton's Museum of the American Frontier, the farmsteads reveal the customs of the area's early immigrant pioneers. Lexington also gives you a taste for one of Virginia's other passions—horses. If your kids love Black Beauty and dream of riding like the wind, take them to see the thoroughbreds at the multimillion dollar Virginia Horse Center.

Tidewater Virginia takes you back to 1607 and the days of Jamestown's first settlers. The plantations along the James River reflect the pomp and pleasures that came with life in the prosperous new world. Colonial Williamsburg affords a more detailed glimpse of our nation's fledgling years. Walk along the cobbled streets and you can almost feel the presence of George Washington and hear the fiery words of Patrick Henry.

Hampton offers the saga of different kinds of American pioneers. The Virginia Air and Space Center details the history of the astronauts and the American space program. The Mariner's Museum in Newport News displays ship models, figureheads, and a small craft collection that runs the gamut from a gondola to a Chinese sampan. In Norfolk you can tour the naval base and experience hands-on high-tech naval encounters at Norfolk's Nauticus. Be sure to stop over in Virginia Beach, a bustling ocean town. The heartier members of the family can leave the tourists behind and hike 5 miles through Back Bay National Wildlife Refuge to the secluded beaches of False Cape State Park.

In Alexandria, Northern Virginia's historic and once bustling seaport, you can visit the Torpedo Factory, a renovated World War II plant that once assembled torpedoes but now houses the studios of some of the region's best potters, jewelers, weavers, and photographers. Arlington National Cemetery, resting place of John F. Kennedy and the Unknown Soldier, is not far from Alexandria. Civil War buffs won't want to miss the battlefields of Fredericksburg, Chancelorsville, and Manassas. If you are in the area on a clear summer night, pack a picnic and head for Wolf Trap Farm Park For the Performing Arts. Kids enjoy exploring the grounds and listening to outdoor concerts.

Virginia's Eastern Shore, a popular getaway for Washingtonians, offers a relaxing escape. A hike along Assateague Island National Seashore treats you to a wild beach, a loblolly pine forest, and marshes. You might see white-tailed deer, snow geese, and the island's famous wild ponies. Towns like Onancock continue a fishing tradition that dates from the seventeenth century. Wachapreague, the Flounder Fishing Capital of the World, serves up a scenic waterfront and, of course, great fresh fish.

Central Virginia offers families a wide variety of attractions. In Charlottesville, you can tour Monticello, Thomas Jefferson's home. You sense his revolutionary vision and his love of the Piedmont's rolling hills. In Richmond the heart of the Civil War still beats. The Museum of the Confederacy houses swords, uniforms, and paintings of this era. The White House of the Confederacy gives you insight into the lives of Jefferson Davis and his family. Richmond glitters with other treasures, such as a large collection of Fabergé jewels housed at the Virginia Museum of Fine Arts. For pure escapist pleasure head to

TimeTravelers is a statewide program that rewards students in kindergarten through twelfth grade for visiting museums and historic sites. Any student who visits six of the over one hundred participating sites receives a certificate from the governor of Virginia and a TimeTravelers t-shirt (a handling fee is required for each t-shirt). Students participating are also entered in drawings for special prizes. The program runs from March to November of each year, and all students—not just Virginia residents—are welcome to join the fun. Museums and sites participating in the program are indicated in this book with **(TT)** next to the name.

the movie-themed fun of Paramount's Kings Dominion. Older kids get their thrills on ten roller coasters, while younger tots play with such favorite pals as Yogi Bear and Fred Flintstone at Hanna-Barbera Land.

The Southwest Blue Ridge Highlands serves up down-to-earth simplicity. As you drive back country roads, take time to hike to a waterfall, skip rocks in the streams, walk through the pine groves of Cumberland Gap National Historic Park, and fish for pike in the 108-acre lake of Hungry Mother State Park.

Information centers and resources that apply to just one region are included within the pertinent chapter. Here are some additional resources that are helpful in planning:

- Virginia Division of Tourism: (800) 932-5827; www.virginia.org.

- Virginia Disabilities Guide, Virginia Tourism Corporation: (800) 742-3935; www.virginia.org.

- Virginia State Park Reservation system for cabins and campgrounds: (800) 933-PARK or (804) 225-3867, or TDD (804) 786-2121.

- Virginia State Parks website: www.dcr.state.va.us

- Skiing information: (800) THE-SNOW; www.virginia.org.

- Virginia Department of Game and Inland Fisheries, 4010 West Broad Street, P.O. Box 11104, Richmond, VA 23230-1104; (804) 367-1000; Web address: www.dgif.state.va.us. Provides information on where to find what kinds of fish. Helpful for anglers and snorkelers.

In the sections "Where to Stay" and "Where to Eat," rates are represented with dollar signs and offer a sense of the price ranges at press time.

Rates for Lodging		Rates for Restaurants	
$	up to $60	$	most entrees under $10
$$	$61 to $85	$$	most $10 to $15
$$$	$86 to $105	$$$	most $15 to $20
$$$$	$106 and up	$$$$	most over $20

Whatever your changing fancy, Virginia offers sweet family treats. Enjoy the pleasure of each other's company as you embark on these family adventures.

The prices and rates listed in this guidebook were confirmed at press time. We recommend, however, that you call establishments to obtain current information before traveling.

Attractions Key

The following is a key to the icons found throughout the text.

 Swimming

 Animal Viewing

 Boating / Boat Tour

 Food

 Historic Site

 Lodging

 Hiking / Walking

 Camping

 Fishing

 Museums

 Biking

 Performing Arts

 Amusement Park

 Sports/Athletic

 Horseback Riding

 Picnicking

 Skiing/Winter Sports

 Playground

 Park

 Shopping

Nature

(TT) TimeTravelers

The Shenandoah Valley

The Shenandoah Valley stretches for some 200 miles between the Blue Ridge and Allegheny mountain ranges in northwest Virginia. The scenic mountains and valleys make this region one of the most beautiful in the East. In the valley towns visitors can enjoy an array of country culture as down-home and as lively as apple blossom festivals, bluegrass concerts, and square dances and as unique as Staunton's presidential museum and historic farmsteads.

The Shenandoah Valley boasts another ingredient vital for a family vacation destination: an abundance of recreational opportunities. Hike along park trails where tree branches form lush canopies. Go underground to explore the eerie and awesome formations found in water-carved limestone caverns. Enjoy the pastoral views of ridges and valleys offered by the 105-mile Skyline Drive which runs along the mountain's crests the entire length of Shenandoah National Park. Both this and the Blue Ridge Parkway offer splendid vistas; in fall they turn into glorious, although crowded, leaf-peeping routes.

This trip through the Shenandoah Valley begins about 18 miles north of the beginning of Skyline

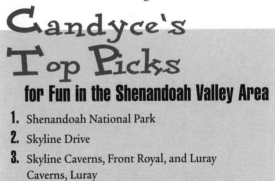

Candyce's Top Picks
for Fun in the Shenandoah Valley Area

1. Shenandoah National Park
2. Skyline Drive
3. Skyline Caverns, Front Royal, and Luray Caverns, Luray
4. The Frontier Culture Museum, Staunton
5. The Homestead Resort, Hot Springs

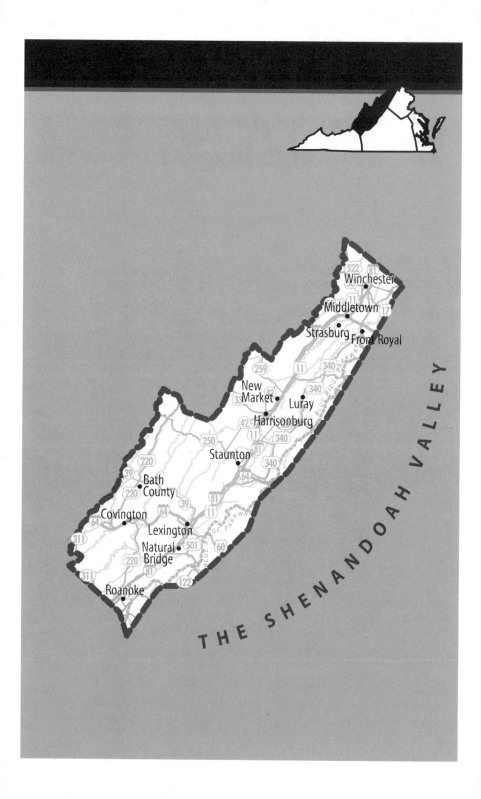

THE SHENANDOAH VALLEY

Drive in Winchester and leads through Middletown to Front Royal, a gateway for the Shenandoah National Park. Towns near Skyline Drive include Luray, New Market, Staunton, Lexington, and Roanoke. Strasburg and Natural Bridge are nearby and make for convenient day trips. For information on Culpeper and Lynchburg, also in the Shenandoah Valley region, see the Northern Virginia and Central Virginia chapters.

For Civil War Buffs The Shenandoah Valley was the site of several battles and an area through which both Union and Confederate troops passed throughout the war. The brochure, "The Civil War Campaigns of Virginia's Shenandoah Valley," available at area visitor centers, includes a map and detailed information about Civil War sites throughout the valley.

Winchester

Located 140 miles northwest of Richmond, and 18 miles north of the start of Skyline Drive, Winchester is a good starting point for exploring the Shenandoah Valley and the Virginia highlands. This city, population 22,000, played a significant role in both the French and Indian and Civil Wars. During the latter, the town changed hands more than seventy times, including thirteen times in one day. If your family comes in the spring, you'll be treated to the heavenly sight of apple blossoms at the Shenandoah Apple Blossom Festival, whose parade includes marching bands, floats, and the Fire Fighter's Parade, the nation's largest display of fire-fighting equipment.

Discount block tickets may be purchased for Abram's Delight, Stonewall Jackson's Headquarters Museum, and George Washington's Office Museum at each of the three locations.

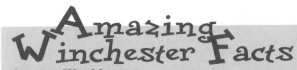

Amazing Winchester Facts

George Washington slept in Winchester. He began his surveying career here in 1748. Later he helped build Fort Loudon and was headquartered in town as commander of the Virginia frontier.

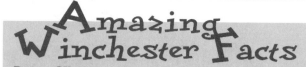

Patsy Cline, country music's sweetheart of the 1960s, was born in Winchester. U.S. Highway 522 has been named the Patsy Cline Memorial Highway in her honor.

ABRAM'S DELIGHT (ages 6 and up) (TT)

1340 South Pleasant Valley Road, right next to the visitors center; (540) 662–6519. Web address: www.winchesterhistory.org. Open from April through October. Admission.

This home, the oldest house in town, was constructed in 1754 of native limestone. (The owner, Isaac Hollingsworth, lived here only a few years before moving to Waterford, Virginia, because of his fear of Indian attacks. Parents may enjoy the house's lakeside location, along with its gardens and gazebo, while kids will like the authentically furnished 1780s log cabin.

STONEWALL JACKSON'S HEADQUARTERS MUSEUM (ages 10 and up) (TT)

415 Braddock Street; (540) 667–3242. Web address: www.winchesterhistory.org. Open daily April through October, weekends November through March. Admission.

This house looks much as it did when General Thomas J. "Stonewall" Jackson coordinated his valley campaign here from November 1861 to March 1862. On display are maps, memorabilia, photos, and artifacts of Jackson and other Civil War soldiers, including the table Jackson used as a desk and his prayer table, which was taken into the field with him. A small shop sells coloring books, Confederate hats, and children's books about the Civil War. Fans of the Nickelodeon network and its reruns of classic television shows might be interested to know that this building was originally owned by Colonel Lewis T. Moore, great-grandfather of Mary Tyler Moore; the colonel invited Jackson to use it while he was headquartered in Winchester.

GEORGE WASHINGTON'S OFFICE MUSEUM (ages 10 and older) (TT)

32 West Cork Street, on the corner of Cork and Braddock; (540) 662–4412. Web address: www.winchesterhistory.org. Open daily April through October. Admission.

This small log cabin served as Washington's office from September 1755 to December 1756, while he built Fort Loudon to defend the 300-mile frontier of Virginia during the French and Indian War. Memorabilia, including some rare surveying tools, are on display, but kids will probably be more interested in the detailed table model of the city of Winchester in the 1750s, plus the two authentic cannons. One is from Fort Loudon and the other was used by the British General Braddock in the French and Indian War. (Legend has it that Braddock's cannon was fished out of the Potomac River, where his soldiers had tossed it. An exhibit, "George Washington and the West," demonstrates that the frontiers of Virginia were where Washington gained his military experience.

JIM BARNETT PARK (all ages)

Adjoins the visitors center and Abram's Delight; (540) 662–4946. Open year-round, dawn to dusk.

The city's major recreation area with 174 acres, this park gives you and your kids a chance to play and picnic. Try the fitness trail, swim in the indoor or outdoor pools, play tennis, basketball, horseshoes, and miniature golf. There are also a fitness room and a racquetball court. Admission to the park is **Free**, but there is a cost for some of the activities.

THE STATE ARBORETUM OF VIRGINIA (ages 5 and older)

On U.S. Highway 50 in Boyce, about 9 miles east of Winchester; (540) 837–1758. Web address: www.virginia.edu/~blandy. Open year-round, dawn to dusk. **Free**.

Also called the Orland E. White Arboretum, these 170 acres of trees and meadows offer families a tranquil place to unwind. Walking and driving trails are available as well as guided bird-watching. Call for schedule.

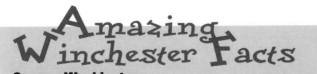

George Washington left another legacy in Winchester: As a landlord, he required each tenant to plant four acres of apples. As a result, ample apple orchards surround the town.

SHENANDOAH VALLEY DISCOVERY MUSEUM (ages 2 to 7)

54 South Loudoun Street, between Boscawen and Cork Street, Winchester; (540) 722–2020. Web address: www.discoverymuseum.net. Open year-round. Closed Monday. Admission.

Although a small facility, this museum appeals to young children by offering hands-on activities in art, science, and natural history. The climbing wall is popular as well. Kids love the paleontology exhibit, where a staff person works on a dinosaur skull, preparing it for display, and answering questions about how the work is done and what the skull tells paleontologists about the dinosaur. Throughout the year, the museum offers special programs and workshops. Past classes have covered the steps of dissecting a brain, Mayan archaeology, as well as readings offered by a well-known author of children's books. The Visiting Artist Series (second weekend of each month; **Free** with admission) offers families the chance to work on art projects together. The museum's web site has interesting interactive experiments and puzzles.

DINOSAUR LAND (ages 2 to 5)

3848 Stonewall Jackson Highway (Route 1) in White Post, between Winchester and Front Royal; (540) 869–2222. Web address: www.dinosaurland.com. Closed January and February. Admission.

Located about 10 miles from Winchester, Dinosaur Land intrigues preschoolers, who have fun posing in front of the more than forty life-size reproductions of prehistoric predators, including a stegosaurus, triceratops, and the ever-fierce tyrannosaurus. Then there is the 20-foot King Kong, the 60-foot shark, and the 70-foot octopus. Older kids may not find these models as exciting as scenes from *Jurassic Park* or the high-tech animated models of Dinamation.

VIRGINIA FARM MARKET (all ages)

Route 522, 1 mile north of Winchester, 1881 North Frederick Pike; (540) 665–8000. Open daily April through mid-December.

In the summer, fresh fruits such as peaches and cantaloupes and vegetables from Shenandoah Valley and nearby areas are for sale, along with pies, muffins, and cookies baked fresh daily. In the fall, enjoy the Pumpkin Patch, with a maze, photo area, a 40-foot-long toy train for kids to play in, and pumpkins galore. Fresh cider and hot apple pie, too.

WILSON'S WILD ANIMAL PARK (all ages)

985 West Parkins Mill Road (Route 644); (540) 662–5715. Open May through October. Admission.

Once a small petting farm, this property has expanded into an eight-acre park with more than 200 mammals, birds, and reptiles. Kids can see gazelle, antelope, lions, monkeys, lemurs, pythons, and the unusual Brazilian tapir, a mammal that looks something like a very large anteater.

JAMMIN' GYM (ages 5 to 10)

1107 Berryville Avenue; (540) 667–JAMM. Open year-round. Admission.

This commercial playground has games, rides, a cafe, and a playground.

SHENANDOAH SUMMER MUSIC THEATRE (ages 4 and older)

1460 University Drive, Winchester; (540) 665–4569. Open June through August. Admission.

Broadway musical productions with a full live orchestra for the whole family. Coming in 2002: *My Fair Lady*, *Footloose*, and *The Sound of Music*.

BLUEMONT SUMMER FRIDAY COURTHOUSE CONCERTS (all ages)

Near the Judicial Center in historic downtown Winchester; (703) 777–6306. Concerts on Friday nights in July and August. Admission.

The family-oriented performances come with outdoor picnic-style seating.

Where to Eat

Brewbaker's Restaurant, *168 North Loudon Street; (540) 535–0111. Open Tuesday through Saturday for lunch and dinner.* On sunny days, sit outside and enjoy a bountiful barbecue sandwich, plus other standard fare. Children's menu. $–$$

Snow White Grill, *159 North Loudoun Street, Winchester; (540) 662–5955. Open Monday through Friday for lunch and dinner.* This restaurant is another blast from the past with a 1949 soda fountain, counter, and stools. The shakes, ice cream, and silver-dollar-size burgers appeal to kids. $

Triangle Diner, *27 West Gerrard Street, Winchester; (540) 667–3541. Open daily.* This authentic old-time diner has miniature jukeboxes at each table with tunes from Winchester native Patsy Cline. Breakfast, lunch, and dinner offer generous portions of "good home cookin'." Specials of the day generally cost $4.50. $

Venice Italian Restaurant, *231 Sunnyside Plaza Circle (Route 522 North); (540) 722–0992.* This family restaurant serves lunch and dinner, both Italian food and hamburgers. $–$$

Where to Stay

The Cove Campground, *980 Cove Road, Gore (12 miles west of Winchester); (540) 858–2882. Web address: www. wvalley.com/cove.* This facility has more than one hundred campsites and cabins on its 3,000 mountain acres. In season you can fish and swim in the three lakes, bike, go snow tubing (they have tubes for rent), or cross-country ski. There is electricity for campsites and a small store selling supplies.

Hampton Inn, *1655 Apple Blossom Drive; (540) 667–8011 or (800) HAMP-TON. Web address: www.hampton-inn.com.* This property is convenient to restaurants and historic sites. Room rates include a continental breakfast and $ree HBO, plus in-room Super Nintendo. Adjacent to the Apple Blossom Mall, which has eighty-five stores and a food court. There's an outdoor pool.

Quality Inn East, *603 Millwood Avenue; (540) 667–2250 or (800) 228–5151.* Close to downtown, this motel includes continental breakfast and has an outdoor pool and an exercise room. Microwave and refrigerator supplied on request.

Shoney's Inn, *1347 Berryville Avenue; (540) 665–1700 or (800) 222–2222. Web address: www.shoneysinn.com.* Adjacent to Shoney's restaurant. This inn has an indoor pool, fitness room, and spa, plus complimentary continental breakfast and coffeemakers in rooms.

Wingate Inn, *150 Wingate Drive; (540) 678–4283 or (877) 946–3585. Web address: www.wingateinns.com.* The inn attracts business conventions, but it's a good deal for families, too. Children stay for free with parents. Take advantage of the complimentary expanded continental breakfast, indoor pool, fitness center, and whirlpool. Rooms include a coffeemaker, hair dryer, microwave, refrigerator, iron and ironing board, and color TV with a $ree movie channel.

Long Hill Bed & Breakfast, *547 Apple Pie Ridge Road; (540) 450–0341 or (866) 265–8390. Web address: www. longhillbb.com.* A bit more upscale, for those with children over 12. Three rooms (each with private bath), a library, and a recreation room with a pool table, plus hiking and bird-watching.

For More Information

Winchester–Frederick County Visitors Center/Chamber of Commerce, *1360 South Pleasant Valley Road, Winchester, VA 22601; (540) 662–4135 or (800) 662–1360. Web address: www.winchesterva.org. Open daily April through December; Monday through Friday, January through March.* The eighteen-minute film *Welcome to the Top* offers background on the city and the surrounding area at the visitors center. A free tourist information packet is also available.

Middletown

Middletown, a small town 13 miles south of Winchester, sports three attractions for families: the historic Belle Grove Plantation; performances at the Wayside Theatre, and the tastes of the Route 11 Potato Chip Factory.

BELLE GROVE PLANTATION (ages 6 and up) (TT)

1 mile south of Middletown on U.S. Highway 11, then 0.5 mile west on Route 627 (Belle Grove Road); (540) 869–2028. Web address: www.bellegrove.org. Open daily from April through October; weekends in November. Special holiday tours at Thanksgiving and in December. Admission.

This native limestone mansion was built in the late 1700s by Major Isaac Hite for his bride, Nelly Madison, sister of President James Madison. The president honeymooned here with his wife, Dolley. Thomas Jefferson played an active role in the design of Belle Grove after Madison requested his advice.

The house, restored in 1930, suffered damage during the Civil War Battle of Cedar Creek. Union General Philip Sheridan's troops occupied the plantation and Confederate forces attacked. The early-nineteenth-century forge and ice house are particularly interesting, and if you're lucky enough to be here when groups are touring, be sure to see the working demonstrations. Each October the plantation hosts a Civil War Battle re-enactment, complete with encampments, and in November there is a Living History Weekend with craftspeople in period costume giving demonstrations and selling their wares. No matter when you visit, browse the crafts center and gift shop, which sports an array of locally made goods and hand-crafted items. House tours start April 1. At other times guests take self-guided tours. The grounds are spectacular, with sweeping views of the Shenandoah Valley and surrounding Blue Ridge and Allegheny Mountains.

WAYSIDE THEATRE (all ages)

7853 Main Street, on the corner of Second and Main Streets; (540) 869–1776 or (800) 951–1776. Web address: www.waysidetheatre.org. Open February through December. Ticket prices vary.

For more than forty years the stage performances at the Wayside Theatre have entertained the townsfolk and launched the careers of many well-known actors and dramatists such as Susan Sarandon, Jill Eikenberry, and Peter Boyle. In general, several plays a season are suited to families. The 2002 season includes *Steel Magnolias, All I Really Needed to Know I Learned in Kindergarten,* and *Kiss Me Kate.* In the spring, there are special shows for children.

ROUTE 11 POTATO CHIP FACTORY (all ages)

7815 Main Street (Route 11), Middletown; (540) 869–0104 or (800) 294–SPUD. Web address: www.route11.com. Open Friday and Saturday.

This factory offers the potato chip aficionado the delight of watching how these flaky delectables are made. (Best time to see production is in the morning.) Following the tour be sure to sample some of the factory's unusual varieties such as Dill Pickle, Chesapeake Crab, Mixed Vegetable, and Sweet Potato chips.

Strasburg

Strasburg is about 5 miles south from Middletown on Route 11. *Note:* Ask about the special three-for-one package when visiting the Museum of American Presidents, Stonewall Jackson Museum at Hupp's Hill, and Crystal Caverns at Hupp's Hill.

THE MUSEUM OF AMERICAN PRESIDENTS (ages 7 and up)

130 North Massanutten Street, Strasburg; (540) 465–5999. Web address: www.waysideofva.com. Open daily. Admission.

This museum features information and portraits of our presidents as well as memorabilia. One-of-a-kind items include James Madison's desk and George Washington's Rising Sun chair, the one in which he sat when he signed the Declaration of Independence. In the one-room schoolhouse, kids can dress up in period clothes and play with colonial toys and books.

 ## STONEWALL JACKSON MUSEUM AT HUPP'S HILL (ages 7 and up) (TT)

33229 Old Valley Pike, Strasburg; (540) 465–5884. Web address: www. waysideofva.com. Open daily. Admission.

This museum portrays Stonewall Jackson's military career through exhibits. Kids see a soldier's wool jacket, swords, and other military items. A highlight for younger kids is the hands-on Civil War camp complete with tents, tin cups, muskets, kid-size soldier's clothing, and wooden horses with authentic calvary saddles and bridles. Older kids will enjoy using "discovery boxes" to explore an historic topic through games, puzzles, and artifacts. There is also a Haversack Tour for kids that features haversacks hung from the ceiling from which kids can pull out an item related to a nearby exhibit.

CRYSTAL CAVERNS AT HUPP'S HILL (ages 3 and up)

33229 Old Valley Pike (Route 11), just north of Strasburg; (540) 465–8660. Web address: www.waysideofva.com. Open daily. Admission.

Discovered in 1775, Crystal Caverns is the oldest cave open to the public. Its 0.25-mile trail includes unusual crystal formations and an interpretive museum with exhibits on the cave's geology, paleontology, and history. Native Americans, local settlers, and Civil War soldiers have used the cave. Lantern and Candlelight Living History tours with guides in period costumes are available by reservation.

Where to Eat

Hotel Strasburg, *213 South Holiday Street, Strasburg, about 5 miles from Middletown; (540) 465–9191 or (800) 348–8327. Web address: www.hotel strasburg.com. Open daily for dinner and Sundays for lunch and dinner; weekends for breakfast.* Converted from a hospital to an Edwardian hotel in 1915, the restaurant serves local specialties (split-pea soup, butter-pecan chicken, and Smithfield ham in apple brandy) in a dining room accented with antiques and collectibles. $$–$$$

Where to Stay

The Wayside Inn, *7783 Main Street; (540) 869–1797 or (877) 869–1797. Web address: www.waysideofva.com.* This rambling inn dates back to 1797. Each of the twenty-four air-conditioned rooms (including several suites) are individually decorated with antiques and collectibles (a television is in each room). A visit here can be somewhat intimidating if your kids are young and restless. Well-behaved, older children are welcome, however. Some teens especially appreciate the setting.

The Inn at Narrow Passage, *on U.S. 11 South, Woodstock; (540) 459–8000 or (800) 459–8002. Web address: www.inn anarrowpassage.com.* This cozy, historic inn has been welcoming travelers since the 1740s. Most rooms have private baths and working fireplaces and all are air-conditioned. Well-behaved children of any age are welcome, but not pets.

Super 8–Middletown, *2120 Reliance Road, on I–81, Exit 302; (540) 868–1800 or (877) 978–7278.* Complimentary continental breakfast, plus HBO and an indoor pool.

Additional lodging is available in nearby Winchester.

For More Information

Shenandoah County Tourism, *600 North Main Street, Suite 101, Woodstock, VA 22664; (540) 459–6227 or (888) 367–3965.*

Front Royal

The town of Front Royal is the gateway to the Shenandoah National Park and Skyline Drive. Skyline Drive starts here at Front Royal and continues for 105.4 miles until it ends at Rockfish Gap where the Blue Ridge Parkway begins. Front Royal is worth a pre- or post-park visit to see Skyline Caverns or to find a place to stay or eat while visiting Shenandoah National Park.

SKYLINE CAVERNS (ages 5 and up)

10344 Stonewall Jackson Highway, 1 mile south of Front Royal on U.S. Highway 340 (just beyond the entrance to Shenandoah National Park); (540) 635–4545 or (800) 296–4545. Web address: www.skylinecaverns.com. Open daily year-round. Admission.

Although the region features several caverns, Skyline Caverns is notable for being one of the only places in the world that has caverns with clusters of shimmering white calcium carbonate crystals called anthodites. These rare formations, nicknamed "the orchids of the mineral kingdom," are also slow growing, gaining only 1 inch every 7,000 years, compared to the 120 to 125 years required for similar growth in stalagmites and stalactites.

On the guided one-hour tour the twelve stairs going down and the forty-eight going up are "doable" by younger kids. Just don't attempt this singlehandedly before a tot's nap time, because carrying a child up the steps can be hard, slippery work. Kids like Rainbow Falls, which plunges more than 37 feet from one of three underground streams that flow through the caverns, as well as the 1-mile miniature train ride around the grounds. The ten-minute train ride, a special delight for wee tots, is offered daily, weather permitting. There's a snack bar, and the gift shop has lots of trinkets. Remember, the temperature in the caverns is a cool 54 degrees, so bring jackets.

FRONT ROYAL CANOE COMPANY (ages 8 and up)

P.O. Box 473, Front Royal, VA 22630; (800) 270–8808 or (540) 635–5440. Web address: www.frontroyalcanoe.com Open April through October.

Paddle down the Shenandoah River on a guided outing or rent canoes, kayaks, rafts, and tubes. Also available are guided Full Moon Floats at night.

Seeing It All from Way up There

- **CASS Aviation** (540–635–3570) offers scenic rides leaving from the Front Royal/Warren County Airport on weekends throughout the year.

- **Fighter Command** (540–635–2203 or 800–809–5482), based at Winchester Regional Airport (15 miles north of Front Royal), offers the thrill of riding in an authentic World War II fighter airplane. Web address: www.giftflight.com

- **Blue Ridge Hot Air Balloons** in Front Royal; (540) 622–6325. Web address: www.balloon@rideair.com. For a more gentle trip across the valley, try a hot air balloon ride, available year-round, depending on the weather.

SHENANDOAH RIVER TRIPS (ages 8 and up)

P.O. Box 145, Bentonville, VA 22610; (800) RAPIDS–1 or (540) 635–5050. Web address: www.shenandoah.com. Open April through October.

Offers affordable family rafting trips on the Shenandoah River with professional, certified staff. Also rents canoes, kayaks, rafts, and tubes. Ask about the hayrides.

Where to Eat

Riley's Family Restaurant, *10 Commerce Avenue; (540) 622–2768. Open daily for breakfast, lunch, and dinner.* Locals come here for "cheap eats." Riley's serves up crab-cake sandwiches, Philly cheese steaks, ribs, and spaghetti. Children's menu offered. $-$$

Grapevine Restaurant, *915 North Royal Avenue; (540) 635–6615. Open daily for lunch and dinner.* Enjoy a wide selection of seafood, pastas, steaks, and pizza. Children's menu available. $-$$

The Main Street Mill, *500 East Main Street (next to the Front Royal Visitors Center); (540) 636–3123.* Enjoy the atmosphere of a remodeled 1800s feed mill with chestnut beams and hand-painted murals. The restaurant specializes in pasta, steak, seafood, and desserts. $-$$

Royal Dairy Ice Cream Bar & Restaurant, *241 Chester Street; (540) 635–5202. Open daily for breakfast, lunch, and dinner.* This old-fashioned dairy bar started serving ice cream in 1947 and has kept the antique bar and stools hopping with customers since. Lunch and dinner items include burgers, hot dogs, barbecue, and sandwiches. $

China Jade, *213 East South Street; (540) 635–9161.* Buffet lunches and take-out. $-$$

Where to Stay

Quality Inn, *10 Commerce Avenue; (800) 821–4488 or (540) 635–3161.* Moderately priced lodging with an outdoor pool and an on-site restaurant.

Relax Inn, *1801 North Shenandoah Avenue; (540) 635–4101 or (877) 4URELAX.* This lodging has an outdoor pool, HBO, and a complimentary continental breakfast.

Super 8, *111 South Street; (800) 800–8000 or (540) 636–4888.* A complimentary breakfast is included in the room rates. Cable and suites also available.

Twilite Motel, *53 West Fourteenth Street; (540) 635–4148 or (800) 230–7349.* Moderate prices, with an outdoor pool, HBO TV, and continental breakfast.

For More Information

Front Royal Visitors Center/
Chamber of Commerce, *414 East*
Main Street, Main Street Station, Front
Royal, VA 22630; (540) 635–5788 or

(800) 338–2576. Web address: www.
ci.front-royal.va.us. Stock up on bro-
chures for this area at this renovated
train depot.

Shenandoah National Park

"Shenandoah" is believed to mean either "daughter of the stars" or "river of high mountains" in a Native American language. Whatever the real meaning, the area's beauty is legendary and best preserved in Shenandoah National Park with its 196,000 acres of forests, mountains, and streams. The park is unofficially divided into three main sections: The northern area, just 72 miles from Washington, D.C., receives the most visitors; the central section features the park's main overnight lodging,

Elevation in the park ranges from 600 feet at the north entrance to 4,050 feet at the summit of Hawksbill Peak, among the highest points in northern Virginia.

which, park officials say, attracts more long-term visitors than overnighters; and the southern section features gorgeous backcountry, plus a visitor information center, with restaurant and gift shop, and campground.

SHENANDOAH NATIONAL PARK
Park Superintendent at 3655 U.S. Highway 211 East, Luray. General informa-
tion line: (540) 999–3500 or (800) 999–4714. Web address: www.nps.
gov/shen.

The famous scenic two-lane route, **Skyline Drive,** stretching 105 miles from Front Royal to Rockfish Gap, cuts through the park and can be accessed from all four park entrances. Once on this road use the mile markers on the west side of the drive to find your locale, as well as the nearest facilities, services, and areas of interest.

The countdown for the mile markers starts after the Front Royal Entrance Station in the north, at mile 1, and ends at the Rockfish Gap

Entrance Station in the south, mile 105. The northern park entrance is easily reached; it's just south of Front Royal, close to the junction of Interstate 81 and Interstate 66, and

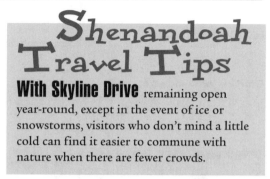

Shenandoah Travel Tips

With Skyline Drive remaining open year-round, except in the event of ice or snowstorms, visitors who don't mind a little cold can find it easier to commune with nature when there are fewer crowds.

accessible via U.S. Highways 340 and 55. Other entrances to Skyline Drive are at Thornton Gap (mile 31.5, accessible via U.S. Highway 211), and at Swift Run Gap (mile 65.5, accessible via U.S. Highway 33). In this section the mile markers are listed along with the sites and trails to make them easy to find when you are traveling along Skyline Drive.

Ranger programs, hikes, and walks explore the natural beauty and cultural history of the park. Most kids' programs are designed for ages 7 and older. In summer at the visitor centers and gift shops, pick up a Junior Ranger Explore Notebook. After kids complete the activities (two of which may include attending a ranger-led program), the kids receive an official Junior Ranger badge or patch, a nice reward and a worthwhile keepsake.

Shenandoah National Park offers families wonders literally as big as all outdoors plus various ways to enjoy them. Remember that Skyline Drive comes with many curves and a 35 m.p.h. speed limit, as well as crowds and many cars in leaf-peeping season. As a result, plan ahead and allow more time than usual when calculating driving distances. If you only have one day to spend in the park, officials recommend driving along Skyline Drive, admiring the scenery, and scouting for animals

Prime Leaf-Peeping During the autumn, the mountainsides blazing with red, yellow, and gold leaves draw crowds. The park is beautiful but crowded. If you visit during leaf-peeping season, prepare to go slow and have patience. Call ahead to these "hotlines" for the latest update on foliage:

- Shenandoah Valley, (800) 434–LEAF

- Skyline Drive/Shenandoah National Park, (540) 999–3500

- Virginia portion of the Blue Ridge, (540) 427–5871.

(maybe even a bear). But be sure to get out of your car to stroll a nature trail or two. Check the park brochures to see which of the short trails are nearby. More advanced

Shenandoah Travel Tips

Winter Visits Don't rule out a winter visit. With fewer crowds, the park seems to open up. And winter, if there's snow—or even mud—is the best time to look for animal tracks.

hikers can try a segment of the Appalachian Trail, 101 miles of which cut through the park. Along the park's trail you can rest awhile at one of the five shelters for day use. These come with a table, fireplace, pit toilet, and water.

If swimming is what your family loves to do, be aware that while it is permitted in all the park streams, it is also done at your own risk.

When conditions are right, the park allows cross-country skiing and snowshoeing, but bring your own gear; the park has no rental facilities. (And remember, winter storms often close Skyline Drive for safety reasons.)

Fishing enthusiasts can also try their luck year-round. The park's twenty-five streams offer great angling opportunities. Anyone 16 and older must have a valid Virginia fishing license and use only artificial lures with a single hook. A temporary five-day license can be purchased at Panorama, Big Meadows Wayside, or Loft Mountain Wayside.

Bird-watching and wildlife-viewing opportunities abound throughout the park. Best hours for viewing are usually in the early morning or early evening.

POTOMAC APPALACHIAN TRAIL CLUB

118 Park Street Southeast, Vienna; (703) 242–0315. Web address: www. patc.net.

Contact this organization for more information on hiking the Appalachian Trail, which runs through the Shenandoah National Park on its way from Maine to Georgia.

SKYLAND STABLES (mile 41.7)

Located near Skyland Lodge; (540) 999–2210. Open from April through October.

A great way to enjoy the trails is from atop a horse. This stable offers one-hour guided trail rides for adults and children at least 4 feet 10 inches tall April through November. Your best bet is to reserve ahead, either through the lodge or by calling the stables.

Hiking Trails

The first five of these popular trails are easy enough for families with young, but energetic, kids. Doyles River Falls is more difficult and best suited to older gradeschoolers who like hiking.

- **Little Stony Man** (milepost 39.1), *0.9 miles with a 270-foot elevation gain to a far-reaching westward view.* Allow one hour round-trip.
- **Blackrock Summit** (milepost 84.8), *1 mile-long round-trip hike with a 175-foot elevation gain to a 360 degree view.* Allow one hour round-trip.
- **Fox Hollow Trail** (milepost 4.6), *1.2-mile circuit hike near Dickey Ridge Visitor Center with a 310-foot elevation gain.* Allow about one and a quarter hours. This trail leads past ruins of old farm fences and a cemetery, one of the many remnants of the homesites of the mountaineers who lived here decades ago.
- **The Story of the Forest Families Trail** (milepost 51), *near Byrd Visitor Center 1.8-mile route with a 290-foot elevation gain.* Allow about one and a half hours. The trail gives visitors a sense of the natural and cultural history of the forest and swamp. You may see deer, chipmunks, and birds along the way.
- **Dark Hollow Falls** (milepost 50.7) *near the Byrd Visitor Center, a 1.4-mile-long round-trip hike with a 440-foot climb back to the start.* Allow one and a half hours. This popular trail leads to the beautiful cascading waterfall, the nearest waterfall to Skyline Drive.
- **Doyles River Falls** (milepost 81.1), *Near Loft Mountain Information Center, a 2.7-mile round-trip trail with an 850-foot change in elevation.* Allow at least three hours. The trail leads to a waterfall surrounded by trees. Some places are steep. Pack a picnic lunch and linger.

Annual Events

The *Shenandoah Overlook* also lists information about seasonal special events.

MAY

Wildflower Weekend in Shenandoah National Park**,** *generally the second weekend in May.* Special walks and exhibits highlight the park's spring flowers.

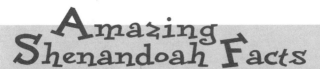

Amazing Shenandoah Facts

Appalachian Trail About 101 miles of the Appalachian Trail, which stretches 2,100 miles from Maine to Georgia, is located within Shenandoah National Park.

Shenandoah Apple Blossom Festival, *135 North Cameron Street, Winchester; (540) 662–3863. Web address: www.sabf.org.* More than thirty events over one weekend, including dances, parades, a 10K run, a circus, food, and fun.

SUMMER

Shenandoah Valley Music Festival, *held on selected weekends between Memorial Day and Labor Day; (800) 459–3396. Web address: www.musicfest.org. Admission.* The last two weekends in July are the symphonic weekends and are held at the Orkney Springs Hotel in Orkney Springs, with juried arts and crafts shows. On Saturday afternoons of both weekends cross-cultural events are held for children to teach them about different cultures' music.

JULY

New Market Fourth of July celebration, *(540) 740–3132.* The celebration is held in the town park with activities for kids such as face painting and pony rides. There are also picnics, food concessions, live music, and great fireworks.

AUGUST-SEPTEMBER

Shenandoah County Fair, *Woodstock; (540) 459–3867.* For more than eighty years, this county fair has had it all: midway rides, greased pig contests, prize livestock, country music concerts, harness races, and bubble gum contests.

SEPTEMBER

Apple Harvest Festival, *every September in Mount Jackson; (540) 477–3275.*

OCTOBER

New Market also has a **Heritage Days Fall Festival** in late October every year, with food, crafts, and games. For information call (540) 740-3132.

Where to Eat

Within Shenandoah National Park there are several informal restaurants as well as snack shacks. Still, the easiest way to eat in the park is al fresco; pack your own picnic and pause where you like to enjoy the food and the scenery. There are seven picnic grounds.

Big Meadows Dining Room (*milepost 51.2, 1 mile off Skyline Drive*), *open from early May through late fall.* Local specialties such as fried chicken and mountain trout as well as burgers are served.

See if your kids want the special dessert: blackberry ice cream pie topped with blackberry syrup.

Panorama Restaurant (*milepost 31.5*). *Open mid-April through October for lunch and late afternoon fare.* Features salads, sandwiches, and pizza.

Skyland Dining Room (*milepost 41.7*), *usually open from late March through November.* Offers the same fare as Big Meadows Dining Room.

Where to Stay

Park lodges don't charge for cribs or for children under 16 who share a room with parents. Reserve far ahead (nine months to one year depending upon the season) for the following park lodgings. Call (800) 999-4714 or (540) 743-5108 to make your reservation.

Campsites are available on a first-come basis, except for Big Meadows. Call (800) 365-CAMP or use the Web site: reservations.nps.gov. There are no hookups at any campground.

Big Meadows Campground (*milepost 51.2*). There are 217 tent or trailer sites, flush toilets, and showers. Reservations required from Memorial Day weekend until the end of October.

Big Meadows Lodge (*milepost 51.2*), *open from late April through early November.* An historic park lodge, Big Meadows offers great views of wildflowers and often of deer, particularly in the evening and early morning. Accommodations

range from twenty-one rooms in the main lodge to eighty-one rustic cabins and multi-units with modern suites. The facility has a playground, televisions in some rooms, and nightly entertainment.

Big Meadows Wayside (*milepost 51.2*). *Open late March through November.* Restaurant, snack bar, souvenirs.

Elkswallow Wayside (*milepost 24.1*). *Open mid-April through fall.* Lunch counter, snack bar, souvenirs.

Lewis Mountain (*milepost 57.6*). The campground has 32 tent sites, flush toilets, and showers, and is open May to November.

Lewis Mountain Cabins (*milepost 57.3*), *open early May through November.* Features semi-rustic cabins with private baths and heat; linens are provided. Cooking facilities include a fireplace, grills, and picnic tables in the connecting outdoor area. A coin-operated Laundromat is nearby.

Loft Mountain Campground *(milepost 79.5). Open mid-March through November.* Campers can use 219 tent or trailer sites, flush toilets, and showers.

Loft Mountain Wayside *(milepost 79.5). Open late spring through late fall.* Lunch and snack foods, souvenirs.

Mathews Arm Campground *(milepost 22.1).* Open June through October. There are 179 tent or trailer sites, flush toilets, no showers.

Skyland *(milepost 41.7). Open from the end of March usually to late November.* Established in the late 1880s, Skyland offers 177 guest units, including modern rooms and rustic cabins. Facilities include a restaurant, craft shop, naturalist programs, horseback activities, playground, television in some rooms, and nightly entertainment.

Accommodations are also available in neighboring communities (see the Luray section).

Overlooks: Great Views

The park delights visitors with about seventy-five scenic overlooks along Skyline Drive and many others on mountain peaks.

- **Shenandoah Valley Overlook** (milepost 2.8). Children especially like Signal Knob, used by Confederate troops in the Civil War to convey semaphore signals. You can see it on Massanutten Mountain across the Shenandoah River and Valley.

- **Range View Overlook** (milepost 17.1). The spot boasts the best view in the park's northern region. At 2,800 feet this area gives you a view to the southwest of the ridgetops of the Blue Ridge, Massanutten, and Allegheny mountains.

- **Stony Man Overlook** (milepost 38.6). This offers panoramas of cliffs and the surrounding Shenandoah Valley to the west.

- **Thoroughfare Mountain Overlook** (milepost 40.5). At approximately 3,600 feet this is one of the highest overlooks, offering views of several mountains to the east and northeast, including Old Rag Mountain.

- **Big Run Overlook** (milepost 81.2). Elevation 2,860 feet. This overlook, one of the most beautiful in the park, looks out over the Big Run watershed (part of the largest federally designated wilderness area in the park) to the mountains, ridges, and slopes.

For More Information

The Dickey Ridge Visitor Center *(milepost 4.6), near the Front Royal Entrance Station. Open daily (later hours during the summer season), but closed from the end of November through the end of March.* Exhibits explain the park's activities and available services. Maps, books, and other items for sale.

The Byrd Visitor Center *(milepost 51)*, *open daily (later hours during the summer season), from April through the end of November.* This center has interpretive exhibits, plus a good selection of books.

Left Mountain Information Center *(milepost 79.5), open Thursday through Tuesday, mid-May through mid-October. (Summer season open daily.)* The center provides visitor orientation information and has publications for sale.

Park Entrance Stations sell passes and provide visitors with a park map and, in season, a copy of *The Shenandoah Overlook*, the visitor guide. Along with the visitor centers' hours, the *Overlook* and park bulletin boards contain listings of the park's numerous ranger-led activities for adults and kids, most of which take place in and around visitor centers and campgrounds.

The Blue Ridge Parkway

The Blue Ridge Parkway connects the Shenandoah National Park (Skyline Drive) to the Great Smoky Mountains National Park. The Blue Ridge Parkway, starting at Rockfish Gap near Waynesboro, Virginia where Skyline Drive ends, continues to Cherokee, North Carolina, at milepost 469.

For almost 470 miles from the southern end of Virginia's Shenandoah National Park to North Carolina's Great Smoky Mountains, the Blue Ridge Parkway straddles mountain peaks and dips into scenic valleys, twisting by overlooks and dappled hillsides. Because of the lower speed limits, drivers sometimes alternate between the Blue Ridge Parkway and Interstate 81, which runs parallel to it and also traverses scenic areas.

BLUE RIDGE PARKWAY ASSOCIATION

P.O. Box 2136, Asheville, NC 28802; (828) 298–0398; 2551 Mountain View Road, Vinton; (540) 857–2213 or (540) 427–5871. Web address: www.blueridgeparkway.org.

For a complete list of the trails and their difficulty levels, as well as attractions, obtain the *Blue Ridge Parkway Information Guide* from the visitor center. Although the parkway is open all year, winter may bring icy conditions that temporarily close the roads, so call ahead.

Like Skyline Drive, this toll-free, 469-mile-long, non-commercialized mountain route offers a great scenic drive. With a speed limit of 45 m.p.h. on meandering mountain roads, the drive is slow; many cars stop at the scenic overlooks to gaze out across the valleys. Allow plenty of time. The most popular and crowded times are spring through summer and fall. The road also offers a number of hiking trails, some of them easy enough for young children.

Because the Blue Ridge Parkway is non-commercialized, there are no accommodations, gas stations, or restaurants directly on the parkway. Find these in the historic towns along the way.

There are five visitor centers (Web address: www.nps.gov) along the parkway in Virginia, each providing information on activities and facilities in the area as well as general information about the Parkway:

- **Humpback Rocks** (milepost 5.8) has a small museum recently renovated to include a new exhibit on late nineteenth- and early twentieth-century life. A U.S. Forest Service campground is located 4 miles south of the Center, off of the parkway and a ninety-one-site picnic area is located at milepost 8.5. The center maintains a reconstructed pioneer mountain farmstead accessible via an easy, quarter-mile, self-guided trail. During the summer, costumed rangers demonstrate mountain crafts and skills.

- **James River** (milepost 63.6) has picnic tables located downhill from the center. Otter Creek (milepost 60.8) has a campground with sites for forty-two tents and twenty-six trailers, a restaurant (804–299–5862), and a handicapped-accessible dock at milepost 63 for fishing. From the center, hike the half-mile Trail of Trees and the easy James River Trail that leads to the restored Kanawha Canal Lock. In the summer, there are guided lock tours, as well as the James River Batteau Festival.

- **Peaks of Otter** (milepost 86) has a visitor center, service station, and small gift shop. Nearby is the sixty-four-room Peaks of Otter Lodge (540–586–1081) and restaurant, open year-round. Nearby is the Johnson Farm, a living history farm where kids can play period games and help work the garden.

- **Roanoke Mountain** (milepost 120.3) is a 4-mile, one-way loop road (no trailers allowed) that affords beautiful views of Roanoke Valley and Mill Mountain, and is adjacent to a campground (milepost 120.4) with sites for seventy-four tents and thirty-one trailers. (Three sites are handicapped-accessible.) There are evening country music programs during the summer.

- **Rock Knob** (milepost 167) has a campground with sites for eighty-one tents and twenty-eight trailers, with a one hundred-capacity campfire circle where interpretive programs are given on summer weekends. There are also demonstrations of crafts, black-smithing, spinning, and weaving.

■ **Mabry Mill** (milepost 176.2) has a coffee shop and a gift shop (540–952–2947).

Luray

Luray is located 9 miles west of Skyline Drive on U.S. Highway 211.

LURAY CAVERNS (ages 4 and up)

9 miles west of Skyline Drive on U.S. Highway 211; (540) 743–6551. Web address: www.luraycaverns.com. Open daily year-round. Admission. Call for reservations for the motel accommodations on property.

Luray Caverns is the largest cavern in Virginia and the most popular in the East. Remember to bring along a sweater; no matter how hot the surface temperature, the underground rooms are cool. The subterranean chambers range from 30 to 140 feet high and feature thousands of colored formations. Even the most blasé of teens will turn off the headphones to listen to chords played on the **Great Stalacpipe Organ,** billed as the world's largest natural musical instrument. The tunes resonate throughout the chamber when plungers tap the stalactites. One-hour cavern tours begin every twenty minutes, and the admission fee also includes a self-guided tour of the on-premises **Car and Carriage Caravan** of Luray Caverns. The 140 vehicles include such finds as an 1892 Mercedes Benz, a Rolls Royce Silver Ghost, and other vehicles and costumes dating back to 1727. There's also a 1-acre **Garden Maze** in which to get lost (and found).

Horseback Riding in George Washington National Forest

Fort Valley Stable, (540) 933–6634 or (888) 754–5771. Web address: www.fortvalleystable.com. Offers guided trail rides through 80 miles of George Washington National Forest trails, with views from some of the highest ridges in the Massanutten Mountains. Riders must be 7 years of age and older. All skill levels are accommodated; no previous riding experience required. Trail guides lead one- and one-and-a-half-hour rides, or half-day and full-day trips with a trail lunch. The stable is at 299 South Fort Valley Road, Fort Valley.

SHENANDOAH RIVER OUTFITTERS (ages 6 and up)

6502 South Page Valley Road; (800) 6CANOE2 or (540) 743–4159. Web address: www.shenandoah-river.com. Open from April through mid-November.

Splash along the river with this company whose canoeing and tubing trips on the Shenandoah River provide a playful and pleasing outing, especially in the heat of summer. Take advantage of the Eleven O'Clock Special for families midweek from April until the end of October, with a discount rate for an 8-mile canoeing trip. Spend the night in a cabin built on the river or canoe all day and then enjoy a charcoal-cooked steak and chicken dinner in an open-air pavilion.

LURAY REPTILE CENTER, DINOSAUR PARK, AND PETTING ZOO (all ages)

1087 U.S. Highway 211 West; (540) 743–4113. Web address: www.lurayzoo.com. Open daily year-round, except when icy; then open only on weekends. Admission.

For slithery things, visit this park whose residents include huge pythons, alligators, rattlesnakes, and cobras. These will either elicit an "awesome" or an "Aggh—get me out of here" shriek. For younger children (and squeamish adults), there's a petting zoo featuring African pygmy goats and fallow deer from Europe.

Skiing at Massanutten In winter the locals ski at Massanutten Resort in McGaheysville (800–207–6277 or 540–289–9441). Web address: www.massresort.com. Virginia skiing isn't like skiing out West, but it's a lot closer to home. Massanutten offers Slope Sliders classes for ages 4 to 12 and snowboarding group instruction for ages 9 to 14. The mountain has seventy skiable acres and a vertical drop of 1,110 feet. Hotel and condominium accommodations are available on-site. Child care programs available for children ages 3 to 12.

Annual Events

MAY

Mayfest on Main Street, an annual spring festival with crafts, games, activities, and antique vendors.

OCTOBER

Heritage Festival, a Blue Ridge tradition commemorating the mountain history of Page Valley with crafts, food, and entertainment.

DECEMBER

Christmas Bird Count *in Shenandoah National Park. Volunteers call (540) 999–3282.*

Where to Eat

Brookside Restaurant and Gift Shop, *2978 U.S. Highway 211 East; (540) 743–5698. Open daily for breakfast, lunch, and dinner; closed from mid-December through mid-January.* This homestyle restaurant features such entrees as pork barbecue, Virginia ham-steak, catfish, as well as a large salad bar and daily buffets. Brookside bakes its own bread and desserts. $–$$

Tastee Freeze, *402 West Main Street, Luray; (540) 743–6196. Open daily year-round.* This eatery is handy for a quick lunch of burgers and fries followed by ice cream. $

Anthony's Pizza, *1432 West 211 Bypass, Luray; (540) 743–9300. Lunch and dinner daily.* Fresh pasta, pizza, salads, and subs.

Where to Stay

Best Western Intown of Luray, *410 West Main Street; (540) 743–6511 or (800) 528–1234. Web address: www. bestwesternluray.com.* This motel property has an outdoor pool and a restaurant on premises plus a swingset and a grassy play area.

Brookside Cabins, *2978 U.S. Highway 211 East; (800) 299–2655 or (540) 743–5698. Web address: www. brookside-cabins.com.* Four and a half miles from the entrance to Skyline Drive. Morning coffee is served at your log cabin overlooking a brook. No television.

Budget Inn, *320 West Main Street, Luray; (800) 858–9800 or (540) 743–5176.* These motel accommodations offer basic rooms at moderate prices. Rooms newly renovated.

Deerlane River Cabins, *P.O. Box 188, Luray, VA 22835; (800) 696–DEER or (540) 743–3344. Web address: www.deer lane-cabins.com.* Rent one- to three-bedroom rustic cabins with kitchenettes, air conditioning and television/VCR.

Jordan Hollow Farm Inn, *326 Hawksbill Park Road in Stanley (6 miles south of Luray); (540) 778–2285 or (888) 418–7000. Web address: www.jordanhollow. com.* A combination horse farm and inn on 150 acres, this lodging offers country views and horseback rides. Choose to stay in either Mare Meadow Lodge, a contemporary hand-hewn log building where all the rooms have gas fireplaces and whirlpool jets in oversize tubs, or the vine-covered Arbor View Lodge, whose sixteen motel-style rooms are furnished in Victorian decor. Breakfast is included in the room rate and is served in a wood-paneled dining room. Most accommodations come with balconies or decks. Enjoy watching foals frolic in the pastures and the views of the soft peaks of the surrounding mountains. Guests can saddle up and take a scenic trail ride through the pastoral landscape of wildflower-filled meadows.

The Mimslyn Inn, *401 West Main Street; (800) 296–5105; (540) 743–5105. Web address: www.svta.org/ mimslyn.* This centrally located and casual inn has family accommodations. Kids will find The Farmhouse Restaurant interesting. Two of its four dining rooms are restored 1700s log cabins.

For More Information

Luray–Page County Chamber of Commerce, *46 East Main Street, Luray, VA 22835; (540) 743–3915 or (888) 743–3915. Web address: www.luraypage.com.*

New Market

New Market is just off Interstate 81, 12 miles west of Luray on U.S. Highway 211.

NEW MARKET BATTLEFIELD STATE HISTORICAL PARK (ages 7 and up)

Off Route 305 (George Collins Parkway); (540) 740–3101. Web address: www.vmi.edu/museum/nm. Open daily, closed major holidays. Admission.

School-age children interested in the Civil War connect with this park because it commemorates the corps of 257 Virginia Military Institute students, some as young as 15 (although the average age was 18), who were called to active duty. Although the cadets were supposed to be kept in reserve until needed to fill a gap in the advancing line of badly outnumbered Confederate troops, these schoolboys were accidentally put on the front lines to face the Union soldiers. The cadets managed to hold the line for thirty minutes, forcing the Union troops to retreat. Ten VMI students were killed, and their troop's heroism is honored here. The Hall of Valor Civil War Museum shows a film about the battle and another about Stonewall Jackson's Shenandoah campaign. Models and dioramas also describe the Civil War. A self-guided, 1-mile-long battlefield tour brings alive the story of the cadets' bravery. A reenactment of the battle takes place here every May, the weekend following Mother's

Day. Inside the museum, look for Camp Discovery, an interactive learning area, and ask about the scavenger hunts for children throughout the museum.

THE NEW MARKET BATTLEFIELD MILITARY MUSEUM (ages 9 and up)

9500 Route 305 (George Collins Parkway) in New Market, 8895 Collins Drive; (540) 740–8065. Web address: www.newmarketmilitarymuseum.com. Open daily mid-March to October and weekends during November. Admission.

The museum is on the battlefield but is a separate, privately run entity requiring additional admission. In this replica of General Robert E. Lee's home, more than 2,500 military artifacts from American wars (beginning with the Revolutionary War up through Operation Desert Storm) are displayed. A thirty-minute-long film about the Civil War is intriguing; the bookshop sells more than 500 titles. Fifteen markers on the grounds denote Union and Confederate troop positions.

ENDLESS CAVERNS (ages 3 and up)

Take exit 264 off Interstate 81, then travel 3 miles south on U.S. Highway 11, New Market; (540) 740–3993, (540) 896–2283, or (800) 544–2283. Web address: www.endlesscaverns.com. Open every day except Christmas. Admission.

Discovered by accident in 1879 when two boys were rabbit hunting, these caverns have now been mapped to stretch more than 5 miles, and there's no end in sight. Guided tours take approximately seventy-five minutes.

Take a Shopping Break

Look for something old and something new in New Market's antiques and crafts shops. You can find some fine crafts by local artisans.

- **Bedrooms of America Museum-Pottery-Antiques** (540–740–3512) is a combination pottery outlet, gift shop, and museum of America's bedrooms, from 1650 to 1930. Also for sale are collectible dolls.

- **Paper Treasures** (540–740–3135) sells used and rare books, magazines, comics, prints, newspapers, postcards, and paper collectibles of all kinds.

- **Shenandoah Valley Crafts and Gifts** (540–740–3899) has local handcrafts, oak baskets, Virginia hams, and a rock shop.

SHENANDOAH VALLEY POWWOW

1371 Caverns Road, Quicksburg, off I–81 at exit 269; (540) 477–9616. Admission.

This annual weekend powwow, held in late June, brings Native Americans from dozens of Indian nations across the country to the Silver Phoenix Indian Trading Post to honor Native American traditions. It's a wonderful opportunity for kids to see and experience Indian dancing, drumming, and singing, as well as Native American food.

Where to Eat

Johnny Appleseed Restaurant and Applecore Country Store and Gift Shop, *Interstate 81, exit 264, New Market; (540) 740–3141. Open for breakfast, lunch, and dinner.* Restaurant offers fried chicken, country-fried steak, biscuits-and-gravy, and apple fritters for dessert. Children's menu. The store has a large assortment of Virginia specialty foods and collectibles. $–$$

Southern Kitchen, *U.S. 11, 3 blocks south of Route 211; (540) 740–3514. Open for breakfast, lunch, and dinner.* Steaks, Virginia ham, seafood, Lloyd's Virginia fried chicken, peanut soup, plus carry-out.

Where to Stay

Shenvalee Golf Resort, *1 mile south of Interstate 81, exit on U.S. 11; (540) 740–3181. Web address: www.shenvalee. com.* The resort has a 27-hole golf course (package plans available), tennis courts, outdoor pool, and restaurant.

Blue Ridge Inn, *U.S. 11, 1 mile north of New Market; (540) 740–4136 or (800) 545–8776. Web address: www.blue ridgeinn.com.* Cozy, country-decor rooms, children stay **Free**. Playground, basketball, horseshoes, barbecue, and picnic area. In-room coffeemakers, refrigerators, and cable.

Budget Inn–New Market, *U.S. 11, 1 mile north of New Market; (540) 740–3105 or (800) 296–6835.* The HBO is **Free** and so are children; refrigerators in the rooms, playground outside.

Quality Inn–Shenandoah Valley, *Interstate 81 at exit 264, New Market; (540) 740–3141 or (800) 228–5151.* In-room coffeemakers, outdoor pool, sauna, and minigolf. Johny Appleseed Restaurant and Applecore Village Gift Shop on site.

The Widow Kip's Country Inn, *1355 Orchard Drive, Mount Jackson, 7 miles north of New Market; (540) 466–2400 or (800) 478–8714. Web address: www. widowkips.com.* A restored 1830s inn with a view of the Massanutten Mountains has two restored cottages that welcome children and pets. Family-style breakfast, outdoor pool, and bikes for rides through apple orchards.

For More Information

Shenandoah Valley Travel Association, P.O. Box 1040, New Market, VA 22844; (540) 740–3132.

New Market Chamber of Commerce, 9184 John Sevier Road, New Market, VA 22844; (540) 740–3212.

Staunton

Staunton (pronounced *stanton*), 42 miles south of New Market and 11 miles west of the southern end of Skyline Drive at Waynesboro, is the birthplace of Woodrow Wilson and one of the oldest cities west of the Blue Ridge Mountains. Since Staunton survived the Civil War intact, the town boasts some splendid nine-

Amazing Staunton Facts

Staunton celebrated its 250th anniversary in 1997.

teenth-century buildings. This is a pleasant place to take a stroll; walking tour maps are available weekdays from the chamber of commerce.

THE WOODROW WILSON BIRTHPLACE AND MUSEUM (ages 7 and up) (TT)

18–24 North Coalter Street (888) 496–6376 or (540) 885–0897. Web address: www.woodrowwilson.org. Open daily year-round. Admission. **Free** admission on December 28, Wilson's birthday.

This building has been restored to look the way it did when the former president was born here in 1856. The twelve-room house features memorabilia of the Wilson family, including Wilson's crib. His father was a Presbyterian minister and the family moved when Wilson was 2. At the museum building, which contains seven galleries, school-age kids learn about Wilson's life and career and American history during his presidency from 1913 to 1921, including our entry into World War I. Kids particularly enjoy a glimpse of the presidential limousine in the garage: a 1919 Pierce-Arrow. There's even a nineteenth century mousetrap on view. Children touring the museum are given a clipboard and a list of questions about objects in the museum and Wilson's life and career. Those who answer all the questions correctly are given a counterfeit $100,000 bill with Wilson's face on it.

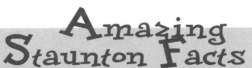

In 1745 the first courthouse was constructed here out of logs.

FRONTIER CULTURE MUSEUM (all ages) (TT)
U.S. Highway 250, 1250 Richmond Road; (540) 332–7850. Web address: www.frontiermuseum.org. Open daily, closed Thanksgiving, Christmas, and New Year's Day.

Staunton, a prominent stop for pioneers on their journey west, pays tribute to this heritage at this museum. Plan to spend several hours at this living-history museum; your kids will love it. Although while touring this 185-acre complex you can still hear the traffic on the nearby highway, the four seventeenth-, eighteenth-, and nineteenth-century homes transport you to a preindustrial time. The buildings, laced along a 0.6-mile dirt loop, illustrate the hopes and the customs that these hardy immigrants from Germany, Scotland, Ireland, and England brought with them and planted in the fertile Virginia soil. As you look across the rolling hills, you can imagine the promise that these pioneers sensed in the wind. By 2004, the museum plans on two new additions: a farm from West Africa that will reflect the ancestry of many African-Americans, and an eighteenth-century Virginia farm reflective of those built in the Shenandoah Valley.

The interpretative guides and the hands-on history lessons make learning fun. A bonneted matron at the eighteenth-century German home sits in the *stube* (the family room) carding wool. She carefully teaches kids to pick the straw and hay from the fibers. Outside, another *hausfrau* knits fingerless gloves, which kept workers' hands warm while still enabling them to toss grain to the animals. The stone fence, thatched roof, and Prudence the pig rooting in the mud endear the Scotch-Irish farm to city kids. In this proverbial cottage of yore dating to the mid-nineteenth century, pull up a "creepie stool" (because you crept closer to the fire as the night wore on) and learn how to cook Donegal pie in the open-hearth fireplace. At the seventeenth-century English farm, a poor man's one-room abode with a cattail roof and mud cob walls, you can practice your darning. At the log American house with its double-pen log barn, flail wheat on the central threshing floor, then try your hand at the "new-fangled" fanning mill, which cleaned a bushel a minute. As you look into the sunset, imagine women cooking a country supper, and the folks readying for a barn dance to celebrate the harvest.

Amazing Staunton Facts

Staunton is the home of the country singers The Statler Brothers.

The museum offers more than fifty programs a year, many of them geared to the seasons. In May, Wool Days has costumed staff members shearing sheep by hand, cleaning the fleeces, and spinning the wool. Autumn hosts a special celebration of fall and a music festival in September. A Halloween tour takes visitors to the Scotch-Irish farm to hear ghost stories and folktales. Special programs for children are also held throughout the year. In July, programs for 4- to 10-year-olds include a variety of crafts, farm visits, and recreation, and there is a Children's Holiday Party in December. Reservations (made at least two weeks in advance) are necessary for the children's programs; call (540) 332–7850, ext. 159.

SHOPS AND STOPS

- The **Staunton Fire Department** (500 North Augusta Street; 540–332-3885) displays a 1911 Jumbo Antique Fire Engine, the only surviving fire engine of its type in the world.

- **Robert L's Coins & Stamps** (128 West Beverly Street; 540-885-7767) also sells baseball cards.

- **Staunton Trains & Hobbies** (123 Beverly Street; 540-885-6750) sells Lionel trains, and right behind that shop is a shop called **Perspicacity** (3 North Lewis Street; 540-886-1186) that is operated by a high school student.

Shenandoah Shakespeare *11 East Beverley Street; (540) 885–5588*. Web address: www.shenandoahshakespeare.com. Even kids who have never heard of Shakespeare (and those who think it's all boring) will enjoy the Shenandoah Shakespeare theater company. This is MTV-generation Shakespeare, but with respect for the work and contagious enthusiasm. Experience the Bard as Medieval audiences did: a simple stage, minimal sets, and with the lights up on the audience as well as the stage. Plays are performed without intermission and kept under two hours. In September 2001, the company is opening an authentic indoor Elizabethan playhouse modeled after Shakespeare's Blackfriars Playhouse.

Annual Events

Unless otherwise noted, information about these events can be obtained from the Staunton Convention and Visitors Bureau at (540) 332-3865.

APRIL–OCTOBER

The Staunton–Augusta Farmers' Market in Staunton. Seasonal fruits and vegetables, baked goods, and other locally grown products are available Saturdays from 7:00 A.M. until noon at the Wharf Parking Lot, Johnson Street and Central Avenue.

JUNE–AUGUST

Stonewall Brigade Band Concerts, Monday at the Gypsy Hill park bandstand. (540) 332-3972.

JUNE–OCTOBER

Guided walking tours of historic Staunton, Saturday 10:00 A.M., leaving from the Woodrow Wilson Birthplace and Museum; (540) 885-7676.

SEPTEMBER

Annual African-American Heritage Festival with live music and dance performances, arts and crafts, and historic exhibits; (540) 332-3972.

Where to Eat

Baja Bean Co. Restaurant & Cantina, *9 West Beverly Street; (540) 885–9988. Open daily for lunch and dinner.* The standard Mexican fare includes tacos, chimichangas, and enchiladas. Charbroiled chicken, steak, and shrimp are also served. Children's menu available. $-$$

The Beverley Restaurant, *12 East Beverley Street; (540) 886–4317. Open Monday through Saturday for breakfast, lunch, and dinner, closed Sunday.* The restaurant serves southern home-style meals, as well as boxed lunches and hot meals to go. Breakfast is served all day, and English tea is served on Wednesdays and Fridays from 3:00 to 5:00 P.M. $-$$

The Depot Grille, *42 Middlebrook Avenue; (540) 885–7332. Open daily for lunch and dinner.* Located in the railroad station, the restaurant is decorated with train memorabilia. Ask if you can reserve a table in the old boxcar. American cuisine of steak, seafood, and pasta. Children's menu available. $$

Heavenly Bake Shop and Café, *101 West Beverly Street; (540) 886–4455. Open daily for lunch and dinner.* Sandwiches, salads, and baked goods. $-$$

Luigi's Pizza, *111 North Augusta Street; (540) 886–6016. Open daily for dinner.* Pizza, salads, and sandwiches. $–$$

The Pullman Restaurant, *30 Middlebrook Avenue; (540) 885–6612. Lunch and dinner daily.* Located in the railroad station, includes a restored Victorian ice cream parlor. $–$$

Where to Stay

The Belle Grae Inn, *515 West Frederick Street; (540) 886–5151 or (888) 541–5151; Web address: www.bellegrae.com.* Built as a showcase residence in 1873, this inn offers turn-of-the-century élan in six rooms decorated with antiques and period pieces. It has also expanded to offer thirteen restored Victorian homes, which give families with well-behaved children the added option of flats and cottages in which to stay. All accommodations include breakfast and afternoon tea. House dinner specialties include roast pork tenderloin, roast quail, and broiled stuffed trout with crayfish, and desserts that show the valley's apples to advantage, apple crisp, apple dumplings, and apple pie. For more Southern cuisine, try smudge pie (chocolate and vanilla ice cream in a chocolate pie shell) and buttermilk pie. Not open for lunch.

The Frederick House, *28 North New Street; (540) 885–4220 or (800) 334–5575. Web address: www.frederickhouse. com.* With fourteen rooms in five separate town houses along Frederick Street and no central lounge for guests to greet and mingle in, the Frederick House offers the anonymity of a small-town hotel, with the homespun warmth of a bed and breakfast. At Frederick House the rooms are plain and comfortable; many have simple, country-style furnishings such as spool bedsteads and serviceable pine bureaus. Rates include a full breakfast at Chumley's Tearoom. Spacious accommodations include the Fred Morgan and the Frances Bell suites. Kids also like the inn's edible landscaping. Ask for permission first, but in season, you can generally pick and eat blueberries, raspberries, gooseberries, cherries, and pears.

For More Information

Staunton–Augusta Visitors Center, *exit 222 off Interstate 81, (near the entrance of the Museum of American Frontier Culture), (800) 332–5219 or (540) 332–3972. Open daily.*

Staunton Convention and Visitors Bureau, *116 West Beverley Street; (540) 332–3865. Web address: www.stauntonva. org.* There's also a visitor center at the Woodrow Wilson Birthplace and Museum. At any of these, ask for the brochure "Kool Stuff 4 Kids," which has information on activities, stores, and restaurants for children.

Lexington

Lexington, 35 miles south of Staunton, is a college town with two venerable institutions located next to one another: the **Virginia Military Institute** (VMI) and **Washington and Lee University.** The lively college atmosphere and the Civil War history make this area an appealing place to visit with kids, but maybe not for too long. Judge your kids' patience with historic settings and war lore.

VIRGINIA MILITARY INSTITUTE (VMI) (ages 7 and up)

Located at the intersection of Interstate 64 and Interstate 81. VMI Visitor Center; (540) 464–7306. Web address: www.vmi.edu.

Founded in 1839, VMI lays claim to being the nation's first state-supported military college. Stonewall Jackson taught here for ten years before the Civil War, which may have been part of the reason Union forces shelled and burned this institute. Another possible contributing factor was the cadets who fought in the Battle of New Market (see New Market section). Every May 15, a solemn New Market Day Ceremony honors the cadets who died in that battle.

If you come during the academic year, take the cadet-led guided tour, which begins at Lejeune Hall. Even if you don't take a tour, the cadets in uniform and the Friday afternoon full-dress parades appeal to kids. (No parades in the summer.)

THE VMI MUSEUM (ages 7 and up)

Jackson Memorial Hall, VMI campus; (540) 464–7334. Web address: www.vmi.edu/museum. Open daily year-round. Donations requested.

The museum displays uniforms, weapons, and memorabilia, including the coat Stonewall Jackson wore at VMI and the bullethole-riddled raincoat he was wearing at the Battle of Chancellorsville. Kids gravitate to the typical cadet's room in the barracks and to Little Sorrel, Jackson's war horse, mounted and preserved forever. There's a scavenger hunt questionnaire to help children learn more about the exhibits. Those who complete the questionnaire get a cadet bookmark.

LEE CHAPEL AND MUSEUM (ages 10 and up)

On the campus of Washington and Lee University; (540) 463–8768. The chapel is open daily except for Thanksgiving, Christmas, and New Year's Day.

The chapel, now used for concerts and other special events, was built in 1867 under the supervision of General Robert E. Lee, president of the college from the end of the Civil War until his death in 1870 (when the name of the college was changed to include his name). The brick chapel contains Lee's office, Lee family memorabilia, and a famous portrait of George Washington by Charles Willson Peale. A white marble sculpture of the recumbent Lee by Edward Valentine is behind the altar, a solemn but impressive sight. Lee and his family are buried beneath the chapel on the museum level. Lee's beloved horse Traveler is interred in a marked plot outside Lee's office.

STONEWALL JACKSON HOUSE (ages 9 and up) (TT)

8 East Washington Street; (540) 463–2552. Web address: www. stonewalljackson.org. Open daily, except major holidays. Admission.

This was the home of the general from 1859 until he went to war in 1861 (he died in 1863). Just 5 blocks from the Virginia Military Institute campus where he taught, the house has period furnishings and a reproduction of Jackson's vegetable garden. Youngsters are given a small slate listing household items to find, such as the upright desk where Jackson stood to prepare his lessons or his razor resting on the bedroom bureau. There's also a museum shop on the premises.

HORSE-DRAWN CARRIAGE TOURS OF HISTORIC LEXINGTON (all ages)

Headquartered at the Visitors Center, 106 East Washington Street; (540) 463–5647. Open daily April through October. Admission.

Children who don't have the attention span or don't like to walk through houses may brighten up at the prospect of a narrated ride on a horse-drawn carriage. The tour passes by the Jackson House, the restored historic downtown district, Washington and Lee University, Lee Chapel, the historic residential district, and the Stonewall Jackson Memorial Cemetery.

GHOST TOURS OF LEXINGTON (all ages)

Leaves from the Visitors Center, 106 East Washington Street; (540) 348–1080. Tours run from late May through October.

Experience the eerie transformation of the charming city of Lexington after the sun goes down. This walking tour lasts about one hour and thirty minutes and begins at 8:30 P.M. Reservations advised.

VIRGINIA HORSE CENTER (all ages)

On State Highway 39 west near the intersection of Interstate 64 and Interstate 81; (540) 463–2194. Web address: www.horsecenter.org. Open year-round, shows on selected dates. Admission.

Call ahead to see if there's anything special going on during your visit. This nearly 400-acre center presents horse shows throughout the year and also offers English and Western riding demonstrations, rodeos, and drill team exhibitions, as well as miniature horse shows and pony club shows.

Annual Events

JULY

Rockbridge Regional Fair, *mid-July at the Virginia Horse Center; (540) 463–6263.* This festival has lumberjacks, horses, art, a rodeo, and an antique car show, as well as food and music.

Lexington Hot Air Balloon Rally and Fourth of July Celebration, *at the VMI parade grounds; (540) 463–3777.* Enjoy hot-air balloon rides, tethered balloon rides, food, games, and entertainment. Fireworks on the Fourth cap off the two-day event.

AUGUST

Rockbridge Community Festival, *late August. Check with the Lexington Visitors Center for more information; (540) 463–3777.* The community gathers together in the streets of Lexington to celebrate and enjoy the summer with crafts, food, and entertainment.

JUNE, JULY, AND AUGUST

Lexington Alive, *most Fridays in June, July, and August; (540) 463–7191.* Summer concerts in Davidson Park.

SEPTEMBER

Annual Labor Day Festival in Glen Maury Park; *(540) 463–3777.*

Annual Rockbridge Mountain Music and Dance Festival, *Glen Maury Park; (540) 463–3777.*

DECEMBER

Downtown Lexington Holiday Parade.

Where to Eat

Harbs' Bistro, 19 West Washington Street; (540) 464–1900. Open for breakfast and lunch Tuesday through Saturday. A casual cafe, Harbs' has a patio for outdoor dining in nice weather. At breakfast select from homemade muffins or freshly baked croissants; lunch brings a wide selection of sandwiches. Children's portions. $–$$

Sweet Things Ice Cream Shoppe, 106 West Washington Street; (540) 463–6055. Open daily. Take a milkshake, sundae, or frozen yogurt break at this dessert haven where the ice cream and cones are homemade. $

Wilson–Walker House, 30 North Main Street; (540) 463–3020. Open Tuesday through Saturday for lunch and dinner. Reservations requested. This 1820s home, decorated with period antiques, serves Southern-influenced cuisine. Children's menu available. $$–$$$.

Country Café, 1476 West Faulkner Highway, Natural Bridge Station; (540) 291–2843. Breakfast, lunch, and dinner daily. Sandwich and full dinner menu, homemade biscuits, salads, desserts, 1950s soda fountain, and children's menu. $–$$

Where to Stay

Llewellyn Lodge, 603 South Main Street; (540) 463–3235 or (800) 882–1145. Web address: www.LLODGE. com. A bed-and-breakfast choice for families with kids age 10 or older, this brick colonial-style house offers a room with a separate sitting area and television (just in case your kids can't miss their favorite shows). The lodge is known for its delicious breakfasts, as well as its guided fly-fishing trips and hiking trips around the area.

Maple Hall, U.S. Highway 11, 7 miles north of Lexington; (540) 463–6693 or

(877) 463–2044. If your kids are older (teens), well-behaved, and awed by manor houses try Maple Hall. This 1850-plantation on fifty-six acres features antiques-furnished rooms, including some suites. A fishing pond, outdoor pool, tennis court, and 3-mile hiking trail provide ample recreation.

Country Inn and Suites, 875 North Lee Highway, Lexington; (540) 464–9000 or (800) 456–4000. A new hotel offering complimentary continental breakfast, indoor pool, exercise room, in-room refrigerator, and coffeemaker.

For More Information

Lexington Visitors Center, 106 East Washington Street, Lexington, VA 22450; (540) 463–3777. Web address: www. lexingtonvirginia.com. Open daily. The center has walking tour brochures.

Bath County

The drive to Bath County, some 40 miles from Lexington along State Highway 39, includes the former stagecoach route into Lexington, whose scenic highlight is the 3-mile-long Goshen Pass. This pleasant drive winds through the mountains along the Maury River. There are no incorporated towns and no traffic lights in Bath County, but there are several small communities. For centuries visitors—especially the socially prominent and ambitious—have ventured to Warm Springs for the thermal waters sheltered in eighteenth-century bathhouses. Urbanites are still coming for relaxation. The Homestead, an upscale resort, offers fine dining and family activities.

THE HOMESTEAD RESORT (all ages)

U.S. Highway Route 220, Hot Springs; (540) 839–1766 or (800) 838–1766. Web address: www.thehomestead.com.

Soaking, supping, or simply relaxing is easy here. This year-round resort, long favored by the rich, politically influential (including presidents), and famous, offers families lots of recreational possibilities, including a snowboard park. Most activities cost extra, so a stay here can get pricey, especially for an active family. Adults can reenergize at the expanded spa, which employs the county's famed healing waters in a variety of tub and rub combinations. Kids and teens can receive facials as part of the kids' spa program. In season families enjoy golf, tennis, mountain biking, fly-fishing, horseback riding and pony riding for smaller children, skiing, and ice skating. Outdoor activities include paintball games, hay rides with campfires, sunset hikes, and a rope-climbing course, as well as a new outdoor pool.

The Homestead KidsClub, for ages 3 to 12, operates year-round from 9:00 A.M. to 4:00 P.M. Monday through Saturday, evening dinners from 6:30 to 9:30 P.M. and 9:00 A.M. to 1:00 P.M. on Sunday. Activities include computer games, arts and crafts, science projects, kite flying, pottery making, swimming, pole fishing at the Children's Pond, and hiking. Homestead offers package deals for families during the off-season that include KidsClub for **Free**; otherwise, there is a charge.

Shops include the Homestead Market, with fresh foods and upscale gourmet items, and Fiddlesticks, a toy shop that also features specialty ice cream snacks.

HOMESTEAD SKI AREA

U.S. Highway Route 220, Hot Springs; (540) 839–1766 or (800) 838–1766. Web address: www.thehomestead.com.

In winter, the Homestead Resort's Ski Area sells lift tickets on a first-come basis, but resort guests have the option of purchasing ski packages to avoid the lines. There are nine slopes and trails covering forty-five acres, with a Bunny School for children ages 5 to 11. The skiing here is basic and the resort also offers snowboarding and snow tubing.

NATURAL BRIDGE (TT)

Take exit 175 or exit 180 from Interstate 81 to get to Natural Bridge, which is located on U.S. Highway 11; (800) 533–1410 or (540) 291–2121. Web address: www.naturalbridgeva.com. Admission.

Natural Bridge can be a pleasant day trip from the Homestead Resort or a half-day trip from Lexington (it's in the same Rockbridge County, which, in fact, was named for this rock bridge). It also makes a good stop on the way to Roanoke. The bridge is a limestone arch, 215 feet high and 90 feet wide, that has been carved by Cedar Creek, which flows beneath it. It contains 450,000 cubic feet of rock, and its estimated weight is about 36,000 tons. Like almost everything else in Virginia, the Natural Bridge has a historic past. George Washington surveyed it for Lord Fairfax (you can see where he was believed to have carved his initials), and Thomas Jefferson, so taken by its beauty, bought the arch and the surrounding land.

The arch is the centerpiece for a complex of attractions. Natural Bridge of Virginia puts on "The Drama of Creation" a nightly light show, and has caverns, a hotel, and a museum (540–291–2121 or 800–533–1410) whose 150 lifelike replicas of historic people take you on a three-dimensional trip through early American history. Kids will enjoy the forty-five-minute self-guided tour of the factory where visitors can see the wax figures being made.

Besides the bridge itself (which has guides on site to answer questions and make presentations throughout the day), the most interesting attraction here may be the **Monacan Indian Living History Village,** reached by a beautiful Nature Trail (complete with waterfall and caves). Children are invited to participate in canoe-building, shelter construction, hide tanning, mat and rope weaving, fishing, and lots more. The Monacans are one of Virginia's oldest Native American tribes and they welcome the opportunity to explain and demonstrate their culture to visitors. At the

Fall Festival every year, visitors are welcome to learn songs and dances and to sample Monacan vegetables grown at the village.

There is also a Civil War Living History encampment every spring and fall, and in 2002 there are plans to establish several butterfly gardens along the nature trail.

THE NATURAL BRIDGE CAVERNS (all ages)

U.S. Highway 11; (800) 533–1410 or (540) 291–2121. Open daily, closed mid-December through mid-March. Admission.

Descend three levels on steps and inclines. The lowest level is thirty-four stories below the top. On the forty-five-minute guided tour, you see one of the largest flowstone formations on the East Coast. Older kids might like to hear that some persons believe these caverns are haunted. The temperature is 54 degrees year-round, so bring a light sweater or jacket.

VIRGINIA SAFARI PARK

229 Safari Lane, Natural Bridge; (540) 291–3205. Open daily April through October, weekends March through November.

Drive through the 180 acres and free-roaming elk, bison, zebra, antelope, and ostrich come close to your vehicle. Little one enjoy the petting zoo.

THE WILDERNESS CANOE COMPANY

U.S. 11 and State Highway 130, Natural Bridge; (540) 291–2295. Web address: wilderness-canoe.com.

Canoe rentals for self-guided trips and some guided canoe expeditions. Overnight trips use a fifty-acre basecamp from which you hike and canoe.

Roanoke Valley

Roanoke, 54 miles south of Lexington, is a great town for families, offering recreational and educational attractions.

CENTER IN THE SQUARE (all ages)

One Market Square; (540) 342–5700. Web address: www.centerinthesquare. com.

This five-story renovated warehouse located on the Historic Farmers' Market houses museums, performing arts (such as the Roanoke Ballet Theatre and Opera Roanoke), and gift shops. Check the web site for a calendar of events.

SCIENCE MUSEUM OF WESTERN VIRGINIA (all ages) (TT)

Center in the Square, corner of Campbell and Market Streets, Levels 1, 4, and 5; (540) 342–5710. Web address: www.smwv.org. Open Tuesday through Saturday. Admission.

Tops on the list of attractions at Center in the Square is the Science Museum. Hands-on explorations range from broadcasting weather on closed-circuit television to fingering critters in a Chesapeake Bay "touch tank" and playing an environmentally themed computer game. In the Geology Gallery kids can unearth clues about how old the Earth is and in Body Tech explore the body's circulatory system. The Science Arcade is an interactive exploration of color, sound, and light. Throughout the year, national touring exhibitions might include anything from giant robotic dinosaurs to laser shows.

The William B. Hopkins Planetarium, part of the Science Museum, has star shows, lectures, concerts, and movies, and there's a MegaDome Theatre with a 40-foot dome and a wrap-around screen with surround sound. The museum shop has a good array of educational toys and games with kid-appeal.

THE ART MUSEUM OF WESTERN VIRGINIA (ages 5 and up)

Center in the Square, Levels 1 and 2; (540) 342–5760. Web address: www. artmuseumroanoke.org. Open every day except Monday.

The museum's collection includes modern Appalachian folk art, a genre that never fails to impress children. But the real treat for kids is:

ART VENTURE (ages 3 and up)

Open Saturday and Sunday, except major holidays. No reservations necessary.

This **Free** 2,000-square-foot space on the first floor of Center in the Square (directly below the Art Museum) offers kids a chance to explore their creativity and imagination. They can make their own three-color print, create a circus using puppets and costumes, make clay animals, and listen to stories told by Pocahontas, Captain John Smith, and Powhatan. Eight interactive stations offer open-ended hands-on activities related to the Art Museum's collection, helping parents introduce art to their children.

HISTORY MUSEUM AND HISTORICAL SOCIETY OF WESTERN VIRGINIA (ages 5 and up) (TT)

Center in the Square, Levels 3; (540) 342–5770). Web address: www. history-museum.org. Open daily except Monday. Admission.

This museum presents the area's cultural heritage. Peruse prehistoric artifacts, Native American relics, colonial costumes, and an 1890s dry-goods store. "A Crossroads of History" features a Native American wigwam, a land grant deed signed by Thomas Jefferson, Civil War surgical implements, and a 1925 Marshall & Wendell baby grand player piano. In "Ships & Shipmates," visitors learn about Roanoke Valley's maritime legacy. Kids can try their hand at knot tying, map reading, raising a sail, and sounding the boatswain's calls. The museum's store, The History Shop, sells old-fashioned toys, handmade quilts, historical maps, and books.

VIRGINIA MUSEUM OF TRANSPORTATION (ages 3 to 9) (TT)

303 Norfolk Avenue; (540) 342–5670. Web address: www.vmt.org. Open daily; closed on Monday in January and February. Admission.

Located in a restored railway freight station next to the Norfolk Southern main line downtown, this museum emphasizes rail transportation as Roanoke got its start as a railroad town. The collection includes examples from railroad's golden past such as steam and vintage electric locomotives and classic diesels. Kids step into a caboose, walk through a railway post-office car, and try out several hands-on exhibits, including one that shows how a steam engine works. Although the museum is primarily devoted to rail, other eye-catchers include aviation exhibits as well as horse-drawn buggies, buses, and streetcars. There's also a 1920 Buick touring car (a new Automobile Gallery is in the works) and a 1942 Ford/American LaFrance Fire Engine. Every weekend special **Free** tours of the museum can include hands-on activities such as learning Morse code and taking part in a scavenger hunt. Check for special events and performances.

ROANOKE STAR/OVERLOOK (all ages)

Off the Blue Ridge Parkway at milepost 120; follow Jefferson Street to Walnut Avenue.

The city's most visible attraction, the 100-foot-high illuminated star made out of steel, concrete, and 2,000 feet of neon tubing shines from the top of Mill Mountain, less than a ten-minute drive from downtown.

MILL MOUNTAIN ZOO (all ages)

Off U.S. Highway 220 south, milepost 120 on the Blue Ridge Parkway; (540) 343–3241. Web address: www.mmzoo.org. Open daily except for Christmas. Admission.

Along with its great view of the valley, the zoo exhibits fifty species of exotic and native animals, such as red pandas, a Siberian tiger, hawks, snow leopards, and reptiles. Educational programming and fun can be found in "Camp Wildcat," a discovery area. Young children particularly like the goats in the "contact area," which is generally open weekends only. There are picnic facilities on the grounds and, in summer, a concession stand. If you visit in the summer, check the schedule of live programs in the zoo's amphitheater.

 VIRGINIA'S EXPLORE PARK (all ages) (TT)

Roanoke River Parkway, 1.5 miles from milepost 115 on the Blue Ridge Parkway; (540) 427–1800 or (800) 842–9163. Web address: www.explorepark.org. Open Wednesday through Sunday, May through October. Admission.

This 1,100-acre living history museum recreates three Blue Ridge settlements, ranging in time from 1671 to 1850. The 1671 Native American Village recreates aboriginal woodland culture and lifestyle. At the 1740 settler's cabin, visitors learn about gardening, tool making, cabin repairs, and hunting. The 1850 settlement takes you to a one-room schoolhouse, a blacksmith's shop, and a farmstead. Costumed interpreters do chores and tend to true-to-the-period farm animals and crops, including antique pear and apple trees. The Historic Brugh Tavern offers lunch and dinner in an authentic nineteenth-century tavern setting. In addition, there are 12 miles of mountain bike trails and 6 miles of hiking trails, plus fishing, canoeing and kayaking, and picnic facilities.

ARTS COUNCIL OF THE BLUE RIDGE

20 East Church Avenue, Level 1; (540) 342–5790. Web address: www. theartscouncil.org. Open Tuesday through Friday.

Use this resource center to see if anything is going on during your visit. Regular programs include the Roanoke City Art Show, the High School art exhibition, and Real Art/Real Cheap. A toll-free Culture Hot Line helps out-of-town visitors plan their trip; call (877) SWVTODO; locally (540) 224–1248.

MILL MOUNTAIN THEATRE

*Center in the Square, downtown Roanoke; (540) 342–5740 or (800) 317–
6455. Web address: www.millmountain.org.*

This professional year-round theater offers children's and family
musicals, dramas, comedies, and regional premieres on two stages,
Tuesday through Sunday. There are regularly scheduled signed and
audio-described performances, and both theaters are handicapped
accessible. Coming in 2002, *The Jungle Book.*

DIXIE CAVERNS AND POTTERY SHOP (ages 4 and up)

*5753 West Main Street, Salem; (540) 380–2085. Web address: www.
dixiecaverns.com. Open daily year-round. Admission.*

If you haven't had your share of caverns yet, take Interstate 81 South
to exit 132 and go to Dixie Caverns. On the forty-five-minute tour see
the Cathedral Room (the main area), as well as the Wedding Bell and
Turkey Wing named after key formations. The temperature is a constant
56 degrees, so grab the sweaters. Souvenirs, if your kids haven't yet
spent all their allowance, are at the miner's shop.

BOOKER T. WASHINGTON'S BIRTHPLACE (ages 7 and up)

*On Virginia Highway 22, 6 miles east of Burnt Chimney (540) 721–2094. Web
address: www.nps.gov/bowa. Open daily except Thanksgiving, Christmas, and New
Year's Day.*

Booker T. Washington was born into slavery in the kitchen of these
slave quarters. He lived here until the age of 9, when he was freed by the
Emancipation Proclamation. Later Washington became a respected educator and founder of the Tuskegee Institute in Alabama, as well as an
adviser to presidents. Start at the visitors center with a fourteen-minute
slide show on Washington's life. An historic 0.25-mile-long trail loops
through this 224-acre restored plantation and leads to several reconstructed buildings, which include a kitchen cabin (showing what the
kitchen looked like when Washington was born) and the tobacco barn
(the cash crop during Washington's days). During the summer, children
can hear African folktales and see living history demonstrations of the
times with costumed interpreters.

HARRISON MUSEUM OF AFRICAN AMERICAN CULTURE

*523 Harrison Avenue; (540) 345–4818. Web address: www.roanoke.com/
harrisonmuseum. Open Tuesday through Sunday.*

Located on the ground level of the 1916 Harrison School, the first high school for African Americans in southwestern Virginia, this museum celebrates African-American culture through both local and regional historic exhibitions, art displays, and special events throughout the year, including the Henry Street Festival in September.

Annual Events

MAY

Roanoke Festival in the Park, *around Memorial Day; (540) 342–2640.* Features music, sports, art, and food at a variety of parks and venues throughout town. This ten-day event draws hundreds of thousands of people to the valley.

Annual Sidewalk Art Show. *(540) 342–5760.* Works by hundreds of regional artists displayed in downtown Roanoke, sponsored by the Art Museum of Western Virginia.

Salem Fair & Exposition. *(540) 375–3004.* Rides, games, food, and music.

JULY

Commonwealth Games of Virginia, *mid-July; (540) 343–0987.* An amateur sports festival for all ages. Recognized by the U.S. Olympic Committee and National Congress of State Games, these are Virginia's Olympics. In the past, over 10,000 athletes have competed in forty-five sports. Gold, silver, and bronze medals are awarded.

AUGUST

Virginia Mountain Peach Festival, *first Friday and Saturday of August; (540) 342–2028.* Peach shakes, sundaes, cobbler, and shortcakes, accompanied by live entertainment.

Annual Vinton Old-Time Bluegrass Festival and Competition, *mid-August; (540) 983–0613.* Features four days of bluegrass, vendors, crafts, kiddie rides, and more.

SEPTEMBER

Appalachian Folk Festival, *at Virginia's Explore Park; (540) 427–1800.* Dedicated to celebrating traditional Appalachian music and folkways.

OCTOBER

Blue Ridge Folklife Festival, *fourth Saturday of the month; (540) 365–4416.* Virginia's largest celebration of authentic regional traditions—crafts, music, food, and the skills of working dogs, mules, and horses.

Where to Eat

Homeplace, *4968 Catawba Drive in Catawba; (540) 384–7252. Open Thursday through Saturday for dinner and Sunday for lunch and dinner.* The family-style meals feature fried chicken, hot biscuits, and mashed potatoes and gravy. $

Market Building, *32 Market Square (directly across from the visitors center); (540) 774–1641.* For a kid-pleasing meal, take a short stroll to the **Market Building.** This historic building, once the city's meat market, now sports an international food court serving kids' favorites such as tacos, burgers, and pizza.

Sunnybrook Inn Restaurant, *7342 Plantantion Road, exit 146 off I–81; (540) 366–4555 or (800) 586–0088. Lunch* and dinner, Tuesday through Sunday. Located in a large, white farmhouse built in 1912, this inviting restaurant uses traditional recipes (some one hundred years old) from the valley of Western Virginia, plus home-cooked favorites like country ham and golden fried chicken. Children's menu. $$–$$$

Carlos Brazilian International Cuisine, *312 Market Street; (540) 345–7661. Lunch and dinner, Monday through Saturday.* If you're in the mood for something a little different, like Paella Valenciana (seafood, chicken, pork, and sausage with rice and herbs), this might be the place. Kids will enjoy trying Guarana, a popular Brazilian soft drink. $$–$$$

Where to Stay

Best Inn Civic Center, *501 Orange Avenue; (540) 342–8961 or (800) 237–8466.* Its downtown location makes this a convenient base from which to explore Roanoke. A pebbled courtyard surrounds the outdoor pool.

AmeriSuites, *5040 Valley View Boulevard, Roanoke; (540) 366–4700 or (800) 833–1516.* Complimentary continental breakfast; indoor pool; refrigerator, microwave, and coffeemaker in rooms; and a fitness center, located at the Valley View Mall, with shopping and food court.

Dixie Caverns Campground, *5753 West Main Street, Salem; (540) 380–2085. Open year-round.* Hookups include electricity, water, cable TV; showers and dump station.

The Patrick Henry Hotel, *617 South Jefferson; (540) 345–8811 or (800) 537–8483.* Located in a circa-1925 building downtown, this hotel has 117 rooms with kitchenettes. Passes to the YMCA for pool and fitness facilities are available.

For More Information

The Roanoke Valley Convention and Visitors Bureau Visitor Information Center, *114 Market Street, Roanoke, VA 24011; (800) 635–5535* or *(540) 342–6025. Web address: www. visitroanokeva.com. The center is open from 9:00 A.M. to 5:00 P.M. seven days a week.*

Tidewater and Hampton Roads

As Washingtonians, we have been escaping to Virginia for years. My family's favorite let's-have-fun foray takes us through Tidewater, an area that combines the earliest history of the American colonies with such hands-on high-tech fun as a nautical center and such sure-to-please vacation spots as Virginia Beach.

Colonial Williamsburg, Jamestown, and Yorktown, known collectively as Virginia's historic triangle, are connected by the Colonial Parkway. As you tour the area, you and your children will see the progression of American history from the first colonial settlement at Jamestown to the flowering of colonial culture and the beginnings of a revolution at Williamsburg to the final triumph over the British at Yorktown.

From here the route leads to Newport News, Hampton, and Norfolk before ending at the sandy shores of Virginia Beach. The region's abundance of family attractions, including Busch Gardens Williamsburg and its sister theme park, Water Country USA, has led this area to be dubbed Virginia's "kids' corner." A long weekend, better yet, a week, in this area is how we like our colonial history, sprinkled with science and salted with sea spray—and in summer—spiced by roller coasters and lightened by water parks.

Candyce's Top Picks
for Fun in the Tidewater Region

1. Colonial Williamsburg
2. Busch Gardens Williamsburg
3. Nauticus, the National Maritime Center, Norfolk
4. Virginia Beach

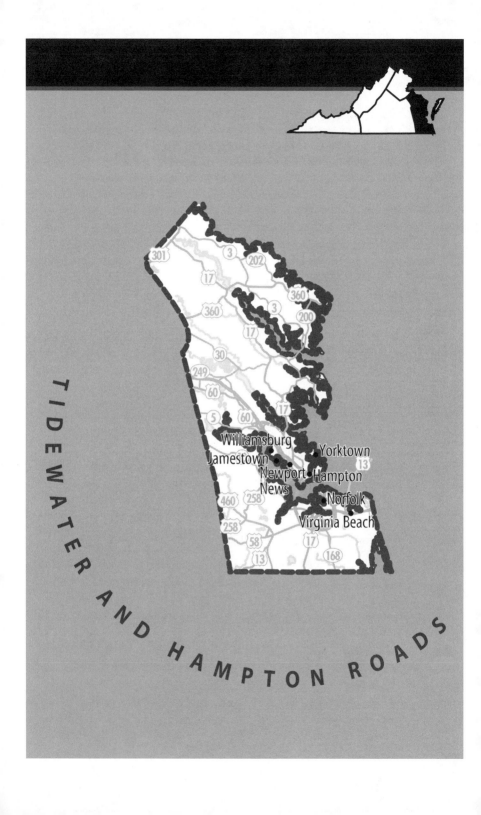

TIDEWATER AND HAMPTON ROADS

Colonial Williamsburg

Colonial Williamsburg is about 150 miles south of Washington, D.C., approximately midway between Richmond and Norfolk on Interstate 64.

Colonial Williamsburg is certainly among America's most well-known living history museums. The area served as the capital of Virginia, England's oldest, largest, most populous, and richest colony from 1699 to 1776. How Williamsburg's leading citizens felt made a great deal of difference in the struggle toward independence. This former Virginia capital bred independent politics and drew revolutionaries such as Thomas Jefferson and Patrick Henry. Colonial Williamsburg recreates life in Virginia as it existed in the 1770s, just before the Revolutionary War. Williamsburg, once the political and cultural center of the new world, has more than 500 buildings on its 173 acres, of which eighty-eight homes, shops, public buildings, and taverns are recreations of original buildings. Two on-site museums provide glimpses into the arts and crafts of the era, and Carter's Grove Plantation includes an interpretation of slave history.

Williamsburg Travel Tips

Colonial Williamsburg is the kind of place you can visit many times because what you do depends on the season and the age and interests of your children.

Historic Williamsburg lets you see life as the colonists did. By visiting the powder magazine, courthouse, wigmaker, milliner, apothecary, shoemaker, and other trade shops, you get a sense of the realities of eighteenth-century life. Most historic buildings and exhibits are open from 9:00 A.M. to 5:00 P.M. In 2001, Colonial Williamsburg celebrated its 75th anniversary, and some of the special programs commemorating that event are continuing into 2002.

The best way to make the most of a visit and to see the beyond the area's commercialism is to take part in several special programs. During these you get to interact with "a person of the past." The clash between the characters' eighteenth-century world and ours makes the time travel lively. Check the *Visitors Companion,* available at any Colonial Williamsburg ticket outlet, for times. At selected times you can enjoy activities such as meeting a printer at his office, listening to a grandmother tells stories about her life, and finding out about a soldier's life at a military encampment. Favorite programs of ours include Welcome, Little Stranger, an interactive talk about colonial clothing for kids at the Milliner and Order In the Court, trials at the courthouse.

CHILDREN'S PROGRAMS (ages 5 to 12) (TT)

Special children's programs allow kids to experience Colonial Williamsburg as a child of that era by providing interactive fun. During the day, kids can help the colonial fire brigade put out a fire, or march in musket drills. Evenings bring a pirate trial, candlelight tours (the only ones that take you inside homes and trade shops), or ghost stories. These programs are open to children ages 5 to 12 but are likely to be best appreciated by kids between 5 and 10. Advance reservations are not necessary. Additional fees required; inquire at the visitors center.

- **Remember Me.** Children spend the evening with the slave Paris, an old man recalling his life in Africa, his enslavement, and how he's managed his cultural and spiritual survival.

- **Bill and Betsy's Pirate Adventure.** Bill, Betsy, and their gang rescue Granny Epps from a band of fun-loving pirates.

- **The Military Encampment.** For physically active children, a chance to "enlist" and experience eighteenth-century military life, with marching, musket drills, and a chance to learn how a cannon is fired, all in an authentic Revolutionary War campsite.

- **Peyton Randolph Kitchen,** located behind the Peyton Randolph House in the Historic Area. Children are invited to listen in on discussions about the Randolph family and their newly reconstructed kitchen. There are also a dairy and a smokehouse to explore.

- **Musical Traditions of African Americans.** Children and parents can join in the storytelling traditions of early African-Americans through dance and vocal and instrumental music.

Older children will enjoy The Subject is Murder: Williamsburg's Most Wanted, an evening program in the candlelit General Court in the Capitol. Audience participation is encouraged as Williamsburg's residents deliberate the guilt or innocence of some of the most notorious accused murderers of colonial Virginia.

Williamsburg Travel Tips
Before coming to Colonial Williamsburg, check out its web site at www.colonialwilliamsburg.org and the section called "Historic Almanack." Here you'll find biographies of the residents and historic figures you'll encounter, details about the buildings and archaeological excavations, and information about the roles of women, children, and African-Americans in the 1700s.

LEGENDS OF THE PAST (ages 10 and up)

This program allows visitors to "drop in" on several eighteenth-century characters. Lanterns light the way, partly for atmosphere and partly so that guests won't step in the authentic horse poop. In the taverns you may meet Mrs. Jonathan Edwards, a merchant's

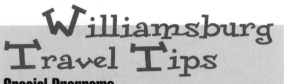

Williamsburg Travel Tips

Special Programs Take part in the historic area's special programs. These make history fun by putting the "living" in living history. At these regularly scheduled events, costumed interpreters interact with guests.

wife, who relates a Cherokee legend of how the Milky Way came to be; a tipsy sailor who tells a tall tale of Blackbeard, booty, and pirates; and Emma Johnston, who gossips about a woman who puts on airs by wearing French fashions.

WYTHE HOUSE (ages 4 and up)

The house's back yard is the setting for hands-on activities such as stitch books, water coloring, puzzles, and writing. At the stable and laundry, you can learn how the Wythe family traveled, raised livestock, and perfected household crafts.

DUKE OF GLOUCESTER STREET (all ages)

A stroll along this main street conveys the ambience of this bustling town. Pause to peek into the stores, chat with costumed interpreters, and—a kid favorite—shop for keepsakes from clay wig curlers to quill pens.

THE COURTHOUSE (ages 8 and up)

With kids middle-school age or older, a good choice is the special program, "Order In the Court." When the clerk at the courthouse calls out for jurors, if you are, as required by law, a man, over 21, Protestant, white, and a landowner, you can serve. Others can be plaintiffs, defendants, and witnesses. Cases vary. On one visit we observed a husband, whose tipsy wife sang a ditty belittling the king, receive a two-pound fine. The poor man, played by a visitor reading from cue cards, complained that such a fee is beyond his means. How then is justice served?

The judge ordered the wife to be lashed to a stool and dunked six times. "As you grow wet, may you grow wise," he intoned. As the guests filed out, a teenage girl in the audience wondered why the husband wasn't dunked instead.

Williamsburg Travel Tips

In the Lamplight Be sure to walk through the historic area at night. In the lamplight it's easy to imagine that inside the frame and brick houses women are stirring kettles over open-hearth fireplaces and schoolchildren are puzzling out their "'rithmetic" by candlelight.

THE POWDER MAGAZINE (ages 4 and up)

Kids like touring this building, built in 1715, to see where shot, powder, and flints were stored.

THE GUARDHOUSE (ages 4 and up)

This reconstructed building was used in the colonial period to store military equipment such as tents.

THE SHOPS (all ages)

A visit to the harness and saddlemaker, apothecary, and shoemaker presents the everyday necessities of eighteenth-century life. Favorite stops of ours are:

- The **Greenhow Store:** This store, we think, offers the most interesting assortment of allowance-affordable souvenir goodies reflecting the colonial era. Kids can buy items such as wax animals, scented soaps, chalk, ostrich plumes, initial seals, and clay wig curlers.
- The **Milliner:** Along with providing hats for ladies, the milliner created clothes for women and children. On display are gowns, bonnets, bolts of cloth, and children's dresses (also worn by boys until they were about 4 or 5 years old and graduated to britches).

Check the schedule so you can show up for the special program "Welcome, Little Stranger," good fun for kids of all ages and informative as well. When James Slate, a tailor at the Milliner's discusses children's clothing, kids in the shop make those "I-can't-believe-it" faces. Mothers (or servants) used "diapers," or linen cloths, to fold "clouts," what we think of as diapers, fastening them with straight pins. In reply to a visitor's question about safety pins, Mr. Slate, after a long perplexed look, says, "Indeed, they are safe, Madam, if fastened correctly." We also learn that toddlers put on "pudding caps," a kind of padded, open helmet to protect their noggins from bumps, and that even tots wore "stays," those corsetlike contraptions.

Amazing Williamsburg Facts

Declaration of Independence On July 25, 1776, a huge crowd gathered outside the courthouse to hear the reading of the Declaration of Independence. Cannons were fired to signal the crowd's approval.

PUBLIC GAOL (ages 4 and up)

For a look at another aspect of Williamsburg society, visit these small dark cells with their shackles and leg irons that once held pirates, runaway slaves, Indians, debtors, and the mentally ill. "Family Life at the Public Gaol" tells you about the lives of the gaoler and his family.

THE GEDDY HOUSE AND FOUNDRY (ages 9 and up)

Check out this site, which includes a silversmith shop, a home, and a foundry. There are hands-on activities in the yard, and at the foundry visitors can watch tradesmen craft brass, bronze, silver, and pewter castings.

BENJAMIN POWELL HOUSE (ages 5 and up)

You may come upon the teenage daughters weeding the garden, practicing cross-stitch embroidery with their mother, or taking lessons with their music teacher. Here also meet Benjamin and Sarah, children of Mrs. Powell's personal slave, Rose. Listen to the boys speak in dialect, and watch as they assist with the house laundry. Adults and children can lend a hand with these eighteenth-century household tasks.

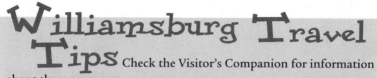

Williamsburg Travel Tips

Check the Visitor's Companion for information about these programs:

- Dance Our Dearest Diversion. "Virginians will dance or die," wrote a diarist in the 1770s. Learn the newest (circa 1776) dance steps and put your best foot forward in the candlelit Capitol.

- Highlife Below Stairs. A delightful eighteenth-century comedy about a master who disguises himself as a servant to discover what is actually going on "below stairs" in his own household. As you might expect, it is nothing like he imagined.

- Tryin' To Get Some Mother Wit. Three African-American women share advice on surviving slavery. Presented in Hennage Auditorium. (This one is too strong for younger children.)

- Clandestine Marriage. A delightful comedy in which two young lovers struggle to keep their marriage a secret, when all the while, their families are attempting to buy and sell their relations to gain wealth and respectability.

- Puttin' Slavin' Aside. Christmas was one of the few times the bonds of slavery were loosened. Guests help or watch as a holiday meal is prepared over an open fire; they talk with single men as they plan to meet their sweethearts or listen in as a father reunites with his young son.

THE CAPITOL (ages 5 and up)

The House of Burgesses met in the east wing. The landowners of each county elected two members to represent them, plus Jamestown, Williamsburg, Norfolk, and the College of William and Mary each had one representative. The Council, which met in the west wing, consisted of twelve leading colonists appointed for life by the king. This imposing building was the site for many of Patrick Henry's impassioned speeches for independence. Check the *Visitors Companion* to see if Mr. Henry and his fiery revolutionaries are speaking during your visit.

GOVERNOR'S PALACE (ages 5 and up)

Decorated with bayonets, muskets, swords, and rifles to reinforce the sense of the Crown's power, the twenty-five-room palace is a highlight of any tour. The finery includes gilt mirrors, black-walnut paneling, marble floors, hand-tooled leather wall coverings, and mahogany and cherry furniture. Guides talk about the last governor, the Earl of Dunmore, and the life he and his wife and six children led. The governor sent his family back to England after just two years in Williamsburg because of the brewing revolution. The tour ends in the ballroom. Thomas Jefferson once danced here and

Williamsburg Travel Tips

Summer In summer Colonial Williamsburg often teams up with other area attractions to offer combined lodging and admission tickets at a reduced fee. Inquire about this when you make your reservations.

didn't leave, reports say, "until the sun came up in the garden." Be sure to allow time to walk through the palace garden. Kids especially like the holly maze. Families are encouraged to join in playing hoops, lawn bowling, pick-up sticks, tops, checkers, and other Colonial-era games.

Colonial Williamsburg and Slavery

Colonial Williamsburg is a good place to talk to your kids about slavery. After downplaying or downright ignoring the issue, Colonial Williamsburg began a Black History program in 1979 that culminated in the creation of "Enslaving Virginia." Day and evening programs (check the *Visitor's Companion* for schedule) explore the impact of slavery on the lives of Colonial Williamsburg's African-American and white residents on the eve of the American Revolution. The reenactments are realistic and may be too frightening for children under 7, but it is a great opportunity for parents and older children to discuss the raw truth about slavery and its legacy in our society today.

Visitors follow several African-American characters through their day, experiencing their pride, fear, and the consequences of their actions. You can meet slaves at several historic buildings, including the Benjamin Powell House, Wetherburn's Tavern, and Carter's Grove Plantation (8 miles from the historic area). A two-hour walking tour of the historic area, "The Other Half Tour," highlights sites important to blacks and talks about the lives of blacks. In February, Black History Month, there are additional lectures, storytellers, and activities.

THE DEWITT WALLACE GALLERY (ages 8 and up)

325 Francis Street, entrance through the Public Hospital at the corner of Francis and North Henry Street, Williamsburg; (757) 220–7724.

This is home to Colonial Williamsburg's art masterworks. More than 8,000 seventeenth-century through early-nineteenth-century decorative delights, from silver and ceramics to linen and lace, are presented here. Although this facility may appeal more to older children, don't avoid it; instead, find something that will catch your child's interest. Go on a treasure hunt here: Let your kids follow their fancies through a door and see what they find. Does your child take music lessons? Then locate the case of eighteenth-century instruments. Is your fifth-grader learning about geography? Browse the gallery of hand-colored colonial maps where the pink for Virginia bleeds all the way past the Mississippi River, and Indian names mark the territory of Michigan. Cafe on the premises.

Amazing Williamsburg Facts

During colonial times the average life expectancy for a white male was 50 to 55 years; for a black male 40 to 45 years; and for a white or a black woman, 25 to 35 years.

ABBY ALDRICH ROCKEFELLER FOLK ART CENTER (ages 5 and up)

307 South England Street, across from the Williamsburg Lodge, Williamsburg; (757) 220–7698.

Kids are intrigued by folk art with its simple lines, bright colors, and easily recognizable figures. More than 400 paintings and objects from the seventeenth through nineteenth centuries are on display. My family's favorites are the whimsical hog and cow weathervanes, the old-fashioned toys, and the portraits of children with fat cats and flower baskets. The ground floor and the outdoor sculpture garden display changing exhibits of contemporary folk art.

CARTER'S GROVE PLANTATION (ages 8 and up)

Located on U.S. 60, about 8 miles from the colonial area; (757) 229–1000, ext. 2973. Open daily March through December.

Take in the fourteen-minute slide presentation, *A Thing Called Time*, which provides a general overview of the plantation's 400 years. My family found the mansion, built by Carter Burwell in the 1750s and restored to its

Williamsburg Travel Tips

A Weekend is the length of a typical visit, although if you want to see nearby Jamestown, Yorktown, and the Busch Gardens theme park, consider a four- to five-day stay.

1920s appearance, boring. More interesting was the plantations's reconstructed **Slave Quarters.**

Although small, these reconstructed quarters reveal the darker side of plantation history. You can see the gang house, where as many as sixty slaves slept, and the slave master's house as well as corn cribs, garden plots, and chicken coops. Costumed interpreters talk with visitors about slavery, focusing on some of the brutalities but also emphasizing sly ways the slaves devised to cope. On one visit we learned that the slaves sang while working to communicate with one another. The verse "I see a buzzard flying high" meant the master was watching, and "little piglets wallowing in the mud" meant that the master's children were nearby.

The plantation site also is home to the **Winthrop Rockefeller Archaeological Museum.** This facility exhibits artifacts discovered on the property and also documents a seventeenth-century village, Wolstenholme Towne, destroyed by Indians in 1622, just three years after its founding. A partial reconstruction of the settlement includes a palisade fort, several homes, and a large barn.

Williamsburg Travel Tips

Williamsburg has a new ticket structure: The Day Pass (least expensive) is valid for one day for all daytime programs and exhibitions, ending with the Grand Event in the late afternoon, plus free parking. The Freedom Pass is valid for one full year and includes all of the above plus evening programs. The Liberty Pass is also valid for one full year and includes all of the above plus special events, a quarterly newsletter, and discounts on shopping, dining, golf, and paid evening programs.

Annual Events

JUNE

Reenactment of 1781, *end of June.* The British return and impose martial law on Colonial Williamsburg, reenacting the 1781 occupation. More than 250 military re-enactors converge on the Historic Area to encamp and drill.

JULY

Fourth of July. You and your family can celebrate the day with all the fervor of a newly independent nation. Enjoy an eighteenth-century garden party and a fireworks display.

JULY–AUGUST

Military Encampment, *summer.* This favorite event makes army folk out of tenderfoot visitors, kids included. After signing up with the Second Virginia Regiment, the new recruits practice drills, learn the bayonet lunge, present arms (using sticks instead of loaded muskets), and assist with cleaning and firing a cannon.

OCTOBER

Washington prepares for Yorktown. The general and his staff use Williamsburg as their base of operations to plan the siege of Yorktown in the fall of 1781. More than 150 military re-enactors encamp and drill, and General Washington talks about the war.

The language of Clothing. A new exhibit at the DeWitt Wallace Museum focuses on how clothes offer clues to understanding people of the past.

DECEMBER

Grand Illumination, *early December.* Winter not only brings fewer crowds than summer, but the colonial streets sport the festive decorations of the eighteenth century. It all begins with this event when fireworks, music, and entertainment mark the beginning of Colonial Williamsburg's Christmas season. Dance the minuet at a candlelight ball (book ahead for tickets), enjoy the carolers, and visit homes tastefully decorated with natural wreaths.

Carter's Grove Mansion, *December.* During Christmas this mansion, restored to a 1920s appearance, is turned out in the splendor of holidays past.

Where to Eat

Colonial Taverns, *within the historic area. Call to make reservations for all the Williamsburg taverns; (729) 229–1000.* Dining at the colonial taverns is popular, so your best bet is to make these reservations when you make your lodging reservations. If you haven't already made reservations for meals, however, do so at the visitors center. Even though the entrees are more adequate than memorable, the wooden tables aglow in candlelight and the costumed staff help transport you back 200 years. Such eighteenth-century southern staples as spoon bread and Carolina fish muddle (a stew) help evoke the era. For the less adventuresome, kid's menus offer hamburgers, fried chicken, and other friendly fare. Each tavern's cuisine (described below) varies and each serves some colonial dishes. $$–$$$.

Williamsburg Travel Tips Colonial Taverns When you book your lodging, make reservations to dine at one of the colonial taverns. We like to dine here the first night to get into the eighteenth-century spirit.

Campbell's Tavern, *120 Waller Street,* features seafood and such noteworthy dishes as clam chowder, jambalaya, and muddle—a tomato-based stew of shrimp, scallops, and fish fillets. Be sure to sample the spoon bread. $$$

Chowning's Tavern, *100 East Duke of Gloucester Street,* specializes in meat (pork chops, prime rib, pork rib, and steak) and is best known for its Brunswick stew. An evening program for adults includes the eighteenth-century gambling game Hazards. $$$

The King's Arms Tavern, *409 East Duke of Gloucester Street,* tends toward Southern fare such as Virginia baked ham, fried chicken, and peanut soup. $$$

Shield's Tavern, *417 East Duke of Gloucester Street*, features fowl plus some seafood items. Get your kids to sample the crayfish soup and such colonial desserts as Indian pudding, or syllabub, a whipped cream and lemon juice treat. Dishes are inspired by recipes from eighteenth- and early nineteenth-century cookbooks. $$$

Merchants Square, *Duke of Gloucester Street*. Adjacent to the historic area, Merchants Square offers a few cafes, many shops, and one really good restaurant, the Trellis.

The Trellis, *403 Duke of Gloucester Street; (757) 229–8610.* Award-winning chef Marcel Desaulniers is known for his creative cooking. At lunch a variety of affordable salads, sandwiches, and light fare are served. Dinner can be pricey, but the food is wonderful. Children will feel more comfortable at lunch, but the restaurant welcomes well-behaved children. Save room for the desserts, especially the chef's signature Death by Chocolate, a rich cakelike concoction that chocoholics "die for." $-$$$

NEARBY RESTAURANTS

Nearby Richmond Road offers a string of restaurants from fast-food to fine dining. Here's a listing of a few reliable family-friendly eateries.

The Whaling Company, *494 McLaws Circle; (757) 229–0275. Open for lunch and dinner.* Discount for early diners and a children's menu available. Fresh seafood is the specialty, and the decor is New England fishing village. $$

Ledo Pizza, *814 Capitol Landing Road; (757) 220–3791. Open for lunch and dinner.* Since 1955 this family-owned restaurant has been making pizza, subs, and pasta. Kids menu. Carry-out. $

Mama Steve's House of Pancakes, *1509 Richmond Road; (757) 229–7613. Open for breakfast and lunch.* Pancakes, omelettes, creamed chipped beef, and plantation platters. $

Pierce's Pitt Bar-B-Que, *477 East Rochambeau Drive; (757) 565–2955. Open for breakfast, lunch, and dinner.* Named one of the best in the nation by *Bon Appetit.* Hand-pulled pork barbecue cooked on site. $

Where to Stay

Williamsburg offers a variety of lodgings within the historical area as well as nearby. *Call 800–HISTORY for reservations at the following lodgings operated by Colonial Williamsburg. Be sure to ask about special packages, of which there are many, offering a variety of discounts. Booking online—www.colonialwilliamsburg. org—offers further discounts.*

Colonial Houses. Within the historic area several properties serve as small inns, accommodating two to twelve people. A stay in one of these colonial houses adds to the fantasy of living in the historic era. Some, like the Chiswell–Bucktrout Tavern, have private gardens, a nice oasis after a day of touring. Renting a house would be fun for a family reunion. The rooms vary and so do the prices; some of these are the most expensive lodgings in the historic area. Some rooms are small and, despite the canopy bed, are more drab than charming.

Governor's Inn. This motel-type lodging just outside the historic area is the most economical choice for families. You can leave your car there and take one of Colonial Williamsburg's shuttle buses into the historic area. Guests at this inn can use the recreational activities at the Williamsburg Woodlands, including children's activities.

Williamsburg Inn. This five-star hotel exudes country elegance. It's an upscale property with fine dining, swimming pool, lawn bowling, tennis courts, and golf. This is one of the most expensive properties on site.

For Children Staying at Colonial Williamsburg Hotels . . .

These programs are available from mid-June through August.

- **Young Colonials Club** (Woodlands and Governor's Inn; ages 5 to 12; extra fee): The fun starts at Chowning's Tavern with lunch, then a special tour of the Historic Area and activities such as lawn cowling, stilt walking, helping with farming or household chores, Fife & Drum Corps parades, or a visit to the Governor's Palace maze. There are also evening programs (for an additional fee) that include a picnic dinner at Woodlands, followed by activities such as swimming, miniature golf, games, table tennis, and arts and crafts.

- **Capitol Kids Club** (Inn and Lodge; ages 5 to 12; extra fee): Kids are given a tour of the Historic Area geared specifically to their interests and take part in children's activities in the area, followed by swimming and pool games at the Inn. In the evening (for an additional fee), the program begins with a light dinner followed by a movie and swimming.

- **Golf Clinics and Tennis Clinics** (ages 8 to 17) are open to everyone, not just those staying at a Colonial Williamsburg accommodation.

Williamsburg Lodge. Family-friendly, this lodge on the edge of the historic area is a bit more expensive than the Woodlands but is still priced to appeal to families.

Williamsburg Woodlands. Located behind the visitors center, in a forty-acre pine forest, this is the most economical lodging within the historic area. (This hotel has been completely renovated and re-opened in 2001.) This hotel's rooms are basic but comfortable. In summer the property offers babysitting services and bike rentals.

Kingsmill Resort, *1010 Kingsmill Road; (800) 832–5665 or (757) 253–1703. Web address: www.kingsmill.com.* Located about five minutes from the historic area on the James River, this condominium and hotel property offers a nice oasis away from the historic area's hustle and bustle. The one-to-three-bedroom condos give families the convenience of kitchens plus more room for the money. The on-site resort facilities include golf, tennis, a very nice spa, and a Sports Club featuring an indoor swimming pool, exercise equipment, racquetball, a recreation room with pool table and video games, and a moderately priced restaurant. In summer the property offers Kingsmill Kampers—a supervised half-day or full-day children's program for kids between 5 and 12, (divided into 5–7 and 8–12), with fishing, nature sessions, golf, tennis, arts and crafts, and swimming.

The War Hill Inn, *4560 Longhill Road, 4 miles from Colonial Williamsburg; (757) 565–0248 or (800) 743–0248. Web address: www.warhillinn.com.* Located on a working farm, this bed and breakfast features country-comfortable furnishings and offers thirty-two acres of fields in which to roam plus see some black Angus cattle. The property offers a separate, two-bedroom cottage that works well for families.

The Williamsburg area also has many chain motels and hotels. These include:

Quality Inn Lord Paget, *901 Capitol Landing Road; (800) 444–4678 or (757) 229–4444.* Indoor and outdoor pool, cable, in-room refrigerator, and microwave.

Embassy Suites, *3006 Mooretown Road; (757) 229–6800 or (800) 333–0924.* Indoor pool, cable.

Best Western Patrick Henry Inn, *249 York Street; (757) 229–9540 or (800) 446–9228.* Outdoor pool, cable, in-room refrigerator, and microwave.

Hampton Inn Williamsburg Center, *201 Bypass Road; (800) 444–4678 or (757) 220–0880.* Indoor pool, cable.

Marriott Hotel–Williamsburg, *50 Kingsmill Road (800) 442–3654 or (757) 220–2500.* Indoor pool, in-room refrigerator.

▲ AREA CAMPGROUNDS

Jamestown Beach Campsites, *2217 Jamestown Road; (757) 229–7609 or (757) 229–3300.* Six hundred wooded campsites.

Williamsburg Resort KOA Kampground, *5210 Newman Road; (757) 565–2907 or (800) KOA–1733. Web address: www.koa.com.* A complimentary shuttle service to Colonial Williamsburg is offered as well as an on-site pool and convenience store. One hundred-fifty campsites, plus forty-three cabins with air-conditioning and heat.

FOR MORE LODGING INFORMATION

The Association of Williamsburg Hotels and Motels. Call the complimentary reservation service; (757) 220-3330 or (800) 446-9244.

For More Information

Colonial Williamsburg's Visitors Center, *Visitors Center Drive, Williamsburg, VA 23185; (757) 220–7645 or (800) HISTORY. Web address: www. colonialwilliamsburg.org.* Obtain maps, guide books, and tickets for attractions and make reservations for lodging and meals if you haven't already. Also see the orientation film *Williamsburg—The Story of a Patriot.*

Williamsburg Area Convention and Visitors Bureau, *201 Penniman Road, Williamsburg, VA 23187 (mail: P.O. Box 3585, Williamsburg, VA 23187); (757) 253–0192 or (800) 368–6511. Web address: www.williamsburg.com.*

Williamsburg—Area Theme Parks

Virginia's "kids' corner" isn't all history, hard facts, Redcoats, and revolution. Two in-season must-dos are Busch Gardens Williamsburg and Water Country USA.

 ### BUSCH GARDENS WILLIAMSBURG (ages 2 and up)

One Busch Gardens Boulevard; (757) 253–3350 or (800) 4–ADVENTURE. Web address: www.buschgardens.com. Busch Gardens is open daily from mid-May through Labor Day. In early April and from Labor Day to the end of October, the park is generally open Friday through Sunday. Hours, however, vary with the season, so be sure to check before you visit. Admission.

At this theme park you get twirled, tossed, drenched with torrents of water, scared by monsters, and still come away giggling for more. The park combines roller coasters and other fun rides with German, French, Italian and—new in 2001, Irish—village themes. The first new village at Busch Gardens in twenty years, the Irish setting has an adventure ride through a land of giants, an enchanted castle, a resident leprechaun stirring up trouble, plus good, shops, and entertainment. For little ones, there's Land of the Dragons, a climb-and-play area with a three-story treehouse, water fountains (you're allowed to get wet), and friendly dragons. At Caribou Pottery Shop, kids can create their own pottery works of art. Busch Gardens Williamsburg adds thrills to the classic water ride with Escape from Pompeii. While traveling on a boat exploring an archaeological dig, you suddenly become caught in the eruption of Mount Vesuvius, complete with flames and a drastic plunge. Older kids and adults should love this; little kids may find the vivid special effects and the plunge a bit too much to handle. Pirates! is a swashbuckling 4-D adventure.

You can also find thrills on one of the park's five roller coasters. Apollo's Chariot, one of the park's newest attractions, hurls riders down nine drops totaling nearly 1,000 feet at speeds up to 73 m.p.h., and gives riders a feeling of "free flight" as they're falling. Alpengeist is billed as the world's tallest, most-twisted inverted steel coaster. It hurtles riders at top speeds of 67 m.p.h., flipping them six times, and dropping them a dizzying 170 feet. The riders' delighted screams echo in waves throughout the park. The Big Big Bad Wolf is a bit more tame, although it's lots of fun. This coaster whizzes through an ersatz alpine village at a top clip of 48 m.p.h. before descending a stomach-wrenching—for us—99 feet. The thirteen-story-high Loch Ness Monster twirls riders through two serpentine

Busch Gardens Travel Tips

Busch Gardens Williamsburg is an exceptionally pretty park. For five years in a row the park has been voted "America's Most Beautiful Theme Park." A relaxing way to enjoy the scenery is to board the **Rhine River Cruise** for a scenic river foray.

loops at up to 60 m.p.h. Wilde Maus, the mildest of the park's coasters, is a good introduction to coaster thrills for grade-schoolers. The Royal Preserve Petting Zoo, home to rare creatures such as baby cinnamon bears, is a nice stop for preschoolers.

To calm down after the coasters, and for a welcome break from walking, take in the shows and see the animals. Jack Hanna's Wild Reserve is a habitat for endangered and exotic animals, such as gray wolves, plus a lorikeet aviary, where you can feed nectar to these colorful, tiny birds.

Each of the themed areas has inexpensive eateries.

 ## WATER COUNTRY USA (ages 2 and up)

176 Water Country Parkway (State Highway 199); (757) 253–3350 or (800) 343–SWIM). Web address: www.buschgardens.com. Open daily from Memorial Day through Labor Day and select weekends in May and September. Admission.

Something else not to miss, especially when the Old Dominion's afternoons get particularly steamy, is Water Country USA, a forty-acre water park with rides, slides, pools, and shows. Partner up with your older kids and slither through the Malibu Pipeline, a slippery chute with a partially enclosed tube. Aquazoid ups the thrills of a water slide by adding a dark section with laser light flashes and eerie howls plus three "water curtains" that douse riders. The whole family can climb onto a giant inner tube and experience a river-rafting race through a 670-foot series of twists and turns on Big Daddy Falls. Cow-A-Bunga, a children's play area, features a 4,500-square-foot heated pool, plus water slides, fountains, and water cannons. Kid's Kingdom, for younger children, offers kid-size water slides and play equipment as well as a dry play area and Minnow Matinee, an outdoor theater.

THE MUSIC THEATRE OF WILLIAMSBURG

7575 Richmond Road; (757) 564–0200 or (888) MUSIC–20. Web address: www.musictheatre.com.

Fun family entertainment with shows highlighting music from the 1940s, '50s, and '60s.

WILLIAMSBURG AREA SHOPPING (ages 9 and up)

We know you didn't come to the Williamsburg area to shop but, if you have time, two outlet malls and a pottery factory offer some good browsing.

■ PRIME OUTLETS AT WILLIAMSBURG

Interstate 64 to exit 234 U.S. Highway 60 West, 5715-62A Richmond Road; (757) 565–0702 or (800) 980–SHOP. Web address: www.primeoutlets.com. Open daily; closed Easter and Christmas.

More than eighty outlet stores offer savings. Well known names include Liz Claiborne, Nike, J. Crew, Jones New York, Eddie Bauer, Carter's, OshKosh B'Gosh, and Big Dogs. Snack at Ben & Jerry's.

■ WILLIAMSBURG OUTLET MALL

U.S. Highway 60 West in Lightfoot at 6401 Richmond Road; (757) 565–3378 or (888) SHOP33. Web address: www.shopwilliamsburg.com. Open daily, except Easter and Christmas.

The sixty outlet stores here include Levi's, Leggs Hanes Bali/Playtex, Dexter Shoes, and Kiddie Koncepts.

■ WILLIAMSBURG POTTERY FACTORY

6692 Richmond Road, Lightfoot, U.S. Highway 60 West, just ten minutes outside Williamsburg; (757) 564–3326 or (800) POTTERY. Web address: www. williamsburgpottery.com. Open daily, except Christmas.

Definitely worth the trip for those who are looking for pottery and tableware, this factory offers 200 acres of pottery, fine china, glassware, stemware, baskets, silk flower arrangements, toys, brass, and crafts, all at discount prices. Be sure to browse some of the other outlet shops here including those selling designer clothes, shoes, and appliances. There's also a restaurant.

Jamestown and Yorktown

From Williamsburg the **Colonial Parkway** leads to Jamestown. The winding road cuts through groves of oaks and elms, winds over creeks, and travels past marshes thick with cattails and green reeds before opening to sweeping views of the James River. While it's only about a 10-mile-long drive, you "go back" to 1607 when the first permanent English settlement in the New World was established.

The 9,316-acre **Colonial National Historical Park** includes Jamestown, the original site of the first permanent English settlement; Yorktown, the scene of the last major battle of the Revolutionary War; and the Colonial Parkway, a 23-mile roadway that connects Williamsburg, Jamestown, and Yorktown. **Cape Henry Memorial,** a one-quarter-acre spot near Virginia Beach, marks the site of the first landing of the Jamestown settlers with a memorial cross. The site provides a superb view of the Chesapeake Bay and Atlantic Ocean. This is an unattended site with no facilities or special services available.

For information on the Colonial National Historical Park, write P.O.Box 210, Yorktown 23690; (757) 898–2410. Web address: www.nps.gov/colo. Note that the Jamestown Settlement and the Yorktown Victory Center are not part of Colonial National History Park. For information about these sites, contact the Jamestown-Yorktown Foundation, P.O. Box 1607, Williamsburg, VA 23187; (757) 253–4838 or (888) 593–4682. Web address: www.historyisfun.org.

 JAMESTOWN NATIONAL HISTORICAL PARK (ages 7 and up)
Located at the westernmost point of Colonial Parkway in Jamestown; (757) 229–1733. Web address: www.nps.gov/colo. Admission.

Although only modern bricks mark the footprints of the first buildings, this is the original site of the 1607 Jamestown settlement, the first permanent English settlement, established thirteen years before the pilgrims landed in Massachusetts.

Although Jamestown Settlement, a living-history museum, is fun, my family finds the quiet of Jamestown, the original site, more compelling. Sitting along the windblown riverbank, listening to the lapping gray waters, we find it easy to imagine the hopefuls who landed here and the hearty few who survived. The visitors center displays pottery shards, bits of buckles, and other period artifacts, and the rangers lead interpretive programs. Visit the museum bookstore, which has a great children's section with books on colonial American history.

Begin your tour at the visitors center by watching a fifteen-minute film about the colony's story. Then take the mile-long self-guided tour of the ruins of New Town, imagining the colonists' life here nearly 400 years ago.

A visit to Old Town (about three-quarters of a mile from New Town) includes the current excavation of James Fort and Confederate Army earthworks. For a more extensive exploration of the island, take the 5-mile-long loop drive and witness the wilderness these first colonists encountered. Before you leave stop by the reconstructed glasshouse of 1608, where a craftsman demonstrates seventeenth-century glass blowing.

For Children Visiting Jamestown

Beginning in mid-June and ending in mid-August each year, there are a number of National Park Service hands-on activities for children, such as the Pinch Pot Program, where they learn about the pottery-making of the English and the Powhatan Indians and make a small pinch pot that they can take with them.

The Junior Ranger Program can include answering written questions about the settlement, walking around the town site, and learning about the materials colonists would have found in the area and how they used them with "environmental bags" containing some of those same materials.

In October, on the Saturday of the Columbus Day holiday weekend, there are activities related to the process of archeology, where kids try to earn a Junior Archeologist Certificate by identifying "mystery artifacts" and how they were used.

Also check out the NPS web site, where there is excellent and detailed information about the settlement, its inhabitants (including African-Americans) and the Native Americans living here at the time.

JAMESTOWN SETTLEMENT (ages 5 and up) (TT)

Next to Jamestown Island on Route 31 South; (757) 253–4838 or (888) 593–4682. Web address: www.historyisfun.org. Admission.

Adjacent to the actual site where the settlers lived, Jamestown Settlement is a living-history museum. The facility depicts the early seventeenth-century by recreating a Powhatan Indian hamlet, the three ships that carried the pioneers there in 1607, and the fort that they built. Start at the museum exhibition galleries. The twenty-minute film, Jamestown: The Beginning, offers a useful overview. The English Gallery, which outlines the events in England that led to the colonization of Jamestown, includes an examination of ship designs, navigational tools, and maps that may interest school-age kids. In the Powhatan Gallery, the British way of life is contrasted with that of the Powhatan Indians, whose way of life is detailed through their food, shelter, religion, and government. The Jamestown Gallery traces the development of the

Jamestown Colony from the colonists' landing to the 1699 movement of the Virginia capital from Jamestown to Williamsburg. The **Powhattan Gallery** explores the culture of this area's Native American people.

Most children, though, find many of these artifacts "boring." What fascinates children lies just beyond the gallery building: the living-history areas complete with costumed interpreters.

At the **Powhatan Indian Village,** families can explore the Powhatan houses, called *yehakins,* and watch and even help prepare food, tan animal hides, and make pottery or tools from bones. Watching an interpreter dressed in buckskin weave storage bags from plant fibers, we wonder if Pocahontas, a Powhatan maiden, ever wove a similar sack.

The path from the galleries leads to the pier on the James River, where full-size replicas of the three ships that sailed to Jamestown are docked. Costumed interpreters recount the four-and-a-half-month voyage, demonstrating piloting and navigational skills. Onboard the ship the *Susan Constant,* try on "slops," the baggy pants worn by sailors, help haul cargo, and try deducing latitude with an astrolabe, an early navigational tool. At the triangular **James Fort** kids can defend the re-created seventeenth-century settlement of homes, church, storehouse, and guardhouse. Children may tend the gardens, try on armor, play games with the costumed colonists, or even be called to duty in the colony's militia.

A new visitor cafe is expected to open in 2002, with a new orientation video, a large cafe, and an expanded gift shop.

YORKTOWN VICTORY CENTER (ages 7 and up) (TT)
Route 238, the Colonial Parkway, Yorktown; (757) 253–4838 or (888) 593–4682. Web address: www.historyisfun.org. Admission.

At the other end of the Colonial Parkway, 23 miles away, is Yorktown, site of the last significant battle of the American Revolution, in 1781. Amid the static displays of maps and timelines, Witnesses to the Revolution captures interest with its real war stories. While looking at a 3-D assemblage of mannequins, gun replicas, clothing, and cookery, viewers hear voices of early pioneers, soldiers, and women. Jeremiah Greenman, a Continental soldier from Rhode Island, complains about the deep snow and the constant hunger while Tigoransera, a Mohawk chief, counsels his people to stay out of this white man's war. (Despite his neutrality, he was captured by the British and died in prison.)

There is a picnic area with vending machines and outdoor seating.

A short film, *Time of Revolution*, set in an encampment at night during the siege of Yorktown, continues the witnesses theme. Costumed interpreters depict eighteenth-century life in a wartime encampment, complete with musket drills, field medicine, and cooking demonstrations, as well as depicting life on a 1780s Tidewater Virginia farm, where kids can lend a hand weeding.

A Children's Kaleidoscope discovery room offers children the opportunity to learn about the Revolutionary era with activities such as trying on eighteenth-century clothing, copying from a hornbook, making rubbings of woodcuts, and playing the African game mancala.

Throughout the Victory Center, there are display panels at a child's eye level asking kids thought-provoking questions about their lives compared to the lives of colonial children. At the recreated encampment, children can ask the camp surgeon about eighteenth-century medical techniques, join a mock military drill, and watch the cannon being fired.

Discovering Pocahontas *Pocahontas,* the Walt Disney Company film that debuted in 1995, fired kids' curiosity about the real Pocahontas, the Indian maiden Captain John Smith credited with saving his life in 1607 by pleading with her father Chief Powhatan. This is the region where the real Pocahontas lived 400 years ago.

YORKTOWN BATTLEFIELD (ages 10 and up)

Located along the Colonial Parkway between Williamsburg and Yorktown; (757) 898–3400. Web address: www.nps.gov/colo. Open daily, except Thanksgiving, Christmas, and New Year's Day. Admission.

Here is the site of the finale of the American Revolution, October 1781. This National Park Service site features the battlefield, which includes Washington's headquarters, the surrender field, and the Yorktown Victory Monument. Park rangers lead tours of the British inner defense line. Stop by the museum at the Visitor Center, and at the center, see a fifteen-minute film on the siege of Yorktown. The Junior Ranger program is available for children up to the age of 12 for a nominal fee.

YORKTOWN—THE TOWN (ages 10 and up)

Yorktown, the town, is nestled along the York River between the Yorktown Victory Center and the Yorktown Battlefield. A **Free** pamphlet guides you on a walking tour of the historic town. Most kids could really skip this except for the restaurants and, for some kids, the small Watermen's Museum. In the summer, there's a hands-on (non-firing) artillery demonstration. The Nelson House, open spring through fall, features a hand-on room for children. The house, built around 1730, still bears the scars from the 1781 bombardment.

Ferry Through History

Aboard the ferries that cross the James River, it's easy to imagine the new world as the first colonists saw it. Car ferries leave from Glass House Point at Jamestown and go to Surry County. It's a twenty-minute ride. **Chippoke's Plantation and State Park**, with its acres of greenery and fields of corn, peanuts, rye and soybeans, makes for a great destination. For information call 800–VA–FERRY.

WATERMEN'S MUSEUM (ages 10 and up)

309 Water Street, P.O. Box 531, Yorktown; (757) 887–2641. Web address: www.watermens.org. Open April through mid-December.

Here's the place to learn the story of the generations of men who have earned their living from Chesapeake Bay through ship models, paintings, photographs, artifacts, and tools. Check out the 100-year-old Poquoson five-log cabin outside the museum, near the steel replica of the *Betsy*, a colonial-era British supply ship.

River cruises depart daily from the museum's dock.

Special Events at Jamestown and Yorktown

The National Park Service sponsors a number of special events throughout the year, including programs in February honoring African-American participation in the Jamestown settlement. Jamestown Day (May 11—in 2002, the 395th anniversary of the founding), Yorktown Civil War Weekend in May, Independence Day Celebration at Yorktown, Virginia Archeological Celebration at Jamestown in October, and Yorktown Victory Weekend in October.

THE JAMES RIVER PLANTATIONS

Several of Virginia's first plantations still thrive a short drive from Williamsburg along the James River. These plantations give a glimpse into the pomp and pleasures of a life grown prosperous in the new world. Two that may especially delight children are Shirley Plantation and Berkeley Plantation;

both boast lawns that sweep to the river and ancestry traced back to England's Queen Elizabeth I.

Combination admission tickets are available for Shirley, Berkeley, Evelynton, and Sherwood Forest plantation.

SHIRLEY PLANTATION (ages 9 and up)

35 miles west of Williamsburg on State Highway 5, 501 Shirley Plantation Road, Charles City; (804) 829–5121 or (800) 232–1613. Web address: www.shirley-plantation.com. Open daily, except Thanksgiving and Christmas, reduced hours in January and February. Admission.

This is Virginia's oldest plantation and dates to 1613. The imposing brick Queen Anne–style manor house built in 1723, sits like a crown jewel, flanked by its dependencies. Shirley exudes a genteel hospitality and lived-in practicality and is still a working plantation, home to the ninth generation of Hill-Carters (Ann Hill Carter was the mother of Confederate General Robert E. Lee), whose scion may sometimes be seen dressed in blue jeans as he oversees farm chores. The tour highlights history, antique furniture, paintings, and silver, and may well bore many kids who are nonetheless impressed with the manor house's size and gardens. In June, there's an American Revolution Encampment weekend and in September a Civil War re-enactment and Living History Weekend.

BERKELEY PLANTATION (ages 7 and up)

2 miles down the road from Shirley Plantation, State Highway 5, 12602 Harrison Landing Road, Charles City; (804) 829–6018. Web address: www.berkeley plantation.com. Open daily, except Thanksgiving and Christmas; reduced hours in January and February. Admission.

Discover the site of some unusual historic firsts. Birthplace of Benjamin Harrison, a signer of the Declaration of Independence, and William Henry Harrison, ninth president of the United States, this brick Georgian manor house, built in 1726, hosted the first "Thanksgiving" in 1619 and witnessed the composition of "Taps" during a Civil War encampment. In spring and summer Berkeley's gardens are especially nice. Although furnishings and antiques are emphasized, the site's firsts make this stop appealing to younger children.

EVELYNTON PLANTATION (ages 10 and up)

6701 John Tyler Highway; (804) 829–5075 or (800) 473–5075. Web address: www.evelyntonplantation.org. Open daily, except Thanksgiving, Christmas, and New Year's Day. Admission.

If you are interested in other plantations, try this one. A Georgian-revival house with many antiques, the home is named after the daughter of the founder of Richmond, Virginia. The 2,500-acre farm is still family-owned and operated.

SHERWOOD FOREST (ages 10 and up)

14501 John Tyler Highway, Charles City; (804) 829–5377. Web address: www.sherwoodforest.org. Open daily except Thanksgiving, Christmas, and New Year's Day. Admission.

This was the retirement home of President John Tyler, at more than 300 feet considered to be the longest frame house in the U.S. It has nice grounds and picnic facilities, and also claims a ghost called the Gray Lady. On March 29, President Tyler's birthday, there are special events and free birthday cake. Each May, there is a re-enactment of the first successful defense by the U.S. Colored (African-American) Troops on May 24, 1864.

PINEY GROVE AT SOUTHALL'S PLANTATION (ages 10 and up)

16920 Southall Plantation Lane, Charles City; (804) 829–2480. Web address: www.pineygrove.com. Grounds open daily except major holidays; house tours by appointment only.

A rare surviving example of early Virginia log architecture representative of Virginia's typical plantation. Civil War re-enactments are held here in the summer, and there are special events at Christmas.

Where to Eat

In Yorktown and its vicinity you can find several fast-food places, including Pizza Hut, Kentucky Fried Chicken, and McDonald's. For other kinds of choices, see Williamsburg.

Hampton

Hampton, an interesting city with much history, is home to Hampton University. The area is part of Hampton Roads, a southeastern section of Virginia that stretches from Williamsburg to Virginia Beach to the Chesapeake. The kid-pleasing attractions are centered on the waterfront; the most notable is the Virginia Air and Space Center.

THE VIRGINIA AIR AND SPACE CENTER (ages 7 and up)

600 Settlers Landing Road; (757) 727–0800 or (800) 296–0800. Web address: www.vasc.org. Open daily year-round except Thanksgiving and Christmas. Admission. IMAX movies cost extra.

The Virginia Air and Space Center is not nearly as elaborate as Washington, D.C.'s National Air and Space Museum, but it isn't as crowded either. You don't have to stand in line to see the moon rock or wait to get close enough to the copper-colored Apollo 12 command module to read the astronauts' inscription: "Yankee Clipper sailed with Intrepid to the Ocean of Storms, Moon.

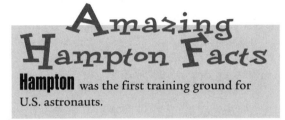

Hampton was the first training ground for U.S. astronauts.

November 14, 1969." This is a great place for adults and kids alike, with more than one hundred interactive exhibits. In "Touch and Tornado," kids can watch a tornado form, then touch the funnel to make it change shape. Visitors can stand in front of the blue screen used by TV weather forecasters and see how they use 'invisible' maps. Kids can enter a wind chamber, try on a pair of wings and feel the lift, launch a rocket, or explore Mars. There are also an IMAX theater, and an impressive array of fifteen planes are suspended—as if in mid-flight—in the atrium. Gaze on an F–4E Phantom II fighter used in the Vietnam War and a Corsair F–106B Delta Dart that was struck by lightning nearly 700 times as part of NASA research. The photographic exhibit on the first black aviators, the Tuskegee Airmen, is informative.

HAMPTON ROADS HISTORY CENTER (ages 7 and up)

Inside the Virginia Air and Space Center; (757) 727–0900 or (800) 296–0800. Hours and admission are the same as for the center.

This one-room exhibit takes you back to the colonial past and forward to the 1960s, the days of the Mercury astronauts. View artifacts from a pirate skeleton to a reproduction of the U.S.S. *Monitor*.

FORT MONROE AND THE CASEMATE MUSEUM (ages 7 and up)

P.O. Box 341, Fort Monroe, 23651; (757) 788–3391. Open daily.

This portrays another view of Hampton's military history. Fort Monroe, the largest stone fort ever built in the United States, is currently the only

Amazing Hampton Facts

Hampton was the site of America's first organized school for African–Americans, known now as Hampton University. The great black educator Booker T. Washington was a graduate of Hampton Institute.

moat-encircled fort still in active use. The fort now serves as the headquarters for the U.S. Army's Training and Doctrine Command. A tour includes the Chapel of the Centurion, Cannon Park, and the army quarters of Gen. Robert E. Lee. In a network of caverns once filled with Fort Monroe's massive guns, the Casemate Museum traces the history of the Civil War and the U.S. Coast Artillery Corps. The museum includes the cell in which Confederate president Jefferson Davis was held after the war. A free brochure guides you on a walking tour of Fort Monroe.

HAMPTON CAROUSEL (ages 2 and up)

610 Settlers Landing Road; (757) 727–1102 or (757) 727–6381. Open daily April through September, and Saturday and Sunday from October through mid-December. Closed mid-December through late March.

While you're at the waterfront, take the kids to the restored 1920s merry-go-round with forty-eight prancing steeds. Even if your video-age kids find riding this a bit tame, a spin will probably bring back great memories from your own childhood.

HAMPTON UNIVERSITY MUSEUM (ages 7 and up) (TT)

In the Huntington Building, Frissell Avenue, Hampton University campus; (757) 727–5308. Web address: www.hamptonu.edu (click on "University Services"). Open Monday through Saturday. Free.

Founded in 1868, this is one of Virginia's oldest museums and the oldest African-American museum in the U.S. It houses more than 9,000 objects and pieces of art from around the world, including two new permanent exhibits, one on African tribal art, the other on Native American art. Hampton University has an interesting and important history. Opened in 1868 as the Hampton Normal and Agricultural Institute, the school was dedicated to the education of the thousands of newly freed slaves, providing them with manual and agricultural skills. From

1878–1923, the school also educated Native Americans from more than sixty-five tribes who were brought here under a federal program geared at assimilation through education. Today the school has 6,000 students and 150 buildings.

Blackbeard's Point on the Hampton River was named for the infamous pirate. Legend has it that this was where Blackbeard's head was displayed on a pike as a warning to would-be pirates.

Where to Eat

Bennigan's, *2029 Coliseum Drive; (757) 838–9261. Open daily for lunch and dinner.* $-$$

Captain George's Seafood Restaurant, *2710 West Mercury Boulevard; (757) 826–1435. Open daily for dinner, plus lunch on Sundays.* $$$

Chi-Chi's Mexican Restaurante, *1119 West Mercury Boulevard; (757) 838–4155. Open daily for lunch and dinner.* Known for its seafood buffet. $-$$

Grate Steak, *1934 Coliseum Drive; (757) 827–1886. Open daily for dinner, plus lunch on Sundays.* Here you grill your own steak, chicken, and seafood. $-$$

Where to Stay

Courtyard by Marriott, *1917 Coliseum Drive; (757) 838–3300 or (800) 321–2211.* Offers a restaurant and indoor and outdoor pools.

Days Inn, *1918 Coliseum Drive; (757) 826–4810 or (800) 325–2525.* Offers a restaurant and indoor and outdoor pools.

The Hampton Inn, *1813 West Mercury Boulevard; (757) 838–8484 or (800) HAMPTON.* Offers complimentary

continental breakfast and an indoor-outdoor pool.

Quality Inn & Suites, *1809 West Mercury Boulevard; (757) 838–5011 or (800) 228–5151.* Indoor pool and exercise room.

Todd's Cottages, *200 Point Comfort Avenue; (757) 851–7700.* This offers an away-from-downtown choice on the bay. The property has an outdoor pool.

On the Water

Want to spend some time out on the water? Check out these boating opportunities:

Spring through fall *The Miss Hampton II* cruises the Hampton Roads Harbor, passing the world's largest naval base and Fort Wool, a pre–Civil War island fortress. Catch the boat at 764 Settlers Landing Road; (757) 722–9113 or (888) 757–BOAT. Cruises sail at 10:00 A.M. from early April to late May and from early September to the end of October; from late May to early September departure times are 10:00 A.M. and 2:00 P.M.

From December through March the *Venture Inn II* takes passengers in search of whales. Be the first to shout "thar she blows." The boat docks at 764 Settlers Landing Road; (757) 850–8960 or (800) 853–5002. Twenty passengers are required for whale watching cruises. This is most appropriate for kids 7 and up.

For spine-tingling ghost stories and an exciting historical tour of the harbor, try the James River Ghost Fleet Cruise (www.ventureinncharters.com), a five-hour twilight cruise that beckons "those brave souls brave enough to dare it" to come aboard the *Venture Inn II*, April through Halloween (Mondays only), and hear tales about the battle of the ironclads and the ghosts of Castle Calhoun, not to mention stories of spies, pirates, lost loves, and poets. Call (757) 850–8960 or (800) 853–5002.

For More Information

Hampton Visitors Center, *710 Settlers Landing Road, Hampton, VA 23669; (757) 727–1102 or (800) 800–2202. Web address: www.hamptoncvb.com.* Pick up brochures and city information at this conveniently located center.

Newport News

Located along the James River near Virginia Beach, Norfolk, and Williamsburg, Newport News is home to the world's largest privately owned shipyard and Virginia's largest employer, the Newport News Shipbuilding and Dry Dock Company. Newport News has some family-friendly attractions of its own.

THE MARINERS' MUSEUM (ages 7 and up) (TT)

100 Museum Drive; (757) 596–2222 or (800) 581–SAIL. Web address: www.mariner.org. Open daily. Admission.

This museum explores the sea's use for transportation, warfare, food, and pleasure. Examine miniature and handcrafted ship models, carved figureheads, scrimshaw, maritime paintings, and working steam engines. The museum features several galleries. Favorites with kids include the Age of Exploration Gallery with its hands-on replicas of early maps and navigational tools and its fifteen short videos; the Crabtree Collection of Miniature Ships' sixteen detailed miniatures; the Great Hall of Steam's history of steamships (plus an exhibit on the HMS Titanic); the Chesapeake Bay Gallery, which details this body of water's history and has an exhibit on shipbuilding (plus interactive computer games). A permanent exhibit on U.S. Navy history uses lively audio-visual displays to explore the history of sea power in Defending the Seas, from sailing ships to nuclear-powered submarines.

In 2001, the museum, working with the U.S. Navy and the National Oceanic and Atmospheric Administration, recovered the steam engine of the Civil War ironclad USS *Monitor,* currently resting 16 miles off the coast of Cape Hatteras, North Carolina, at 240 feet below sea level. The engine is now on display in a conversation tank outside the museum, surrounded by more than one hundred other artifacts (such as the propeller) from the *Monitor.* Preparations are now underway to recover and display the ship's turret at the museum in 2002.

Allow time to enjoy the museum's parklike setting on 550 acres. You can rent boats, picnic, and walk a 5-mile-long trail that surrounds Lake Maury.

VIRGINIA LIVING MUSEUM (ages 5 and up)

524 J. Clyde Morris Boulevard; (757) 595–1900. Web address: www. valivingmuseum.org. Open daily. Admission.

The exhibits look back at you at this indoor–outdoor museum. Outdoor paths lead you by raccoons, beavers, river otters, foxes, bobcats, deer, a bald eagle, beavers, forty species of birds, and many other animals in their natural habitats. Indoor highlights include a living replica of the James River, a touch tank where kids handle sea stars and horseshoe crabs, an authentic dinosaur footprint made by a kayentapus (measure your foot size against its), plus a planetarium theater and observatory. In 2001, the museum opened the first exhibit of its $21 million expansion—a 5,500-square foot Coastal Plain Aviary, with more than sixteen species of birds that can be viewed from an 800-foot boardwalk that takes visitors 11 feet above Deer Park Lake and into the treetops. In summer, look for Butterflies, Bugs 'n Blooms in the butterfly house, where kids will enjoy surrounding themselves with colorful fluttering butterflies and learning how to create a butterfly garden at home. Every third Saturday, year-round, is Story Time at the museum.

Newport News Travel Tips

Newport News has twelve stops that are part of of **Virginia's Civil War Trails** driving tour. Ask about guided tours at the Newport News Visitor Information Center.

PENINSULA FINE ARTS CENTER'S CHILDREN'S INTERACTIVE GALLERY (ages 3 to 7)

101 Museum Drive; (757) 596–8175. Web address: www.pfac-va.org. Open year-round. Admission.

While this small art center may interest all ages, little ones especially like it. Kids can color, paint, and craft collages and other artistic works. Check the calendar for the facility's special classes.

U.S. ARMY TRANSPORTATION MUSEUM (ages 9 and up)

10 miles east of Williamsburg on Interstate 64 (Washington Avenue). Building 300, Besson Hall, Fort Eustis; (757) 878–1115. Web address: www.eustis.army. mil/dptmsec/museum.htm. Open Tuesday through Sunday. **Free**.

See an array of military transportation vehicles, including a flying saucer, the first helicopter to land at the South Pole, and the army's largest helicopter, the "Flying Crane." This facility traces more than 200 years of Army transportation history through film, miniature models, life-size displays, and nearly one hundred actual vehicles, aircraft, amphibians, rail equipment, and experimental craft. The gift shop has a nice selection of souvenir items that cost less than a dollar.

VIRGINIA WAR MUSEUM (ages 10 and up) (TT)

9285 Warwick Boulevard; (757) 247–8523. Web address: www.warmuseum.org. Open daily. Admission.

The memorial also traces military history, chronicling America's wars from 1775 to the present. In addition to uniforms, weapons, and vehicles, this facility features one of the largest propaganda poster collections in the United States and a 12-by-12-foot section of the Berlin Wall. Reproductions of posters and other interesting items are available at the Duffle Bag gift shop. Ask about children's camps, Civil War re-enactments, and ghost walks sponsored by the museum.

NEWPORT NEWS REGIONAL PARK (all ages)

13564 Jefferson Avenue; (757) 888–3333 or (757) 886–7912. Open year-round.

If the weather's wonderful, pack a picnic lunch and head for Newport News Park. At 8,000 acres it's one of the country's largest municipal parks. After lunch hike the trails, take a paddleboat for a spin, bike ride, golf, canoe, or fish. Campsites are also available. Call (800) 203–8322.

The White Oak Trail is a nice stroll. Along its 2.6 miles you'll find bayberry shrubs, white oak trees, and Sycamore Creek (a good place to look for frogs and tadpoles).

Stop by the Newport News Park Discovery Center, 13560 Jefferson Avenue (757-886-7916), which serves as a temporary shelter for animals being rehabilitated. More than 400 orphaned and injured animals are cared for each year at this facility. Exhibits feature wildlife found in the park and Civil War artifacts.

New in 2001: an eighteen-hole disc golf course located near the entrance to the park.

SPCA PETTING ZOO (all ages)

523 J. Clyde Morris Boulevard; (757) 595–1399. Open Monday through Saturday.

Younger children will love making friends with the ducks, turkey, sheep, goats, ostrich, and llama.

Amazing Newport News Facts

The battle for control of Hampton Roads during the Civil War saw the first fight between two ironclad ships: the USS *Monitor* and the CSS *Virginia (Merrimack)*. At **Monitor–Merrimack Overlook,** Sixteenth Street, you can view the site of this historic battle fought on March 9, 1862. After three hours of combat, both sides claimed victory.

FORT FUN (all ages)

Just want to play? Then head to Fort Fun in Huntington Park. This 13,500-square-foot play area complete with mazes, towers, slides, swings, and lots of ladders makes for a great break from the rigors of touring. Here your kids are likely to find some local children with whom to romp.

Annual Events

MAY

Annual Children's Festival of Friends, Newport News Park; (757) 926-8451. Children and their families are the focus of one fun-filled day centered around ten theme pavilions providing pony rides, make-and-take crafts, rides and clowns, music, and food.

OCTOBER

Annual Fall Festival of Folklife, Newport News Park; (757) 926-8451. South-east Virginia's largest celebration of traditional crafts, trades, and entertain-ment, with **Free** children's activities, food as well.

Where to Eat

What's a shore vacation without some seafood? Be sure to sample some of Newport News' many restaurants.

Captain D's Seafood Restaurant, *10158 Jefferson Avenue; (757) 596–1027. Open daily for lunch and dinner.* $-$$

Cheddar's Casual Cafe, *12280 Jefferson Avenue; (757) 249–4000. Open daily for lunch and dinner.* Offers a variety of Mexican–American dishes. $-$$

Monty's Penquin, *9607 Warwick Boulevard; (757) 595–2151. Open for breakfast, lunch, and dinner.* $-$$

Rey Azteca, *10530 Jefferson Avenue; (757) 595–5956. Open for lunch and din-ner.* Mexican fare. $

Second Street Restaurant, *115 Arthur Way (in the Super K-Mart Shopping Center), (757) 872–7887. Open for lunch and dinner.* Casual atmosphere, friendly service, and huge portions. Italian, seafood, chicken, steaks. $$

Gus's Hot Dog King, *10725 Jefferson Avenue; (757) 595–1630. Open daily for lunch and dinner.* $

China Buffet Restaurant, *10776 Jefferson Avenue; (757) 599–0933. Open daily for lunch and dinner.* $$

Carmela's Homestyle Italian Cui-sine, *14501-A Warwick Boulevard; (757) 874–8421. Lunch, Monday through Friday; dinner daily.* $$

Where to Stay

Comfort Inn, *12330 Jefferson Avenue; (757) 249–0200 or (800) 368–2477.* Adjacent to the Patrick Henry Mall, it has an outdoor pool and a fitness center. Complimentary continental breakfast, coffeemakers in rooms.

Days Inn Oyster Point, *11829 Fishing Point Drive; (757) 873–6700 or (800) 873–2369.* The hotel has an outdoor pool and a fitness center. Complimentary continental breakfast, coffeemakers in rooms.

Holiday Inn Express, *16890 Warwick Boulevard; (757) 887–3300 or (800) 248–0408.* Outdoor pool (shared with

the Mulberry Inn) and a fitness center. Complimentary continental breakfast, coffeemakers in rooms.

The Mulberry Inn, *16890 Warwick Boulevard; (757) 887–3000 or (800) 223–0404.* The Mulberry has an outdoor pool and some efficiency rooms. Complimentary continental breakfast and coffeemakers in rooms.

Omni Newport News Hotel, *1000 Omni Boulevard; (757) 873–OMNI or (800) HAMPTON.* This hotel has an indoor pool, a health spa, and restaurant.

For More Information

Newport News Visitor Information Center, 13560 Jefferson Avenue, Newport News Park, VA 23603; (757) 886-7777 or (888) *4–WE–R–FUN.* *Web address: www.newport-news.org.* Call

for a **Free** visitor's guide and information about guided Civil War sites tour. For additional information on the state's Civil War history, call 888-CIVIL-WAR.

Norfolk

Home to the world's largest naval installation, Norfolk's history is tied to the sea. The renovated downtown harbor has many attractions, shops, and a friendly family feel, especially at Waterside Festival Marketplace, a collection of shops and eateries. The city's charms are not confined to port. Good bets to visit include the first-class botanical garden and

Norfolk Travel Tips

The Norfolk Trolley offers one-hour tours of downtown, allowing visitors to get off to explore sites and then reboard. The trolleys depart from Waterside Festival Marketplace, (757–222–6100, listen to Southside message).

the Chrysler Museum of Art. Just twenty minutes west of Virginia Beach, Norfolk is a good stop for families en route to the beach or those taking in Tidewater's attractions.

NAUTICUS, THE NATIONAL MARITIME CENTER (ages 5 and up)

1 Waterside Drive; (757) 664–1000 or (800) 664–1080. Web address: www.nauticus.org. Open daily, reduced hours Labor Day to Memorial Day, closed Thanksgiving, Christmas, and New Year's Day. Admission.

This $52 million facility is devoted to exploring the sea's importance and power as a commercial and military force. A highlight is the USS *Wisconsin* battleship moored at the center. (There is no admission to the ship itself, only to the center.) Two new exhibits complement the experience of seeing the battleship: "Battle Scopes," overlooking the bat-

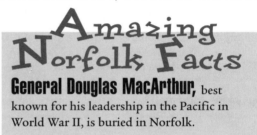

Amazing Norfolk Facts

General Douglas MacArthur, best known for his leadership in the Pacific in World War II, is buried in Norfolk.

tleship, lets kids see the virtual result when laser cannon are fired at the ship, and "City At Sea" shows what it's like living with 2,900 other people on a ship at sea.

More than 150 hands-on exhibits make learning about the world's seas oceans of fun. Thrown overboard are static museum displays in favor of "interactive theater," which explores the marine environment as well as maritime consumers, technology, and the modern U.S. Navy. Some of the fun includes landing a navy warplane on an aircraft carrier, piloting a merchant vessel through dangerous waters, designing a seaworthy ship, and discovering how an octopus travels.

At the Aegis Theater, live actors and video involve the audience in a high-tech naval battle aboard a destroyer, thus demonstrating how the Aegis weapons system makes crucial decisions. Some of the battle booms and special effects may scare preschoolers, so exhibits are recommended for ages 6 and above.

Kids can also stand atop a real ship's bridge (USS *Prebble* destroyer) in the traveling exhibits gallery, touch sharks in Aquaria (a gallery that includes a Chesapeake Bay exhibit), and tape their own weather forecast in Natural Power. May through September 2002 in the traveling exhibits gallery, "Adventures in 3-D" will show how the eyes and brain work together to create the 3-D effect.

Norfolk Travel Tips

Try the Harborlink Ferry that travels between Nauticus in Norfolk and the Virginia Air & Space Center in Hampton. Packages include exhibit admission, one IMAX film at the center, and roundtrip ferry ride. Call (877) HRFERRY or check out the web site at www.harborlink.com.

Nauticus also houses the **Hampton Roads Naval Museum** (757– 444–8971), one of the U.S. Navy's ten official museums. This one highlights naval battles and events in the Norfolk area through detailed ship models, naval artwork, and underwater artifacts. Admission is **Free.**

THE TUGBOAT MUSEUM (ages 5 and up)

Docked beside the Nauticus; (757) 627–4884. Open seven days a week Memorial Day Weekend through Labor Day. Open Tuesday through Sunday in fall and winter. Admission.

Looking like a storybook vessel with its red paint, the *Tug Huntington* is a restored 1933 working boat turned into a dockside museum. Aboard you can tour the engine room, visit the crew's quarters and the galley, and view photographs of life on a tugboat.

THE NORFOLK NAVAL BASE (ages 9 and up)

9079 Hampton Boulevard; (757) 444–7637. Bus tours run year-round from the Naval Base Tour Office, 9809 Hampton Boulevard. From March to December, bus tours also depart from the Waterside Festival Marketplace.

Norfolk is home port to more than seventy-five ships of the Atlantic fleet and is the world's largest naval installation. Forty-five-minute-long bus tours go past fleet training centers, the Jamestown Exposition (a group of restored 1907 structures now used as homes), and aircraft carriers. Bellied up to the port, these grey behemoths seem huge.

FORT NORFOLK

On the banks of the Elizabeth River near Ghent, 810 Front Street; (757) 625–1720. Open the second and fourth Sundays from May through October.

The oldest fort on the Virginia waterfront, Fort Norfolk is one of the best-preserved War of 1812 sites in America. Military reenactments are staged throughout the year.

THE CHRYSLER MUSEUM OF ART (ages 12 and up)

245 West Olney Road at Mowbray Arch; (757) 664–6200 or (757) 622–ARTS. Web address: www.chrysler.org. Open Wednesday through Sunday. Admission.

The museum's vast collection includes textiles, ceramics, bronzes, and paintings from pre-Columbian, African, and Asian artists, plus an array of European paintings and American art from the eighteenth to the twentieth centuries. A highlight of the museum's notable glass collection is the many Tiffany items with their lush and elaborate designs. Kids also appreciate the prints of Norfolk by famous photographers such as Ansel Adams and Alfred Stieglitz. Young visitors are given a sheet so they can go on a treasure hunt to see what they can find among the exhibits. In the last three years the museum has undergone major renovations in its galleries featuring European Old Masters, its galleries of modern art, and its photography galleries. Ask about its Family Days and Holiday Fest.

For families interested in viewing historic homes, the museum offers two, both in downtown Norfolk: The Moses Myers House, which shows how a prosperous eighteenth-century merchant and his family lived,

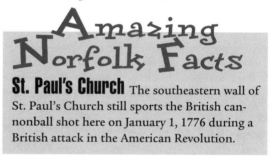

Amazing Norfolk Facts

St. Paul's Church The southeastern wall of St. Paul's Church still sports the British cannonball shot here on January 1, 1776 during a British attack in the American Revolution.

and the Willoughby-Baylor House, which reflects a middle-class family's daily life in eighteenth-century Virginia.

NORFOLK BOTANICAL GARDEN (all ages)

6700 Azalea Garden Road (located near the airport); (757) 441–5830. Web address: www.virginiagarden.org. Open daily. Boat and train tours daily from mid-March through October.

This don't-miss spot outside downtown Norfolk has, in season, 155 acres of garden blooms, including the east coast's largest collections of azaleas, camellias, roses, and rhododendrons. Stroll along 12 miles of garden pathways through more than twenty theme gardens. Kids, especially preschool ones, enjoy the canal boat, horse and carriage rides, and the tram tours, all of which save little feet from lots of walking.

Special events include History Alive! weekends, garden illuminations (Garden of Light), and American Girl gatherings.

CHILDREN'S MUSEUM OF VIRGINIA

221 High Street, Olde Towne Portsmouth; (757) 393–8393 or (800) PORTS– VA. Web address: www.childrensmuseumva.com Open Monday through Sunday. Admission.

This is a fun place for kids, who can test their balance while climbing a rock wall, learn about static electricity with neon tubes, and simulate driving a fire engine through the city. And there's lots more—over eighty hands-on attractions that include being inside a bubble, controlling a construction crane, and landing on the surface of the moon. There are also exhibits of antique toys and a train collection on display.

NORFOLK TROLLEY TOUR

Departs from The Waterside Festival Marketplace in downtown Norfolk; (757) 640–6300. Runs daily Memorial Day through September. First tour leaves at 10:30 A.M., last tour leaves at 3:00 P.M.

See Norfolk's historic neighborhoods the old-fashioned way. Take a one-hour trolley tour of the city, getting off when you want to explore and back on to go to the next attraction.

VIRGINIA ZOOLOGICAL PARK (all ages)

3500 Granby Street; (757) 441–2706. Web address: www.virginiazoo.org. Open daily, except Thanksgiving, Christmas, and New Year's Day. Admission.

Not large compared with some big city zoos, the Virginia Zoological Park offers a nice outing for those with little kids. The zoo features more than 350 animals, including the Siberian tigers, diamondback terrapin, two-toed sloth, Baird's tapi (resembling a miniature elephant), clouded leopard, and white rhinoceros. The zoo's baboon habitat, the Xaxaba African Village, is home to two male gelada baboons. The village features a night house, spacious play area, a waterfall, and a small splash pool for its residents. The habitat will serve as a gateway to the Okavango Delta exhibit, set for completion in April of 2002, which will feature elephants, giraffes, lions, rhinos, and a rock python.

The park's Family Wildlife Adventure Programs include basic introductions to animals and reptiles for ages 2 to 11. Its Keeper for a Day program (age 13 and older) lets kids help prepare diets for the animals, clean exhibits, and work with keepers. There are also family sleepovers and special events throughout the year.

FUN CRUISES

To really enjoy this port town get out on the water. Some of the watery outings include:

AMERICAN ROVER TALLSHIP CRUISES (all ages)

333 Waterside Drive. The ship departs from Waterside Festival Marketplace; (757) 627–SAIL. Web address: www.americanrover.com. Tours run mid-April through late October. Check on times and schedules.

This three-masted topsail schooner offers two- or three-hour-long cruises. Along with seeing the sites, kids can help hoist the sails,

Norfolk is the place credited with the invention of the ice cream cone. Try Doumar's at 1919 Monticello Avenue (757–627–4163).

learn how to navigate, and learn how to tie sailor's knots.

CARRIE B. HARBOR TOURS (all ages)

Cruises leave from both the Waterside Festival Marketplace and North Landing, on the waterfront in Old Town Portsmouth across the Elizabeth River; (757) 393–4735. Tours run April through mid-October and June to Labor Day.

Sail on a replica of a nineteenth-century Mississippi paddlewheel riverboat and view the site of the Civil War battle between the *Monitor* and the *Merrimac*, plus see the mammoth "gray ladies" of the Navy's Atlantic fleet. Children under 6 sail for **Free.**

THE SPIRIT OF NORFOLK (all ages)

Departs from Town Point Park next to Waterside Festival Marketplace; (757) 625–1463. Web address: www.spiritcruises.com.

This ship offers two- and three-hour lunch and dinner cruises, plus specialty cruises geared to children.

THE VICTORY ROVER (all ages)

Departs daily from Nauticus (757–627–7406).

Offers narrated two-hour cruises of the naval base.

HARBOR PARK STADIUM (ages 5 and up)

150 Park Avenue; (757) 622–2222. Web address: www.norfolktides.com.

This park is home to the Norfolk Tides, a Triple A team for the New York Mets. In addition to baseball games, the 12,000-seat stadium hosts concerts and other events.

WHERE TO SHOP

THE WATERSIDE FESTIVAL MARKETPLACE

Norfolk waterfront, 333 Waterside Drive; (757) 627–3300. Web address: www.watersidemarketplace.com.

This shopping mall has become an attraction and gathering place for locals. Overlooking the Elizabeth River, the facility houses more than one hundred shops, stalls, and eateries. In season several boat tours and a tour of the Naval Base leave from here. Your kids will undoubtedly want to come here to shop for take-home treasures.

THE MACARTHUR CENTER

300 Monticello Avenue, Monticello Avenue and East Freemason Street; (757) 627–6000. Web address: www.shopmacarthur.com.

Located in the heart of downtown Norfolk, the MacArthur Center has more than 150 stores, including Nordstrom and Dillard's, plus a food court, restaurants, and eighteen movie theaters.

Where to Eat

Between attractions, sample some of Norfolk's seafood.

Doumar's Drive-in, *1919 Monticello Avenue; (757) 627–4163.* This local landmark is also a legend. The Smithsonian credits this town and this restaurant's owners' ancestors as having invented the ice cream waffle cone. Kids love the eatery's 1950s, hamburger-joint-style complete with curbside tray service, and parents love the inexpensive prices. Everyone likes the ice cream. $–$$

Fisherman's Wharf Seafood Restaurant, *1571 Bayville Street; (757) 480–3113. Dinner only.* Big appetites might like the all-you-can-eat seafood buffet here. $$$–$$$$

Freemason Abbey, *209 West Freemason Street; (757) 622–3966. Lunch and dinner.* Located downtown, this restaurant is a good bet for seafood and steaks. $–$$

Grate Steak, located in the Best Western Center Inn, 235 North Military Highway; (757) 461–5501. Lunch Monday through Friday, dinner daily. Kids will get a kick out of it when you grill your own entrees. $$–$$$

Hong Kong Super Buffet, 1108 East Little Creek Road; (757) 588–8855. Lunch and dinner daily. Chinese/Japanese/American buffet. $

K & W Cafeteria, 7525 Tidewater Drive; (757) 588–7917. Lunch and dinner daily. Southern-style food, lots of variety. $

Where to Stay

Best Western Center Inn, 235 North Military Highway; (757) 461–6600 or (800) 237–5517. Located 3 miles from downtown, it has indoor and outdoor pools.

Hampton Inn Norfolk Naval Base, 8501 Hampton Boulevard, (757) 489–1000 or (800) 426–7866. Close to the naval base, this hotel has an indoor heated pool. Rooms have coffeemakers and refrigerators. Rates include a continental breakfast.

Holiday Sands Motel and Tower, 1330 East Ocean View Avenue; (757) 583–2621 or (800) 525–5156. If you want to stay near the beach, this property is a good bet. Children can play in the gentler surf of Chesapeake Bay,

and parents can relax and enjoy this more peaceful side of town.

Norfolk Waterside Marriott Hotel 235 East Main Street, (757) 627–4200 or (800) 228–9290. Also downtown and family friendly, the hotel offers an indoor pool so that kids (and parents) can swim year-round.

Sheraton Norfolk Waterside Hotel, 777 Waterside Drive; (757) 622–6664 or (800) 325–3535. Located conveniently next door to the Waterside Festival Marketplace, it offers family-friendly lodging.

Radisson Hotel Norfolk, 700 Monticello Avenue; (757) 627–5555. Rooms have refrigerators, microwaves, HBO and Nintendo. Pool and fitness center.

For More Information

Norfolk Convention and Visitor's Bureau, 232 East Main Street, Norfolk, VA 23510; (757) 664–6620 or (800) 368–3097. Web address: www.norfolkcvb.com. For a visitors guide, call (800) 368–3097. Check here about the Big

Ticket package, which has reduced priced tickets to area attractions. Another tourist information office is located in Nauticus, the National Maritime Center, at 1 Waterside Drive, and another off Interstate 64 at exit 273.

Virginia Beach

Virginia Beach lives up to its motto of "all kinds of fun." With 35 miles of coastline and sandy—though sometimes crowded—ocean beaches, the shore and surf bring out the kid in even the most work-weary city dweller. Prime-time is summer; with the high temperatures come crowds, although the completion of the widening of the oceanfront to more than 300 feet spreads out the crowds. A visit in spring and fall can be nice because the crowds are gone. Just please your kids by picking a hotel with an indoor pool.

In Virginia Beach, the Boardwalk has a designated bicycle lane. This no-cars-allowed, long, flat stretch of sidewalk is a great way to get around town. You can rent bicycles as well as inline skates (roller blades) and surreys from the random bike stands set up along the boardwalk. Glide down the board-walk with the sea breeze blowing in your hair.

THE BEACH

Where you stay and where you park your beach blanket depends on what you like. The highest concentration of boombox, bikini, and college crowds are usually found in the resort area from Twentieth through Thirty-fifth Streets. My teenage daughter heads straight into the heart of the action. The bodies can be blanket to blanket and the people-watching is prime, especially along the "boardwalk," the 30-foot-wide paved path edging the sand.

Although Virginia Beach is bustling in summer, there are some relatively quieter spots good for families. These include the strip of sand along the North End, from Forty-third Street north toward **Fort Story.** The southern end of town, the Sandbridge area, has lifeguards and a quieter pace than the hub-bub in the heart of town. For something different, you might try the beach at Fort Story, the army base, which is open to the public. Whatever stretch of sand you pick, time-honored traditions include swimming, sunning, and body-surfing. Here you can look up from your sandcastle and maybe see dolphins breaching the sea. On summer evenings, Atlantic Avenue transforms into a family-style street party called "Beach Street USA," with a variety of entertain-ers, including crooners, strummers, magicians, and jugglers.

Near Virginia Beach's see-and-be-seen strip of sand, you can still view the land as it was seen by America's first settlers. Located at the southernmost end of Virginia Beach, Back Bay National Wildlife Refuge and False Cape State Park share similar topography, but have different functions. Back Bay is mostly a wildlife refuge, whereas False Cape is primarily 10 miles of rustic beach area. At both Back Bay and False Cape one can surf, cast for flounder, or sight white-tailed deer that dart through the thickets. Both serve as havens for nature lovers, because access is primarily by foot, bicycle, private boat, or by an open-air electric tram operated by False Cape State Park.

BACK BAY NATIONAL WILDLIFE REFUGE (all ages)

4005 Sandpiper Road; (757) 721–2412. Web address: www.backbay.fws.gov. Visitor Contact Station open daily, closed Saturdays December through March and on all public holidays except Memorial Day, Fourth of July, and Labor Day. **Free**, *November through March; admission April through October.*

Back Bay's 7,732 acres are a managed area created as a waterfowl refuge. Egrets and herons dance on the water and turtles dive into pools along the 9 miles of dikes built to separate the man-made, freshwater impoundments from the saltwater of Chesapeake Bay. The sounds of geese and ducks echo through these gentle stretches of water. (Approximately 10,000 snowgeese and a large variety of ducks visit here during the peak of their migration, usually in December.) For a quick tour try the 1-mile boardwalk beach loop past dune barriers to the Atlantic, or the 4-mile dike loop through marshlands. Pick up a **Free** brochure at the Visitor Contact Station for information.

FALSE CAPE STATE PARK (all ages)

4001 Sandpiper Road, 5 miles south of Back Bay. For camping and other information, call (757) 426–7128. Web address: www.dcr.state.va.us/parks/falscape. htm. Admission to the park is **Free** *but entry is through Back Bay National Wildlife Refuge, which charges admission April through October.*

Leave behind the tourists and boomboxes for 10 miles of unspoiled beaches, thousands of acres of marshlands, and woods filled with songbirds. False Cape offers the changing interplay of beach, dune, and forest. When here, think about the unspoiled beaches of False Cape and how this spot of what came to be Virginia Beach lured the New World dreamers.

To enjoy False Cape, you can hike 5 miles through Back Bay, rent a mountain bike from Conte's Bicycle and Fitness, 1721 Laskin Road; 757-491-1900), or take the tram (spring and summer) available from Little Island City Park, Sandbridge; (757) 498-2473. Be sure to bring your own water and lots of it. False Cape is a gift for the eye: 6 miles of beautiful shoreline graced by dunes, gulls, and sandpipers but inhabited by only a handful of people. At the height of the beach season, birds outnumber bathers, and the unspoiled arc of surf and sand stretches for miles. Other delights include walks through loblolly pine forests rising above tiers of blueberry patches, marshes speckled with white hibiscus, and sprays of gold asters. Along the **Barbour Hill Trail,** 2.4 miles, stop to go crabbing at the boat docks (bring your own gear), or dangle your feet into the cool water as you look across at Cedar Island, a 400-acre heron rookery. Camping is permitted year-round; call (800) 933-7275 for information. The park offers programs in astronomy, birding hikes and night hikes, and bus tours as well as special events in conjunction with the Virginia Marine Science Museum and others.

Virginia Beach Travel Tips

If your family is really into nature, in the winter the Back Bay National Wildlife Refuge and Falso Cape State Park offer a one-of-a-kind back-to-nature experience during the winter months on its beach mobile, called the *Terra-gator.* Designed to navigate the shoreline with thirty-six passengers, the *Terra-gator* takes families on a five-hour round-trip excursion, including a stopover at the park, with commentary throughout the journey. The trip is available December through March and there is a fee. Call (800) 933-7275 for information and reservations.

FIRST LANDING STATE PARK (all ages)

U.S. Highway 60 at Cape Henry, 2500 Shore Drive; (757) 412–2320. Web address: www.dcr.state.va.us/parks/1stland.htm.

This park with its 19 miles of hiking trails, is Virginia's most popular state park, attracting more than one million visitors annually, yet it still offers a quiet respite. Paths lead you by freshwater ponds and through thickets of large cypress trees draped with Spanish moss. There is a special bicycle trail and bikes are permitted on park roads. (Bikes can be rented at the Chesapeake Bay Center.) A boat ramp offers access to Broad Bay. Kayaks are available for rental on in-season weekends. The first section of the Bald Cypress Trail is 1 mile long, crosses dunes and ponds, and is handicapped-accessible. Located in the park is the newly opened $1.6 million Chesapeake Bay Center, an environmentally focused interactive visitor information center that can serve as a home base for planning an outdoor vacation. The center also showcases Bay Lab, developed by the Virginia Marine Science Museum. This marine lab features aquariums, environmental exhibits, classroom space, a wet lab, and touch tank. The visitor center includes a staging area for adventure programs and equipment rental, enabling visitors to participate in such programs as sea kayaking and explore the Chesapeake Bay firsthand.

VIRGINIA MARINE SCIENCE MUSEUM (ages 5 and up)

717 General Booth Boulevard; (757) 437–4949 or (757) 425–FISH for recorded information. Web address:www.vmsm.com. Open daily, except Thanksgiving and Christmas. Admission.

The Virginia Marine Science Museum is a must-see. At the Atlantic Ocean Pavilion and Main Building, visitors can see sandtiger, nurse and brown sharks, stingrays, and other open-ocean dwellers in the 300,000-gallon Norfolk Canyon Aquarium. There are also a 70,000-gallon sea turtle aquarium, a sea turtle hatching laboratory, a jellyfish and octopus aquarium, a life-size model of a humpback whale, and lots of hands-on exhibits. The Owls Creek Marsh Pavilion tells the story of Owls Creek salt marsh, the waterway on which the museum is located. The exhibits are clever and have kid-friendly touch-screen computers. In the whimsical Macro Marsh gallery where the "grass" is ten times larger than real life, visitors feel as tiny as hermit crabs. In the Micro Marsh gallery via microscopes little things such as mosquito heads come into view.

The dozens of aquariums and terrariums feature creatures such as river otters, seahorses, and a one-of-a-kind interactive theater where children can test their knowledge about the local environment. Attached is a 0.5-acre aviary featuring more than fifty-five species, including cattle egrets, brown pelicans, turkey vultures, and great blue herons, all viewed from an elevated wooden walkway.

Between the two pavilions is the Nature Trail, a 0.3-mile trail that meanders through ten acres of salt marsh preserve along Owls Creek. On this walk sweet gum and maple trees offer shade and circular loops jut out into the water to provide clear views of the gulls and great blue herons swooping down for fish. (You can almost ignore the steady hum of the traffic on busy General Booth Boulevard just 30 feet away. The contrast makes a powerful case for preserving wetlands such as this one.) A 30-foot observation tower and information boxes help visitors identify what they're seeing.

Informative fifteen-minute programs are held throughout the day in both pavilions and along the nature trail on a variety of topics. In addition, special family programs are held throughout the year at the Bay Lab in the Chesapeake Bay Center at First Landing State Park (see above). These range from simple ones, such as learning how sea stars protect themselves, to "Exotic Aquatics: An Evening of Mystery," where participants (ages 6 to adult) are given clues to solve the mystery of what kind of animal has been pulled from the Chesapeake Bay.

In winter sign on for the whale-watching trips sponsored by the museum. From January till mid-March, look for humpback whales as museum staff tell you about these leviathans. June to October, the museum sponsors dolphin-watching trips. Throughout the year Ocean Collection boat trips give visitors the opportunity to examine sea life up close, with sea creatures pulled from the ocean and brought on deck.

THE OLD COAST GUARD STATION MUSEUM (ages 5 and up) (TT)

Twenty-fourth Street and Atlantic Avenue; (757) 422–1587. Web address: www. oldcoastguardstation.com. Open Tuesday through Sunday; closed Thanksgiving, Christmas, and New Year's Day.

Housed in a 1903 Coast Guard Station, this museum looks at another aspect of sea life: Learn about life-saving techniques from the early days of shipwrecks to the submarine-mined waters of both world wars. Check out its TowerCAM to get an up-close view of the ocean, beach, and nearby objects.

OLD CAPE HENRY LIGHTHOUSE (ages 5 and up)

Northeastern tip of Virginia Beach, on the grounds of the U.S. Army's Fort Story. A photo identification card may be needed to enter Fort Story; (757) 422–9421 Open year-round. Admission.

This lighthouse, built in 1791, marked the entrance to the Chesapeake Bay until 1881. The lighthouse is open for tours and climbs to the top year-round.

PSYCHIC TRAVELS: ASSOCIATION FOR RESEARCH AND ENLIGHTENMENT (ages 9 and up)

Sixty-seventh Street and Atlantic Avenue; (757) 428–3588 or (800) 723–1112. Web address: www.edgarcayce.org. **Free.**

Turn-of-the-century seer Edgar Cayce obeyed instructions he received in a trance to move to Virginia Beach in 1925 to establish a hospital. Cayce, frequently called the "sleeping prophet," garnered his information from higher states of consciousness when he was in a trance-like state. Cayce gave readings in which he diagnosed people's illnesses and prescribed cures, skills he never possessed in his waking state. Visitors here can browse through one of the most extensive metaphysical libraries in the world, containing Cayce's transcribed readings. At the bookstore expand your beach reading with tomes on holistic health, numerology, dream interpretation, meditation, and channeling. Daily tours include films, lectures, meditation classes, and ESP demonstrations. Spa treatments are also available.

HIT THE WAVES! (all ages)

Getting out on the water is a favorite family activity. Blue Moon offers lunch, dinner, moonlight, and sightseeing cruises along inland waterways; (757) 627-7771. You can rent a boat, kayak, or canoe at Sandbridge Boat Rentals, 3713 Sandpiper Road; (757) 721-6210. Want to do more than just sail? Book a day of deep-sea fishing with the Virginia Beach Fishing Center at 200 Winston Salem Avenue at the Rudee Inlet Bridge; (757) 422-5700.

OCEAN BREEZE WATERPARK (all ages)

849 General Booth Boulevard; (757) 422–4444, (757) 422–0718, or (800) 678–WILD.

If your family can't live without a water park even in a town where the beach and ocean are primary, then head here for all the splashy doings, including wave pools like the million-gallon Runaway Bay, water slides (the more adventurous should try the Bahama Mama speed slide), and log-flume rides, plus Rocky Springs, a just-for-adults activity pool with slides (why should kids have all the fun?). The park also offers miniature golf, batting cages, go-carts, three-quarter scale Grand Prix cars at neighboring Motorworld and Dive In Movies that let families enjoy a Disney flick while floating on top of the Runaway Bay Wave Pool.

THE CHESAPEAKE BAY BRIDGE–TUNNEL (all ages)

Even if it costs $10 each way to cross the 17.6-mile-long Chesapeake Bay Bridge–Tunnel, the fee is worth it, at least once. As the structure loops over and under the bay, it's easy to savor the sense of space and joy common to open roads, panoramic water views, and sea breezes. In September and early May, hundreds of bird-watchers come to observe this mid-Atlantic flyway for migratory sea birds. Families also will enjoy the view and menu offered at Seagull Pier and Restaurant, midway across the structure.

SURF AND SAND MOVIE THEATRE

941 Alaskin Drive

On rainy days, head over to the local movie theater where they show extra movies when the weather is bad.

Annual Events

Virginia Beach has many festivals and special events throughout the year. Here are a few of them. For more information call (800) 822-3224.

MARCH

Wildfowl Art Show. You'll have nothing but a fowl time here—bird fowl that is—with decoys, carvers, and photography. Kids also get a chance to do their own decoy painting; (757) 437-8432.

MAY

Memorial Day Weekend. Visitors swing to the live sounds of big band music at the Twenty-fourth Street Park on the oceanfront. (757) 463-2300. For strawberry lovers, there's the **Pungo Strawberry Festival,** with homemade delicacies, live music, and arts and crafts. (757) 721-6001. What better month than May for the **Annual Beach Music Weekend.** Kick off your shoes and dance on the sand; (757) 463-2300.

JUNE

Boardwalk Art Show and Festival. More than 450 artists and craftspeople sell their handmade creations along the boardwalk; (757) 425-0000.

Viva Elvis Festival. Hundreds of hip-swinging, lip-quivering "The King" lookalikes descend on Virginia Beach during this musical competition; (757) 463-2300.

AUGUST

East Coast Surfing Championships. Catch a wave—at least vicariously; (800) 861-7873.

OCTOBER

Blues and Brews bring an Octoberfest atmosphere to the beach, with samplings of beers, microbrews, and cider surrounded by authentic German music, plus the best in local blues bands; (757) 463-2300.

Where to Eat

Virginia Beach offers the hungry the usual array of cheap eats plus some good restaurants.

Aldo's Ristorante, *Le Promenade Shopping Center, 1860 Laskin Road; (757) 491–1111. Open daily for lunch and dinner.* This restaurant serves Italian fare. $–$$$

Duck-In, *3324 Shore Drive; (757) 481–0201. Open daily for lunch and dinner.* Treat your family to the homemade crab cakes or the dinner buffet. $$–$$$

The Happy Crab, *550 Laskin Road; (757) 437–9200. Open daily for lunch and dinner.* Pick crabs or shuck oysters on paper-covered tables. $$

The Jewish Mother, *3108 Pacific Avenue; (757) 422–5430.* This informal restaurant offers deli sandwiches with enough variety for even for the most finicky kid. Breakfast is served all day, lunch and dinner. Some evenings there is live music. $–$$

Mahi Mah's Seafood Restaurant & Sushi Saloon, *615 Atlantic Avenue; (757) 437–8030. Breakfast, lunch, and dinner daily.* This is in the Ramada Inn and offers sushi and seafood. $$–$$$

Mary's Restaurant, *616 Virginia Beach Boulevard; (757) 428–1355. Open daily for breakfast and lunch.* Meals are served in a casual and friendly atmosphere. $

Where to Stay

There are many hotels in the Virginia Beach area. Decide whether you want to be beachfront in the heart of the action on the sand in the quieter northern area, or a few blocks from the water. Here are some family-friendly suggestions. Visitors planning on a longer stay should consider real estate rentals. Several rental agencies are available. Visit www.fam-fun.com for an online review of accommodation choices (and area attractions) found in the scenic 50-mile region from Virginia Beach to Williamsburg.

Affordable Properties (757-428-0432) and **Siebert Realty–Sandbridge Beach** (757-426-6200 or 800-231-3037).

The Barclay Towers, *809 Atlantic Avenue; (757) 491–2700 or (800) 344–4473.* This is an all-suite hotel whose rooms have kitchenettes. Five- and seven-night package plans are available. Complimentary continental breakfast, pool.

The Belvedere Motel, *Oceanfront at 36th Street; (757) 425–0612 or (800) 425–0612.* This lodging offers families motel rooms and efficiencies.

The Cavalier Hotel, *Forty-second and Oceanfront; (757) 425–8555 or (800) 446–8199.* This property has two locations, one on the beach and one nearby. Both sites have balconies and children under 18 stay **Free.** Indoor and outdoor pools, bikes, and tennis courts.

The Days Inn Oceanfront, *3107 Atlantic Avenue; (757) 428–7233 or (800) 292–3297.* This is right on the beach and has an indoor pool plus an exercise room.

The Holiday Inn Surfside Hotel & Suites, *2607 Atlantic Avenue; (757) 491–6900 or (800) 810–2400.* In the heart of the "action," this property offers rooms and suites plus an indoor pool.

The Holiday Inn SunSpree Resort On The Ocean, *Thirty-ninth and Oceanfront; (757) 428–1711 or (800) 94– BEACH.* This property has an outdoor pool, and in season, some organized activities for the kids. Also offers refrigerators and coffeemakers in rooms.

The Ramada Plaza Resort, *Oceanfront at Fifty-seventh Street, (757) 428– 7025 or (800) 365–3032.* This beachfront property is a good choice for those who want to stay in the quieter north end of town. The facility has indoor and outdoor pools, plus microwaves, refrigerators, and coffeemakers in rooms.

FOR MORE LODGING INFORMATION

Call 800-VA-BEACH

For More Information

The Virginia Beach Convention and Visitor's Bureau, *2101 Parks Avenue, Suite 500, Virginia Beach, VA 23451; reservations (800) 822–3224. Web address: www.vbfun.com.*

Northern Virginia

Perhaps the best-known attractions in Northern Virginia are Arlington National Cemetery, Mount Vernon, George Washington's plantation, and Alexandria; the latter is both an historic colonial town as well as a bustling urban neighborhood. The region offers additional historic sites, battlefields, and monuments as well as parks and a great, kid-friendly museum dedicated to news.

Arlington

Arlington, just across the Memorial Bridge from the District of Columbia, is well known for Arlington National Cemetery. The area has many other historical attractions and war memorials, too. Visit the ones most likely to interest your kids. Remember, seeing all of them might cause your children to rebel, while a little bit of well-chosen history goes a long

Candyce's Top Picks
for Fun in Northern Virginia

1. Arlington National Cemetery, Arlington
2. Women in Military Service for America Memorial, Arlington
3. Newseum, Arlington
4. Mount Vernon Bicycle Trail, Alexandria
5. Mount Vernon Estate, Mount Vernon
6. Great Falls National Park, Great Falls
7. Wolf Trap Farm Park for the Performing Arts, Vienna

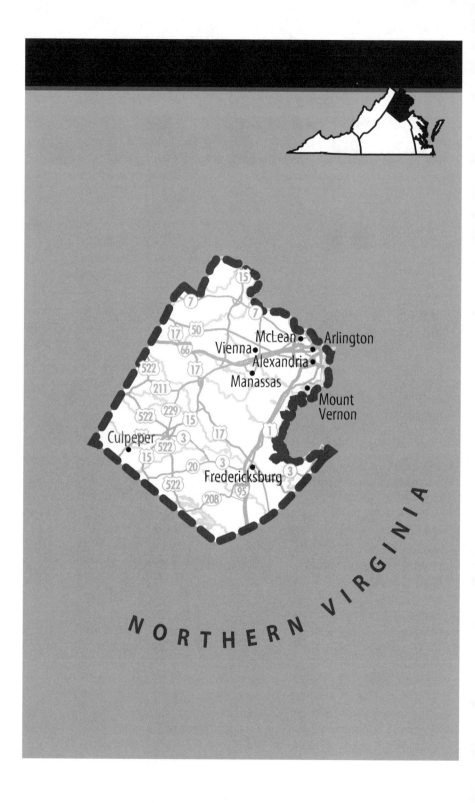

NORTHERN VIRGINIA

way. Along with the well-known sites, be sure to visit the less well-known Women in Military Service Memorial dedicated to women who have served in the Armed Forces, and the Newseum, devoted to journalism. The Newseum is scheduled to move to Washington, D.C. in 2003.

 ARLINGTON NATIONAL CEMETERY (ages 7 and up)
Take the Metro's Blue Line to the Arlington National Cemetery station; (703) 607–8052. Web address: www.arlingtoncemetery.org. Open from 9:00 A.M. to 5:00 P.M. October through March, and 8:00 A.M. to 7:00 P.M. April through September.

See where America's military heroes, presidents, and other public figures have been honored, memorialized, and buried. This cemetery isn't just historical; there are often fifteen or more military funeral services a day, so don't be surprised if you come upon a service. Start at the visitors center near the Metro stop and obtain historical information, gravesite locations for notables, and information on **Arlington House** (also known as the Robert E. Lee Memorial, 703-557-0613). Tour buses (for a fee) shuttle between four stops inside cemetery gates: the visitors center, John F. Kennedy grave site, Tomb of the Unknown Soldier, and the Arlington House.

Visit the **Tomb of the Unknown Soldier,** which overlooks the Washington, D.C., skyline. The tomb contains the remains of unidentified soldiers from World War I, World War II, and Korea. The tomb itself is guarded twenty-four hours a day by the third United States Infantry. Changing of the guard, a solemn and impressive ritual, occurs every half-hour from April 1 through September 30 and every hour on the hour from October 1 through March 31. The guards change at two-hour intervals during night hours year-round.

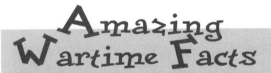

Amazing Wartime Facts

Elizabeth Van Lew, of Richmond, Virginia, received Confederate military plans and encoded them before carrying them to the Union Army. She also smuggled food and clothing to Union prisoners jailed in Richmond's Libby Prison.

Sarah Osborne accompanied her husband Aaron to war during the American Revolution, cooking for him and his fellow soldiers. When General Washington asked her if she was afraid of bullets, she said, "It would not do for the men to fight and starve, too."

As for the guards, there is more method to their marching than one might think. The guard paces from his post and across the crossway in twenty-one steps, turning to pause while facing the memorial for twenty-one seconds. Turning once more, the guard pauses for another twenty-one seconds before repeating the process. "Twenty-one" represents the highest honor of salutation, matching the twenty-one-gun salute.

Additional graves of notables include those of General Philip Henry Sheridan, U.S. Army, a Civil War soldier; Lt. Commander Roger Bruce Chaffee, U.S. Navy, Apollo astronaut, who died while performing test operations for the Apollo One space mission; Lt. Colonel Virgil I. ("Gus") Grissom, U.S. Air Force, Apollo astronaut, the second American in space on the Mercury mission, 1961, and first person to make two space trips on the two-man Gemini flight, 1965; the commingled remains of the seven astronauts who died aboard the space shuttle Challenger in 1986; William Jennings Bryan, presidential candidate, Secretary of State; Oliver Wendell Holmes, Jr., Civil War veteran, Supreme Court Justice; Joe Louis (Barrow), heavyweight boxing champion; Rear Admiral Robert E. Peary, U.S. Navy, explorer; and William Howard Taft, president, chief justice of the United States Supreme Court. Jacqueline Kennedy's and John F. Kennedy's gravesites are home to the Eternal Flame. Your child may well ask how the flame stays lit: There is a constantly flashing electric spark near the tip of the gas nozzle that relights the flame if it should go out in the rain or wind.

The visitors center and parking facility are open during cemetery hours.

Amazing Wartime Facts

Women Airforce Service Pilots (WASP) was a civilian organization of approximately 1,000 women who worked closely with the army during World War II. These women performed essential services such as flying aircraft from factories to air bases and towing, in the air, targets for antiaircraft artillery students to practice shooting at. This task was so dangerous—thirty-eight WASPs died while doing this—that men refused to perform this duty, stating that they'd rather risk their lives in combat.

Amazing Wartime Facts

Phoebe Jeter commanded a platoon of fifteen men assigned to identify incoming enemy SCUD missiles and destroy them during Operation Desert Storm. She became the first woman in her battalion to earn an Army Commendation medal while in Saudi Arabia.

Sybil Ludington rode 40 miles on horseback—farther than Paul Revere—in 1777 to warn the people around Ludington, Connecticut, that the British were attacking.

Grace Banker served in World War I as a telephone switch operator, receiving and sending messages from troops on the front line to soldiers at headquarters. For her work she received the Distinguished Service Cross.

🏛 **WOMEN IN MILITARY SERVICE FOR AMERICA MEMORIAL (ages 7 and up)**

At the entrance to Arlington National Cemetery; (703) 533–1155 or (800) 222–2294. Web addresses: www.womensmemorial.org and www.nps.gov. Open daily year-round, closed Christmas.

This memorial, dedicated October 1997, was built to honor all women who have served in, and with, the military. The education center and 196-seat theater portray the history of women in the armed forces beginning 220 years ago. Children may be surprised to learn that women played important roles in war as far back as the Revolution. The Hall of Honor recognizes women who have made a significant sacrifice, such as those who were prisoners of war or died in service, and those who were recipients of the highest awards for service and bravery. The Computer Registry makes it possible to locate and view the records of friends and relatives who were, or are, servicewomen. Special tours for children are available upon request and the facility is developing programs and materials geared for children.

THE MARINE CORPS WAR MEMORIAL (ages 7 and up)

Marshall Drive between U.S. Highway 50 and Arlington National Cemetery; (703) 289–2500. Web address: www.nps.gov. Open twenty-four hours, year-round.

This Marine Corps memorial, commonly referred to as the **Iwo Jima Memorial,** is not far from the cemetery. The capture of Iwo Jima, a noted incident in World War II, was immortalized on film when news photographer Joe Rosenthal photographed five marines and one Navy corpsman raising a large American flag. Felix W. de Weldon's sculpture of that scene honors not only those marines who fought in World War II but every marine who has died defending America since 1775.

The Netherlands Carillon, a gift from the Dutch people in gratitude for American aid during World War II, is adjacent to the Memorial. Carillon concerts are held on national holidays and on Saturdays. In May and September, the concerts are from 2:00 to 4:00 P.M., and in June, July, and August, from 6:00 to 8:00 P.M. Children may not be thrilled by the concerts, but they (and you) can go up in the tower to watch the carilloneur perform, which they may find interesting. There's also a good view of Washington from up there, too.

PENTAGON (ages 7 and up)

Take the Metro's Yellow and Blue lines to the Pentagon station. **Free** *tours run every hour on the hour from 9:00 A.M. to 3:00 P.M. During the summer tickets usually sell out by 10:00 A.M. Photo I.D. required for all over the age of 16. (703) 695–1776. Web address: www.pentagon.com.*

For more military lore and lessons, visit the Pentagon, the five-sided building housing various offices of the U.S. Department of Defense. (It is currently undergoing a renovation made more necessary by the terrorist attack on September 11, 2001.) The behemoth of a building is interesting to look at from the high-way, but caution: Unless your kids have a particular interest in military history and art, the

Amazing Pentagon Facts

The Pentagon, which covers twenty-nine acres, is one of the world's largest office buildings and has 17.5 miles of corridors.

tour may bore them. An introductory film explains the history behind the building. The tour of the many corridors includes the Military Women's

Corridor, the Flag Corridor, and the Hall of Heroes, which lists Congressional Medal of Honor recipients. You'll see the Pentagon's Time–Life Art Collection, 1,500 works from the army's short-lived 1943 war art program.

DRUG ENFORCEMENT ADMINISTRATION (DEA) MUSEUM AND VISITORS CENTER (ages 10 and up)

This museum is across the street from the Pentagon City Shopping Mall and one Metro stop from Arlington National Cemetery. 700 Army Navy Drive; (703) 307–3463. Web address: www.deamuseum.org. Open Tuesday through Friday, 10:00 A.M. to 4:00 P.M. Tours by appointment only; call between 9:00 A.M. and 5:00 P.M. weekdays to schedule.

This 150-year chronological exhibit on drugs in America is heavy on photographs, but kids will be interested in the items on display about such cultural icons as Coca-Cola, which contained cocaine until 1903 and was advertised as a medicine that would "ease the tired brain," or Bayer Aspirin, whose precursor was Bayer Heroin, advertised as "highly effective against coughs."

THEODORE ROOSEVELT ISLAND (all ages)

Located off the George Washington (GW) Memorial Parkway heading north; (703) 289–2530. Web address: www.nps.gov. Open daily, 8:00 A.M. to dusk.
This island, in the middle of the Potomac river, serves as an eighty-eight-acre bird sanctuary. Its 2.1 miles of walking trails make it something of an oasis if you ignore the jet noise from nearby Ronald Reagan Washington National Airport. You can bird-watch and walk through swamp, marsh, and forest. The upper trail leads through woods filled with elms, tulip poplars, oaks, and red maples. In the center of the island is a 47-foot monument of Teddy Roosevelt. Call ahead to check the schedule for the ranger-led tours.

WHERE TO SHOP

For a break from history, news, and government, Arlington offers three shopping malls.

BALLSTON COMMON

4238 Wilson Boulevard; (703) 243–8088. Take the Metro's Orange Line to Ballston Station.
This facility offers one hundred specialty shops and restaurants.

CRYSTAL CITY

1608 Crystal Square Arcade; (703) 922–4636. Take the Metro's Blue or Yellow line to Crystal City Station.

The underground network of hallways features 125 shops and restaurants.

FASHION CENTRE AT PENTAGON CITY

1100 South Hayes Street; (703) 415–2400. Take the Metro's Blue or Yellow line to Pentagon City Station.

The 150 shops include the usual chains of women's, men's, and kid's clothing stores, plus restaurants, computer, electronics, and toy stores.

Where to Eat

Cafe Parisien Express, *4520 Lee Highway; (703) 525–3332. Open Monday through Saturday for breakfast, lunch, and dinner, Sunday for brunch.* This French bistro features soups, sandwiches, crepes, and quiches. $

Hunan Number One, *3033 Wilson Boulevard; (703) 528–1177. Open daily for lunch and dinner.* Specialties of this Cantonese restaurant are sesame chicken with lemon sauce, sizzling black pepper steak, and the Hunan No. 1, a combination of shrimp, chicken, beef, broccoli, straw mushrooms, and snow peas in a brown sauce. $-$$$

The Little Cafe and Bakery, *2039 Wilson Boulevard; (703) 522–6622. Open daily for breakfast, lunch, and dinner; Sunday for brunch.* The Mediterranean spe-cialties are spinach pie and baklava. Children's menu available. $

Orleans Steakhouse, *1213 Wilson Boulevard; (703) 524–2929. Open daily for lunch and dinner.* This restaurant was here when this area, called Rosslyn, was an undeveloped suburb of Washington, D.C., consisting mostly of vacant lots. The New Orleans cuisine includes blackened catfish and shrimp Creole as well as steaks. Children's menu available. $-$$

Red, Hot, and Blue, *1600 Wilson Boulevard; (703) 276–7427. Open daily for lunch and dinner.* Memphis-style ribs, pulled pork, beans, barbecued chicken, and catfish are staples at this lively restaurant. Children's menu available. $-$$

Where to Stay

Americana Hotel Crystal City, *1400 Jefferson Davis Highway; (703) 979–3772 or (800) 548–6261.* This property offers reasonably priced accommodations 1 block from the Crystal City Metro station. Complimentary continental breakfast and hotel shuttle service.

Days Inn Arlington, *2201 Arlington Boulevard; (703) 525–0300 or (800) 329–7466.* The inn is centrally located and has a restaurant and pool on the property, plus a **Free** shuttle to the Metro.

Embassy Suites Crystal City, *1300 Jefferson Davis Highway; (703) 979–9799.* The suites offer families more space and privacy than a single room. There is a refrigerator in each guest room.

For More Information

Arlington Visitors Center, *735 South Eighteenth Street, Arlington, VA 22202; (703) 228–5720 or (800) 677–6267. Web address: www.stayarlington.com.*

Alexandria

Alexandria was a flourishing seaport long before rebelling from the Crown was even a whisper. It was the river and the promise of riches that lured the first settlers to Alexandria's shores in the early seventeenth century. The area grew with the aspirations of its residents. By 1749 the town became a city as 120 lots were auctioned off. George Washington, a young surveyor's assistant, helped pace off these

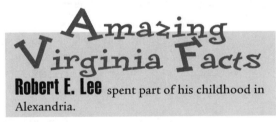

Amazing Virginia Facts

Robert E. Lee spent part of his childhood in Alexandria.

parcels. The heart of this original sixty-acre tract still beats as Old Town, an enclave that wears its historic past with a gracious air.

To see beyond the bustle of Northern Virginia back to colonial times, take a walking tour of Old Town Alexandria and use your imagination to see these streets as the early colonists did. When you stroll along King, Cameron, Queen, and Duke Streets, names that harken back to the town's colonial past, you'll discover amid the modern businesses and traffic the outlines of this thriving river town, which captured the imaginations of its first citizens.

Merchants and money made Alexandria grow. By the eighteenth century this city bustled as the third largest seaport in the colonies. The prosperity created a thriving merchant class who talked business over port in front of fires in tastefully appointed drawing rooms. Remember that with young kids one historic house goes a long way; it's the rare child who wants to see them all. Allow time to browse Alexandria's shops, stroll the waterfront, or take a scenic cruise.

CARLYLE HOUSE (ages 8 and up) (TT)

121 North Fairfax Street; (703) 549–2997. Open Tuesday through Saturday, 10:00 A.M. to 4:30 P.M., Sunday noon to 4:30 P.M., closed Monday. Admission.

Reminiscent of country houses of Scottish gentry, this sandstone manor embodied the dreams of John Carlyle, a prosperous merchant. Completed in 1753, the two-story mansion, built on two choice lots, stands in contrast to the smaller brick townhouses that are flush with the sidewalk. The best view of Carlyle House for many kids may be from the outside. Sparsely furnished with donated period furniture, the rooms seem a bit plain, and a tour often proves bland for kids. An unrenovated bedroom does shed some interesting light on eighteenth-century building techniques, as the old beams reveal the careful carpentry of the era. Be sure to pause amid the aster and foxglove in the gardens. Although not faithful to Carlyle's plan, these flower and herb beds conform to eighteenth-century ideals of symmetry and usefulness.

MARKET SQUARE (ages 4 and up)

On the 300 block of King Street.

The front of Carlyle's house faces what is still among the oldest continuing markets in the country. If you're up early on a Saturday, between 5:00 and 9:00 A.M., browse the stalls set up for fresh bread, pastries, and fruit. Kids like the happy commotion and cheap eats.

THE STABLER–LEADBEATER APOTHECARY SHOP (ages 7 and up) (TT)

105–107 South Fairfax Street; (703) 836–3713. Open Monday through Saturday 10:00 A.M. to 4:00 P.M., Sunday 1:00 to 5:00 P.M. Web address: www.apothecary.org Admission.

Founded in 1792 and in continuous operation until 1933, this shop features patent medicines and blood-letting equipment popular in George Washington's day as well as a letter from Martha Washington requesting cures such as cod-liver oil. There are also displays of hand-blown glass vessels, mortars, and pestles. A brief taped history of the shop available in English, French, Spanish, and Russian.

TORPEDO FACTORY ART CENTER (ages 5 and up)

105 North Union Street; (703) 838–4565. Open daily 10:00 A.M. to 5:00 P.M. year-round. **Free.**

The art center overlooks the waterfront. This space, once a factory for torpedo shells for our fighting men in World War II, now booms as the Torpedo Factory Art Center, where 160 professional artists not only work at their craft but display their

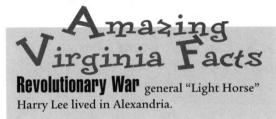

Amazing Virginia Facts

Revolutionary War general "Light Horse" Harry Lee lived in Alexandria.

wares. You can wander through the eighty-three studios, chat with the artists, and watch them at work. Kids and adults enjoy browsing the brightly colored pottery, glass vessels, jewelry, and wearable art.

ALEXANDRIA ARCHAEOLOGY MUSEUM (ages 7 and up)

Number 327, 105 North Union Street; (703) 838–4399. Open Tuesday through Friday, 10:00 A.M. to 3:00 P.M., Saturday 10:00 A.M. to 5:00 P.M., Sunday 1:00 to 5:00 P.M.

Watch archaeologists research Alexandria's history in the museum's laboratory. There might be a volunteer piecing together an eighteenth-century pot or examining bones from a seventeenth-century family's meal.

ALEXANDRIA SEAPORT CENTER (ages 5 and up)

1000 South Lee Street; (703) 549–7078. Web address: www.capaccess.org/asf. Daily 9:00 A.M. to 4:00 P.M.

Built and launched in 1998, the Alexandria Seaport Center is a two-story floating museum nestled among the docks of Alexandria. Inside you'll find a marine environmental sciences laboratory, an extensive maritime history library with accompanying exhibits, and a boatbuilding school. Children may find the boatbuilding especially interesting to watch, since often those working on the boats will be kids their own age. In the future, the museum hopes to offer rides on the river in its boat the *Potomac.*

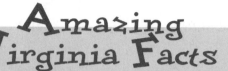

Amazing Virginia Facts

George Washington became the Masonic Lodge's Charter Master in 1788.

LEE–FENDALL HOUSE (ages 9 and up)

614 Oronoco Street; (703) 548–1789. Open Tuesday through Saturday 10:00 A.M. to 4:00 P.M., Sunday 1:00 to 4:00 P.M. Sometimes closed on weekends, so call first.

Find out about the Lee family as you peruse the memorabilia of thirty-seven Lees who resided here over a period of more than 118 years. The house, constructed in 1785 and renovated to an 1850 Greek-revival style, also features a guaranteed-to-please collection of antique doll houses.

THE LYCEUM, ALEXANDRIA'S HISTORY MUSEUM (ages 8 and up)

201 South Washington Street; (703) 838–4994. Open Monday through Saturday 10:00 A.M. to 5:00 P.M., Sunday 1:00 to 5:00 P.M.; closed Thanksgiving, Christmas, and New Year's Day.

A Greek-revival structure built in 1839 and used as a hospital in the Civil War, the Lyceum houses 300 years of historical items, such as Civil War artifacts, photos, ceramics, furniture, and nineteenth-century stoneware. In the South Gallery, materials are provided for children to color pictures of colonial life and draw maps of Alexandria. The gift shop has a nice selection of children's books explaining colonial life and heroes.

The Alexandria Confederate Memorial is just outside the Lyceum at the intersection of Prince and South Washington Streets. A plaque on the corner in front of the Lyceum tells you the statue commemorates the one hundred Alexandrians who died during the Civil War.

ALEXANDRIA'S AFRICAN-AMERICAN HISTORY

Trace Alexandria's African-American History with "A Remarkable and Courageous Journey," a twenty-page, free booklet available at the Alexandria Visitor Center, 221 King Street; (800) 388-9119. Web address: www.funside.com. Learn about Benjamin Banneker, the mathematician who assisted with the survey for the new city of Washington; Moses Hepburn, the wealthiest African-American in Northern Virginia; and Dr. Albert Johnson, the only Africa-American physician practicing in Alexandria in the early 1900s.

Find out about the Bottoms, an eighteenth-century neighborhood where the town's first free slaves lived, and about Hayti, an area established in the early 1800s around the 400 block of South Royal Street, home to the only successful slave uprising in the western hemisphere.

A map pinpoints these sites and others, including the Franklin & Armfield Slave Office & Pen, headquarters for Issac Franklin and John Armfield, owners of one of the largest slave trading companies in the U.S., as well as the 1834 Roberts Memorial United Methodist Church, one of the oldest African-American church buildings in Alexandria.

Another important resource is the Alexandria Black History Resource Center & Watson Reading Room, 638 North Alfred Street; (703) 838–4356. Web address: www.ci.alexandria.va.us/oha/bhrc.

GADSBY'S TAVERN MUSEUM (ages 10 and up) (TT)

134 North Royal Street; (703) 838–4242. Open Tuesday through Saturday 10:00 A.M. to 5:00 P.M., Sunday 1:00 to 5:00 P.M. April through September; Tuesday through Saturday 11:00 A.M. to 4:00 P.M., Sunday 1:00 to 4:00 P.M. October through March.

In the eighteenth and nineteenth centuries, as now, nightlife sparkled. George and Martha Washington danced here in the second-floor ballroom. Frequent guests to this gentlemen's pub, which dates to 1770, included the Marquis de Lafayette, James Madison, and Thomas Jefferson. On the tavern museum tour, you can envision these notables sipping ale and swapping political stories.

Amazing Virginia Facts

George and Martha Washington danced at Gadsby's Tavern.

Gadsby's Tavern is also a restaurant serving lunch and dinner. (See Where to Eat).

CHRIST CHURCH (all ages)

118 North Washington Street; (703) 549–1450. Open Monday through Saturday 9:00 A.M. to 4:00 P.M., Sunday 2:00 to 4:30 P.M. **Free.**

For the warmth of salvation, the locals flocked to this church designed by James Wren in 1767 and consecrated in 1773. It was originally called the Church in the Woods because of its setting on the outskirts of town. The notable parishioners who rode to services here included George Washington, whose family pew is marked and maintained, and Robert E. Lee.

POTOMAC RIVERBOAT COMPANY (all ages)
Alexandria City Marina; (703) 684–0580. Admission.

Another way of seeing Alexandria that is easier on your feet than walking is to take this forty-minute narrated cruise that reveals history, legends, and a view of Captain's Row, where sea captains once lived. The company also offers a narrated boat tour of Washington landmarks, passing the Lincoln and Jefferson Memorials and the Washington Monument and turning around in Georgetown Harbor.

*B*ike the Sites

- **The Mount Vernon Bicycle Trail** totals a hearty 19 miles, but it's only an 8-mile bike trip from Alexandria to Mount Vernon. Trail maps are available at Alexandria's visitors center; call (703) 285-2598.

- **Blazing Saddles,** 1001 Pennsylvania Avenue NW; (202) 544-0055. Web address: www.blazingsaddles.com, rents bikes and offers five mapped routes. The 10-mile Capitol Mall path winds from Capitol Hill to Arlington Cemetery with stops at such major sites as the White house, the Smithsonian museums, and the Vietnam, Korean, Jefferson, and Franklin Roosevelt memorials.

LANTERN LIGHT GHOST TOUR (ages 7 and up)
Doorways to Old Virginia, P.O. Box 20485; (703) 548–0100. Admission. Tours leave Friday, Saturday, and Sunday evenings from March through November and by appointment the rest of the year. Departs from Ramsay House Visitors Center, 221 King Street.

Listen to ghoulish tales about Alexandria's haunts on this walking ghost tour of the historic area.

Annual Events

FEBRUARY

Revolutionary War Encampment and Skirmish, *George Washington's Birthday weekend. 3401 West Braddock Road at Fort Ward Park; (703) 838–9350.* Costumed interpreters re-enact camp life and maneuvers.

George Washington's Birthday Celebration. Alexandria claims to have the largest in the country. The celebration features a parade complete with George Washington himself, plus games, food, and music.

JUNE

Alexandria Red Cross Waterfront Festival, *second weekend in June, Oronoco Bay Park; (703) 549–8300. Admission.* This festival focuses on the city's historic seaport. Check out the visiting ships, arts and crafts, music, and special children's events.

SEPTEMBER

Hard Times Chili Cook-off, *late September, Oronoco Bay Park; (703) 244–7900. Admission.* Lots of chili, from spicy to mild, as well as children's events and live music.

DECEMBER

Scottish Christmas Walk Weekend, *in Old Town; (703) 549–0111.* Honors Alexandria's Scottish heritage.

Where to Eat

Austin Grill, *801 King Street; (703) 684–8969. Open daily for lunch and dinner.* The Tex-Mex cuisine features enchiladas, tacos, and fajitas. $–$$

Bilbo Baggins, *208 Queen Street, Old Town; (703) 683–0300. Open daily for lunch and dinner.* A casual family restaurant set in a 120-year-old townhouse, it is known for its fresh-baked bread and desserts. Kid-size portions are available, and parents will like the thirty-two kinds of wine by the glass and ten micro-brews on tap. $$

The Fish Market, *105 King Street; (703) 836–5676. Open daily for lunch and dinner.* Crabcake sandwiches and seafood stew are two of the noteworthy dishes at this popular seafood restaurant. $–$$

Gadsby's Tavern, *138 North Royal Street; (703) 548–1288). Open daily for dinner, lunch seasonally. Reservations suggested.* This historic tavern, operating in the colonial period, served George Washington and his friends as well as other founding fathers. To evoke the colonial era, the restaurant has period furnishings, pewter dishes, and costumed servers. Period fare includes Sally Lunn bread, colonial game pie, and chicken roasted on an open fire. Fish and pasta are available as well. Ask about half-portions for children. $$–$$$

The Hard Times Cafe, *1404 King Street; (703) 683–5340. Open daily for lunch and dinner.* This cafe offers both Texas- and Cincinnati-style chili and thirty-one brands of beer. $

Le Gaulois Café, *1106 King Street; Alexandria; (703) 739–9494.* This pleasant restaurant serves well-priced French family fare. $$

Lite-N-Fair, *1018 King Street, Alexandria; (703) 549–3717.* This inexpensive eatery serves good food. Try the chocolate mousse. $

Santa Fe East, *100 South Pitt Street; (703) 548–6900. Open daily for lunch and dinner, reservations suggested for dinner.* The Southwestern fare features grilled steaks, chicken, and pasta with Southwestern seasonings. $$

Torpedo Factory Food Pavilion, *5 Cameron Street.* The pavilion offers splendid views of the Potomac and some cheap eats. Besides coffee and ice cream, the food include sandwiches at **Deli by Design,** (703) 683-2827, ($), and good pizza and pasta at **Radio Free Italy,** (703) 683-0361 ($-$$). Also noteworthy is the chilled seafood salad.

West End Dinner Theatre, *4615 Duke Street, in the Foxchase Shopping Center, (703) 370–2500. Open year-round Thursday through Saturday for dinner and Sunday for lunch. Open Tuesday and Wednesday for dinner in spring and fall. Call for reservations and seating.* Play while you eat at this dinner theater where both the food and performances vary in quality. Past plays have included *Little Shop of Horrors* and *Fiddler on the Roof.* Prices include dinner and the show.

Where to Stay

Days Inn, *about 2 miles south of Old Town, 110 Bragg Street; (703) 354–4950 or (800) 241–7382.* This property offers moderately priced lodging within an easy car ride of Old Town.

Embassy Suites Alexandria Old Town, *1900 Diagonal Road; (703) 684–5900 or (800) EMBASSY.* This all-suite hotel includes the cost of breakfast in the room rate and is located across the street from the King Street Metro

station. On weekends the complimentary Kids Corner at the reception desk offers refreshments.

Holiday Inn Select, *480 King Street; (703) 549–6080, (800) HOLIDAY in Virginia, or (800) 368–5047 outside Virginia. Web address: www.hiselect.com/oldtownalex.* Ranked among the top twenty-five Holiday Inns worldwide, this hotel is located in the historic Old Town District.

Princely Bed and Breakfast, *819 Prince Street; (800) 470–5588.* This service books more than thirty rooms in a variety of Alexandria homes, many in the historic Old Town area. Some come with brick courtyards and sitting rooms and a friendly attitude toward well-behaved children. Talk to the reservationist to see which properties might suit your family.

The Radisson Plaza Hotel at Mark Center, *5000 Seminary Road; (800) 333–3333 or (703) 845–1010.* This hotel has a fitness center, racquetball and tennis courts, an indoor and outdoor pool, and two restaurants.

For More Information

Alexandria Convention and Visitors Association, *221 King Street, Alexandria, VA 22314; (703) 838–4200 or (800) 388–9119. Web address: www. funside.com. Open daily 9:00 A.M. to 5:00 P.M. year-round.* Located in historic Ramsay House, the visitors center has brochures for museums, attractions, and walking tours as well as information about restaurants and shops. Out-of-town visitors can get a ℱree parking proclamation here (a very worthwhile item). Constructed in 1724 and rebuilt after a fire in 1942, the building was named for William Ramsay, a Scottish merchant and city founder. This structure was the oldest building in Alexandria.

Mount Vernon Region

Mount Vernon is best known for the attraction after which it's named: George Washington's estate.

GEORGE WASHINGTON'S MOUNT VERNON ESTATE AND GARDENS (ages 5 and up) (TT)

Located at the south end of George Washington Memorial Parkway, 8 miles south of Alexandria; (703) 780–2000. Web address: www.mountvernon.org. Open daily year-round. Admission. The George Washington: Pioneer Farmer exhibit is open year-round, with activities from March through November.

For anyone who hasn't taken the drive to Mount Vernon, the trip is well worth it. Mount Vernon, a lovingly restored riverfront property, was George and Martha Washington's plantation, where the first president lived (although he spent a good deal of his time away from it). The estate has well-kept gardens, an informative mini-museum of eighteenth-century life, and beautiful rooms. In the museum you can see a few of George

Washington's swords, his silver-handled toothbrush, and a sculpted bust made from life bearing a great likeness to Washington. In the mansion much of the furniture is authentic. A newly renovated museum features a changing collection of articles from George and Martha's lives at Mount Vernon and their homes in New York and Philadelphia. The Hands-On Tent for kids, which is open during the summer months, is located at one end of the Bowling Green across from the mansion. Docents are available to help children with hands-on activities. Kids can try on colonial-era clothes, piece together pottery shards similar to those found on the estate by archeologists, and assemble wood blocks and trussing rings to craft buckets as coopers did. Visitors can play games such as sticks and hoops and shoot darts made of corn cobs.

The three gardens on the grounds contain trees, flowers, and herbs selected and planted by Washington himself. Washington chose a nearby setting as the grounds for the family tomb. George and Martha Washington are buried here and nearby is a reminder of another side of eighteenth-century life: the burial grounds of the slaves who served at Mount Vernon and whose hard work made the property the splendid estate that Washington loved.

The plantation also offers the George Washington: Pioneer Farmer exhibit. This features an array of hands-on opportunities such as cracking corn, visiting the animals in the sixteen-sided "round" barn, making a fishnet, or hoeing the fields with "farmers" in period dress. Another fun feature for the kids is the Adventure Map. This colorful brochure is filled with word puzzles that can only be answered from the information found by touring the estate. Upon completing these tasks, kids can go to where "X marks the spot" to find the correct answers.

Picnicking is not allowed on the grounds, but tables and chairs are outside the gates. The property offers a brand-new food court and an expanded Mount Vernon Inn Restaurant (see Where to Eat).

GEORGE WASHINGTON'S GRIST MILL HISTORICAL STATE PARK (ages 7 and up)

Located 3 miles west of Mount Vernon Estate, 5514 Mount Vernon Memorial Highway; (703) 780–2000. Web address: www.dcr.state.va.us/parks/georgwa. htm. Scheduled to reopen when renovations are complete in Spring 2002. (Call before you visit.) Admission.

This reconstruction of a mill once operated by George Washington enables kids to imagine how this important community asset functioned.

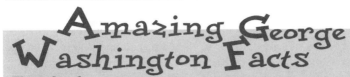

Amazing George Washington Facts

The tale of George Washington chopping down the cherry tree is merely a legend created, perhaps, to portray his honesty.

The myth of George Washington's wooden false teeth is not true; however, he did have false teeth made out of ivory, animal, and human teeth.

🏛 WOODLAWN PLANTATION

Intersection of U.S. Highway 1 and State Highway 235, 9000 Richmond Highway; (703) 780–4000. Web address: nationaltrust.org. Closed in January and February, open daily the rest of the year, closed Thanksgiving and Christmas. Admission.

Designed by the first architect of the U.S. Capitol, Dr. William Thornton, this Georgian-style brick home and its grounds were a gift from George Washington to his nephew Major Lawrence Lewis and adopted daughter, Eleanor Parke Custis ("Nelly"). Visitors can view the Washington and Lewis heirlooms and paintings from the federal period, and enjoy the colonial-revival garden, which features a large array of nineteenth-century rose species.

🏛 FRANK LLOYD WRIGHT'S POPE-LEIGHEY HOUSE

At the Woodlawn Plantation; (703) 780–400. Web address: www.national trust.org. Closed in January and February, open daily 10:00 A.M. to 5:00 P.M. the rest of the year. Closed Thanksgiving, Christmas, and New Year's Days. Admission.

Frank Lloyd Wright designed this home as a model of Usonian architecture—the principle that people of moderate means deserved beautiful, well-designed homes. Made of cypress, brick, and glass, the house is intended to blend in with its natural surroundings, reflecting many of Wright's important contributions to architecture. The furnishings are selected or designed by Wright. Your kids might be surprised how "modern" this house looks, despite the fact that it was built in 1940.

After being saved from demolition, the house was moved to this site in 1964.

🏛 GUNSTON HALL

Six miles south of Mount Vernon. 10709 Gunston Road (State Highway 242), Mason Neck; (703) 550–9220. Open daily. Admission.

George Mason, who drafted the Virginia Declaration of Rights and was a framer of the Constitution, lived at this nineteenth-century manor home originally set on 5,000 acres. Mason, in the end, refused to sign the Constitution because it did not abolish slavery. The film at the visitors center presents some background on Mason's life. The house is known for its intricately carved woodwork, particularly apparent in the Palladian Room. Despite the manor home's grace, children may like the 550 acres of grounds best. The formal gardens, which contain only plants found in colonial times, is noted for its 12-foot-high boxwood. Kids like the nature trail that leads past a deer park and along the river.

Where to Eat

Mount Vernon Inn Restaurant, *3500 Mount Vernon Memorial Highway, located on the grounds of the estate; (703) 780–0011. Open for lunch daily; dinner Monday through Saturday.* This restaurant offers meals in a colonial setting, complete with fireplaces, hand-painted murals, and a costumed staff. Some of the entrees are salmon fillet, stuffed pork roll, and roast venison. The old standby, chicken strips, is available for children as well as smaller portions of the entrees. $$–$$$

Food Court Pavilion, *located on the Mount Vernon estate; (703) 780–0011. Open daily for breakfast, lunch, and snacks.*

If you don't have time—or the kids don't have the patience—for a sit-down lunch, stop by for hamburgers, hot dogs, salads, and sandwiches as well as fresh-baked muffins, cakes, and jumbo hot pretzels. $

RT's Restaurant, *3804 Mount Vernon Avenue in Alexandria; (703) 684–6010. Open Monday through Saturday for lunch and dinner; Sunday for dinner only. Reservations recommended.* The Cajun and Creole dishes draw raves from diners; particularly noteworthy are the crawfish, pasta jambalaya, and pecan-crusted chicken. $$–$$$

Where to Stay

See accommodations listed for Alexandria.

For More Information

Fairfax County Convention and Visitors Bureau, *8300 Boone Boulevard, Suite 450, Vienna, VA 22182; (703) 790–3329. Web address: www.visitfairfax.org.*

McLean

Although McLean is best known as a bedroom community for people who work in Washington, D.C., it has several attractions of its own. Most notable is Great Falls National Park. "Shopoholics" like the upscale shops of the Tysons Galleria and the variety of stores at Tysons Corner Center.

PATOWMACK CANAL AND GREAT FALLS PARK (all ages) (TT)

9200 Old Dominion Drive, McLean; (703) 285–2966 and 11710 MacArthur Boulevard, (at the end of MacArthur Boulevard), Potomac; (301) 299–3613. Web address: www.nps.gov. Open daily year-round; closed Christmas. The entrance fee admits a carful of people to either side for four consecutive days. C&O Canal tours begin during the first two weeks in April and end in early November. Tours run Wednesday through Friday at 3:00 P.M.; Saturday and Sunday at 11:00 A.M. and 1:00 and 3:00 P.M.

Commonly referred to as Great Falls Park, this is a definite must-do. This 800-acre park has 15 miles of hiking trails, ranging from easy to strenuous, and 5 miles of trails for horseback riding and biking. For out-of-town visitors, it may seem confusing as to which side of the park to choose. Separated by the Potomac River, each side offers hiking trails, visitors centers, and snack pavilions, but only the Maryland side of Great Falls Park has the C&O Canal. Both the Virginia and the Maryland sides can be reached easily from the Beltway (Interstate 495) and are just minutes from each other.

I must confess that my family prefers the Maryland side because of the canal towpath. Along this flat, slightly elevated trail removed from any vehicles, we taught our children to ride bicycles. (Bring your own bicycles.) We've spent many pleasant weekends bicycling on the Maryland side and also, sometimes, exploring the Virginia side.

Great Falls, Maryland, also offers canal boat rides from April through October. Mules pull these barges upstream and you can watch a barge going through one of the canal's locks. Claimed as a national monument in 1961, then named a national historical park in 1971, the C&O Canal remains a technological treasure. Its system of lift locks raises the canal's waters from near sea level in Georgetown, Washington, D.C., to 605 feet above sea level at Cumberland, Maryland, 184.5 miles upstream.

At Great Falls, Virginia, take the opportunity to hike the park's trails. The visitors center has maps and brochures, an informative slide show, and artifacts such as a canal lock, a canal boat, and various rocks from the area. There is a snack pavilion, and grills are provided for cookouts (just remember to bring your own charcoal). Ranger-guided walks and special programs are also available on some weekends. Call ahead.

CLAUDE MOORE COLONIAL FARM AT TURKEY RUN (ages 2 to 7)

6310 Georgetown Pike, McLean; (703) 442–7557. Web address: www.1771.org. Open April through December, Wednesday through Sunday.

This living-history museum recreates tenant farm life in the 1770s. The one hundred acres of land are tilled, planted, and cultivated by hand by folks who dress and talk the way tenant farmers did 200 years ago. The best times to visit are during special events such as the fall harvest festival.

COLVIN RUN MILL PARK (all ages) (TT)

Five miles west of Tyson's Corner, 10017 Colvin Run Road (State Highway 7) in Great Falls; (703) 759–2771. Web address: www.co.fairfax.va.us/parks/ history.htm Open daily except Tuesday year-round. Call ahead for a weekly operating schedule.

This site once served as a crossroads for farmers from the Shenandoah Valley and tradesmen from the busy port of Alexandria. A nineteenth-century gristmill and miller's house are on the site. The property also has an early-twentieth-century general store where you can still buy items ground at the mill. In the spring, there's an Easter egg hunt; in the fall, a Halloween program that includes making scarecrows; at holiday time in December, a shopping weekend.

WHERE TO SHOP

McLean has two well-known malls.

TYSONS GALLERIA

2001 International Drive; (703) 827–7700.

This mall has one hundred shops and restaurants, including Macy's, Benetton, Neiman Marcus, and Saks Fifth Avenue.

TYSONS CORNER CENTER

1961 Chain Bridge Road; (703) 893–9400 or (888) 2TYSONS, TDD (703) 893–1761. Web address: www.shoptysons.com.

Nearby, Tysons Corner Center is a true "shop till you drop" place with more than 230 stores, including Nordstrom, Bloomingdale's, Lord & Taylor, JC Penney, Eddie Bauer, Williams-Sonoma, and The Disney Store.

Where to Eat

Kazan Restaurant, *6813 Redmond Drive; (703) 734–1960. Open Monday through Friday for lunch and dinner; Saturday for dinner only; closed Sunday.* The Turkish cuisine includes lamb and chicken shish kebabs as well as shrimp and rice dishes. $$

Maggiano's Little Italy, *Tysons Galleria, 1790-M International Drive (Route 123), Tysons Corner; (703) 356–9000.* Huge portions perfect for sharing and reasonable prices make this chain eatery popular with families. $$

Rainforest Cafe, *located in Tysons Corner Center on the lower level between Lord & Taylor and JC Penney; (703) 821–1900. Open daily for lunch and dinner.* To create the illusion of dining in a rainforest, the restaurant's ceiling is a canopy of leaves; one wall has a waterfall and surrounding you are animatronic alligators, snakes, and elephants. Don't be alarmed if the lights begin to flicker, and you hear the crack of thunder; it is just the ersatz "thunderstorm" that passes through every twenty minutes. The eclectic menu includes pasta, pizza, salads, barbecue ribs, and burgers. This popular place doesn't take reservations, so arrive well before your kids are starving. Children's menu available. $–$$

The Restaurant, *Ritz-Carlton Tysons, 1700 Tysons Boulevard, McLean; (703) 506–4300.* The good quality American fare includes a Friday night seafood buffet. $$$

Tachibana Japanese Restaurant, *6715 Lowell Avenue, McLean; (703) 847–1771.* Teens will like the excellent sushi and tempura dishes. $

Taste of Saigon, *8201 International Drive, Tysons Corner; (703) 790–0700.* Even the fussiest of kids will like the rice, and the rest of the family will enjoy a wide variety of tasty Vietnamese dishes at this popular restaurant. $$

Where to Stay

Holiday Inn McLean–Tysons Corner, *1960 Chain Bridge Road; (703) 893–2100 or (800) HOLIDAY. Web address: www.holiday-inn.com.* This property has an indoor pool and a 𝐅𝐫𝐞𝐞 shuttle to the Metro.

The McLean Hilton at Tysons Corner, *7920 Jones Branch Drive; (703) 847-5000 or (800) HILTONS. Web address: www.hilton.com.* This hotel frequently offers a weekend rate from Thursday to Sunday. Enjoy the indoor pool and a restaurant.

The Ritz–Carlton, *1700 Tysons Boulevard; (703) 506–4300. Web address: www.ritzcarlton.com.* This upscale hotel offers large rooms, concierge service on selected floors, an indoor lap pool, and a spa.

Tysons Corner Marriott, *8028 Leesburg Pike, Vienna; (703) 734–3200. Web address: www.marriott.com.* The hotel features a pool, on-site restaurant, and an exercise facility.

For More Information

Fairfax County Convention and Visitors Bureau, *8300 Boone Boulevard, Suite 450, Vienna, VA 22182; (703) 790–3329. Web address: www.visitfairfax.org.*

Fairfax County Visitor Center, *8180 Silverbrook Road, Lorton, VA 22153; (703) 550–2450.*

Vienna

From May through September Vienna's Wolf Trap Farm Park offers a wide variety of performances on a covered outdoor stage.

WOLF TRAP FARM PARK (all ages)

1624 Trap Road; (703) 255–1916. Web address: www.wolftrap.org. Call the Filene Center Box Office for tickets; (703) 255–1860. Open from late May through mid-September for performances; the park is open year-round. Admission for performances.

An easy drive from both Alexandria and Washington, D.C., Wolf Trap is the only national park for the performing arts. Performances are held at the Filene Center, an outdoor covered pavilion. The National Park Service also offers backstage tours of the Filene Center from October through April. Kids love the concerts, which range from classical to jazz, rock, and pop. Lawn seats allow kids running room (but arrive early with your picnic supper). The informal park atmosphere adds to the fun. From July to August Wolf Trap features the Children's Theatre-in-the-Woods program, with workshops that teach kids how to mime, act like a clown, and become a puppeteer. Each September Wolf Trap hosts the International Children's Festival with outstanding performing artists, including puppeteers, magicians, and storytellers, and children's theater productions.

MEADOWLARK GARDENS REGIONAL PARK

9750 Meadowlark Gardens Court, Vienna; (703) 255–3631. Open year-round; closed Thanksgiving, Christmas, New Year's Day, and when snow or ice cover the trails.

Ninety-five acres of woodlands, park, flowers, and three sparkling lakes make this place a nice respite from sight-seeing. There are picnic areas, a snack room, and a gift shop.

Where to Eat

Amphora Restaurant, *377 East Maple Avenue, (703) 938–7877. Open twenty-four hours a day.* A local landmark, Amphora is the place to go for a snack or a meal, and breakfast is served at any hour. $

Anita's, *147 Maple Avenue West; (703) 938–0888 and 521 East Maple Avenue; (703) 255–1001. Open daily for breakfast, lunch, and dinner.* This predictable, but reliable, Mexican food includes enchi-ladas, tacos, fajitas, and burritos. Traditional American breakfasts are served but so is Mexican-style *chorizo con huevos* (sausage with eggs.) Children's menu available. $

The Olive Garden, *8133 Leesburg Pike; (703) 893–3175. Open daily for lunch and dinner.* There's plenty of pasta, chicken, and lasagna at this Italian restaurant. Children's menu available. $–$$

Where to Stay

Comfort Inn Tysons Corner, *1587 Springhill Road; (703) 448–8020 or (800) 828–3297.* This lodging offers moderately priced rooms.

Residence Inn by Marriott–Tysons Corner, *8616 Westwood Center Drive; (703) 893–0120 or (800) 331–3131.*

An all-suite property, this hotel gives families added space for their money.

Vienna Wolf Trap Motel, *430 Maple Avenue West; (703) 281–2330 or (800) 541–5164.* This lodging offers moderately priced rooms.

For More Information

Fairfax Convention and Visitors Bureau, *8300 Boone Boulevard, Suite 450, Vienna, VA 22182; (703) 790–3329. Web address: www.visitfairfax.org.*

Manassas

Manassas is rich in Civil War history and historical sites.

MANASSAS NATIONAL BATTLEFIELD PARK (ages 9 and up)

12521 Lee Highway, Manassas; (703) 754–1861. Web address: www.nps.gov. Open daily year-round sunrise to sunset; visitor center open 8:30 A.M. to 6:00 P.M. in the summer and to 5:00 P.M. in the winter. Closed Christmas, Thanksgiving, and New Year's Day.

The battlefield is Manassas's most famous attraction. This is the site of the first major land battle of the Civil War, as well as the second Battle of Manassas, better known as the Battle of Bull Run. Begin your battlefield tour at the visitors center where a captioned slide presentation and a battle map illustrate the strategy and tactics behind the campaigns. The First Battle of Manassas is a self-guided, 1-mile-long walking tour along the site up to Henry Hill, the climactic point. Exhibits and audio recordings along the trail provide information. The Second Battle of Manassas route is 12 miles long, so it's best to tour this by car. At the twelve stops along the way, exhibits help you visualize the fighting. Obtain folders, maps, and audio cassettes from the visitors center.

MANASSAS MUSEUM (ages 4 to 7) (TT)

9101 Prince William Street in Old Town; (703) 368–1873. Web address: www. manassasmuseum.org. Open 10:00 A.M. to 5:00 P.M. Tuesday through Sunday and federal holidays; closed Thanksgiving, Christmas, and New Year's Day. Admission.

This small museum details Northern Virginia's history, emphasizing the Civil War. There are exhibits, photographs, artifacts, and videos. Artifacts include Civil War weapons and uniforms, Victorian clothing and quilts, furniture, and store signs from the 1800s. Children can ask for the scavenger hunt sheet at the front desk. Geared to specific age groups, the sheets help kids focus on exhibits. A completed sheet earns them a bookmark.

SPLASH DOWN WATER PARK (all ages)

Take exit 47A off Interstate 66 West to State Highway 234 South and follow the signs to the park in Manassas; (703) 361–4451. Open Memorial Day through Labor Day, daily from mid-June through Labor Day and weekends in mid-June. Admission.

Cool off during Virginia's hot summers at this large waterpark. At this eleven-acre facility, you can float down the lazy river on tubes, twist down slippery slides, and swim in a giant pool. Little ones have their own area, Sandcastle Kid's Club, with child-size slides, climbing equipment, and a kiddie pool.

SKATENATION (all ages)

5180 Dale Boulevard, Dale City; (703) 730–8423. Open daily year-round. Hours vary.

There are two Olympic-size rinks, skate rentals, an arcade, and cafe.

PRINCE WILLIAM FOREST PARK (all ages)

Take State Highway 234 South to Route 619 East for about 7 miles and follow signs to the park; (703) 221–7181. Web address: www.nps.gov. Open daily; closed Thanksgiving, Christmas, and New Year's Day. Park open dawn to dusk; visitor center open 8:30 A.M. to 5:00 P.M. Center located at 18100 Park Headquarters Road, Triangle. Park entrance fee is good for admission for seven consecutive days.

Hike, bike, picnic, fish, and camp at this forest park with 37 miles of trails. Obtain information at the visitors center. If you have a Virginia fishing license, you can try your luck catching bass, bluegills, pickerel, or crappies. The park also offers tent, RV, and backcountry camping year-round. During winter when weather permits, cross-country skiing and snowshoeing are allowed (bring your own equipment).

POTOMAC MILLS

Exit 156 off Interstate 95, 2700 Potomac Mills Circle in Prince William; (703) 643–1770 or (800) VA–MILLS. Web address: www.potomac-mills.com. Open daily year-round.

Potomac Mills is a large off-price mall that advertises shopping discounts of 20 to 60 percent. Some locals swear by the bargains on furnishings and back-to-school clothes. With more than 220 stores, including Ikea, Laura Ashley, Guess, Levi Strauss, American Tourister, Calvin Klein, Gap, Florsheim, and the only East Coast Nordstrom Rack, there's plenty to choose from and a large food court for meals.

Annual Events

APRIL THROUGH NOVEMBER

Farmer's Market, *located in downtown Haymarket.* This open-air produce air market is held every Saturday from spring through fall.

MAY

Sugarloaf SpringCraft Festival, *early May, Prince William County Fairgrounds, Manassas.* Browse the wares of professional artisans and craftspeople selling handmade furniture, clothing, jewelry, musical instruments, and stained-glass items. The festivities include live music, food, and children's theater.

AUGUST

Civil War Weekend, *late August, outside the Manassas museum.* Costumed interpreters talk of warfare and period weapons.

OCTOBER

Fall Jubilee, *early October.* This annual festival in historic Old Town Manassas features music, children's entertainment, food, rides, and crafts.

For additional information about these and other events, call Historic Manassas, Inc. at (703) 361-6599.

Where to Eat

The Sandwich Factory, *9420 Battle Street; (703) 369-6022. Open daily for breakfast, lunch, and dinner.* The cheap eats include a variety of submarine sandwiches. A full breakfast menu is also available. $

Thai Secret Restaurant, *9114 Center Street; (703) 361-2500. Open Tuesday through Saturday for lunch and dinner; Sunday dinner only; closed Monday.* If your kids don't like the traditional spicy Thai cuisine, ask for a rice and vegetable dish. $-$$

Where to Stay

Family accommodations in Manassas include these three moderately priced hotel/motels:

Days Inn, *10653 Balls Ford Road; (703) 368-2800 or (800) 325-2525.*

Holiday Inn, *10800 Vandor Lane; (703) 335-0000 or (800) HOLIDAY.*

Best Western Manassas, *8640 Mathis Avenue; (703) 368-7070.*

For More Information

Prince William County Visitor Center, *200 Mill Street, Occoquan 22125; (703) 491–4045. Web address: www. visitpwc.com*

Prince William County/Manassas Conference and Visitors Bureau, *14420 Bristow Road, Manassas; (703) 792–4254 or (800) 432–1792.*

Historic Manassas Visitors Center, *9431 West Street, Manassas; (703) 361– 6599. Web address: www.VIRGINIA.org.*

Culpeper

If you're traveling from Manassas to Fredericksburg, Culpeper makes for a nice stop. It's about 38 miles south of Manassas on U.S. Highway 29 and features a winery, an equestrian center, and an outdoors outfitter.

DOMINION WINE CELLARS (ages 7 and up)

Number One Winery Avenue; (540) 825–8772. Call for hours; closed Thanksgiving, Christmas, and New Year's Day.

Dominion Wine Cellars is part of Virginia's burgeoning wine industry. The tours are informal and informative. Kids can see the enormous vats where the wine is fermented and learn about wine-making in a casual atmosphere. Wine-tasting is for adults only.

PRINCE MICHEL WINERY & RESTAURANT (ages 7 and up)

U.S. Highway 29, Leon; (540) 547–3707 or (800) 800–WINE. Web address: www.princemichel.com. Open daily, 10:00 A.M. to 5:00 P.M.

The wine-tasting is for adults only, but kids will enjoy the antique wine-making equipment in the museum. There are also luxury suites available and a gourmet restaurant ($$$).

HITS, INC. COMMONWEALTH PARK (all ages)

13246 Commonwealth Parkway; (540) 825–7469. Open March through November, most weekends have shows.

If you're in the area when shows are held, this is definitely worth a visit, especially if you have children who ride or are "in love" with horses.

The riding, hunting, and jumping events in three different rings enthrall kids. Call ahead and check the schedule.

RAPPAHANNOCK RIVER CAMPGROUND (ages 6 and up)

33017 River Mill Road, Richardsville; (800) 784–PADL or (540) 399–1839. Web address: www.canoecamp.com. E-mail: canoe@gemlink.com. Open late March through October. Reservations required.

Rappahannock River Campground can set you up for a self-guided canoe, kayak, or rafting trip down the Rappahnnock or Rapidan Rivers. Opt for either a tranquil float or a stretch with some white water. All participants must know how to swim. Children must be at least 6 years old. A limited supply of child-size life jackets is available. Picnicking in the shade of the pine trees and overnight rustic camping are available.

Where to Eat

Dee Dee's Family Restaurant, *502 North Main Street; (540) 825–4700. Open daily for breakfast, lunch, and dinner.* Known for its down-home cookin', this eatery features hickory-smoked pork ribs, beef barbecue sandwiches, burgers, and seafood platters. Locals like the crab-stuffed mushrooms. Children's menu available. $–$$

It's About Thyme, *128 East Davis Street; (540) 825–4264. Open Tuesday through Saturday for lunch and dinner. The* continental cuisine features staples such as chicken Marsala and Italian pot roast. $–$$

Pancho Villa Mexican Restaurant, *910 South Main Street; (540) 825–5268. Open daily for lunch and dinner.* If you're hungry for something spicy, try the Enchilada Supreme. Kids have the option of creating their own platter of two items plus rice and beans. Children's menu available. $–$$

Where to Stay

Comfort Inn Culpeper, *890 Willis Lane, U.S. Highway 29; (800) 228–5150 or (540) 825–4900.* This property has an outdoor pool and provides a complimentary continental breakfast.

Holiday Inn of Culpeper, *P.O. Box 1206, Culpeper, VA 22701; U.S. Highway 29; (800) HOLIDAY or (540) 825–1253.* This is a moderately priced lodging with a pool and baby-sitting services.

For More Information

Culpeper County Tourism Division,
133 West Davis Street, Culpeper; (540)
825–8628 or (888) CULPEPER. Web
address: www.culpepervachamber.com.
E-mail: culpepercc@summit.net.

Culpeper County Chamber of Commerce & Visitors Center, *109 South*
Commerce Street; (540) 825–8628 or
(888) 285–7373. Web address: www.
culpepervachamber.com.

Department of Tourism, *233 East*
Davis Street; (540) 727–0611. Web
address: www.visitculpeperva.com.

Fredericksburg

If George Washington could visit his birthplace in Fredericksburg, he would probably recognize some of it, because the building facades are restored to their eighteenth- and nineteenth-century appearance. Fredericksburg, situated halfway between the two Civil War capitals of Richmond and Washington, D.C., also served as a critical Civil War locale. The city features historic homes and four Civil War battlefields. The battles took place from 1862 to 1864 within a 17-mile radius of Fredericksburg and are now encompassed in the Fredericksburg and Spotsylvania County Battlefields Memorial National Military Park (more commonly known as Fredericksburg/Spotsylvania National Military Park). Your best bet is to pick and choose carefully to keep your kids' interest. Don't attempt to see all the battlefields and historic homes. Remember, overkill will bore your kids, but a well-chosen tour or two will be welcome.

🏛 FREDERICKSBURG/SPOTSYLVANIA NATIONAL MILITARY PARK (ages 7 and up)

Open daily, visitors centers open year-round except December 25 and January 1. Call one of the visitors centers in Fredericksburg for specific directions or more information on one or all of the four battlefields: Chancellorsville Battlefield Visitors Center, State Highway 3 West; (540) 786–2880; and Fredericksburg Battlefield Visitors Center, 1013 Lafayette Boulevard; (540) 373–6122. Web address: www.nps.gov. The visitors centers can be reached at (540) 371–0802.

The national military park stretches more than 7,800 acres, includes four different battlefields, and is run by the National Park Service. The entire drive is about 75 miles, including driving between and within the parks. In the parks you can see the **Old Salem Church,** the **Spotsylvania Court House,** and the **Marye's Heights National Cemetery** along with trenches, historic buildings, interpretive trails, exhibit shelters, maps, monuments, and of course the landscape where these important battles were fought. The tours take about three hours for each battlefield, so plan a couple of days if you want the full tour. Be selective. For an audio-tape driving tour or other information, stop in one of the two visitors centers that cover all four battlefields in the park.

The battlefields include Fredericksburg, Chancellorsville, Wilderness, and Spotsylvania Court House.

- **Fredericksburg Battlefield,** December 11–15, 1862. The Battle of Fredericksburg took place on Sunken Road and the Stone Wall at Marye's Heights. Look for the Marye's Heights National Cemetery and the Lee Hill Exhibit Shelter, which are located in this battlefield. Also stop by the Old Salem Church on your way to the Chancellorsville Battlefield.

- **Chancellorsville Battlefield,** April 27–May 6, 1863. This was the site of a strategic military maneuver by Robert E. Lee and General Stonewall Jackson. But that same day ended sadly when Jackson was fatally wounded by his own troops. Visit the Wilderness Church, the Catharine Furnace Remains, and the Unfinished Railroad in this battlefield.

- **Wilderness Battlefield,** May 5–6, 1864. This battlefield saw the military confrontation of generals Ulysses S. Grant and Robert E. Lee. You might want to pause at the Wilderness Exhibit Shelter and the Wilderness Tavern. Remains are located on this battlefield.

- **Spotsylvania Court House Battlefield,** May 8–21, 1864. Troops fought for two weeks here in some of the most intense hand-to-hand fighting war called the "Bloody Angle." On view are the **Spotsylvania Court House**, the **Spotsylvania Confederate Cemetery,** and one of three house sites.

Fredericksburg has several historic sites associated with famous people. For many children, especially younger ones, the often static displays and roped-off rooms may be of little interest. Choose carefully.

GEORGE WASHINGTON MASONIC MUSEUM (ages 10 and up)

803 Princess Anne Street; (540) 373–5885. Adult admission. Open by appointment.

This is another place to learn about our first president. Visit the two-room historic lodge where Washington was initiated into the Masons in 1752.

KENMORE (ages 10 and up) (TT)

1201 Washington Avenue; (540) 373–3381. Web address: www.kenmore.org. Open daily except for Thanksgiving, December 25 and 31, and New Year's Day. Admission.

The plantation home of Betty Washington, George's sister, is worth a visit for its eighteenth-century furnishings. Kenmore has a number of tours designed for school children. On the "History Hunt" (kindergarten to grade 2), kids hear stories about George Washington's boyhood. "Steps into the Past" (grades 3 to 5) takes kids into the daily lives of the people who lived on the Kenmore plantation. With "Learning to Read" (grades 6 to 12), kids explore ways to use documents to study the past. Ask ahead about these programs.

JAMES MONROE MUSEUM AND MEMORIAL LIBRARY (ages 10 and up) (TT)

908 Charles Street; (540) 654–1043. Open daily; closed Thanksgiving, December 24, 25, and 31, and New Year's Day. Admission.

The museum contains artifacts from Monroe's law practice, including the desk where he signed the Monroe Doctrine, his collection of Louis XVI furniture, and his wife's gems and gowns.

RISING SUN TAVERN (ages 10 and up) (TT)

1304 Caroline Street; (540) 371–1494. Open daily; closed Thanksgiving, December 24, 25, and 31, and New Year's Day. Admission.

Eighteenth-century life is recreated in the restored taproom with its costumes and artifacts. This house, once owned by George Washington's youngest brother, was later turned into a tavern.

MARY WASHINGTON HOUSE (ages 10 and up) (TT)

1200 Charles Street; (540) 373–1569. Open daily; closed Thanksgiving, December 24, 25, and 31, and New Year's Day. Admission.

This was home of Mary Washington, the mother of George Washington. It offers visitors a chance to see period decorations and a garden with a sundial.

HUGH MERCER APOTHECARY SHOP (ages 7 and up) (TT)

1020 Caroline Street; (540) 373–3362. Open daily; closed Thanksgiving, December 24, 25, and 31, and New Year's Day.

This may interest the kids: Here they can learn about leeches, lancets, snakeroot, crab claws, and other eighteenth- and nineteenth-century treatments and surgeries. You can also see silver-plated pills, a rosewater "still," and hand-blown glass apothecary jars.

 LAKE ANNA STATE PARK (all ages)

Off State Highway 208 in Spotsylvania; (540) 854–5503. Web address: www.state.va.us. Open daily year-round. Parking fee.

For a break from history head to where 9 miles of trails, a boat ramp, and a lifeguard-patrolled beach offer diversions. On summer weekends you can join the interpretive environmental programs.

Fredericksburg is also a place for antiques lovers. The town boasts twenty-two antiques and collectible shops. Your best bet is to meander near the four main blocks of Caroline Street. Some picks are:

 WHERE TO SHOP

PRIVATE STOCK

213 George Street; (540) 371-0999. Open by appointment.

Jukeboxes from the '40s and '50s, antique slot machines, vintage soda machines, and neon signs.

NEAT STUFF

109 Amelia Street; (540) 373–7115. Open Monday, and Thursday through Saturday 10:30 A.M. to 5:00 P.M., Sunday noon to 5:30 P.M.

Antique bottles, tins, military items, fishing equipment, tools, advertisements, and prints.

THE COLLECTOR'S DEN

717 Caroline Street; (540) 373–2430. Open daily 10:00 A.M. to 4:30 P.M.

Memorabilia such as stamps, coins, baseball cards, glassware, and other collectibles.

UPSTAIRS, DOWNSTAIRS ANTIQUES

922 Caroline Street; (540) 373–0370. Open Monday, Tuesday, Thursday, and Friday 10:00 A.M. to 4:00 P.M., Saturday 10:00 A.M. to 5:00 P.M., Sunday noon to 5:00 P.M. Closed Wednesday.

Thirty dealers offer pottery, silver, dolls, furniture, and other collectibles.

THE HIDDEN SHOPS OF FREDERICKSBURG

106 William Street; (540) 371–4588. Open Monday, and Wednesday through Saturday 10:00 A.M. to 5:00 P.M., Sunday noon to 5:00 P.M. Closed Tuesday.

This multidealer area offers 6,000 square feet of antiques and collectibles.

Close to Fredericksburg in Falmouth, visitors can tour the historic home in which George Washington lived as a boy and another home where Detroit-born impressionist painter Gari Melchers resided.

GEORGE WASHINGTON'S FERRY FARM (ages 10 and up) (TT)

240 Kings Highway, State Highway 3 at Ferry Road; (540) 373–3381. Web address: www.kenmore.org. Open daily year-round; closed Thanksgiving, Christmas, and New Year's Day.

George Washington resided here from ages 6 to 20, the period of his formal education and the years in which he taught himself the art of surveying. Only the ice house and surveyor's shack still stand from Washington's childhood. Ask about the schedule (May to October) for the program "I Dig George," which introduces children to the techniques of archaeology.

BELMONT (ages 10 and up)

224 Washington Street; (540) 654–1015). Open daily year-round; closed Thanksgiving, December 24, 25, and 31, and New Year's Day.

Gari Melchers Estate and Memorial Gallery, also known as the eighteenth-century estate where Melchers lived and painted during the last sixteen years of his life.

Where to Eat

623, An American Bistro, *623 Caroline Street; (540) 361–2640. Open Tuesday through Sunday for lunch and dinner; closed Monday.* Located in a 1771 building, the restaurant features contemporary cuisine. $$–$$$

The Riverview Room, *1101 Sophia Street; (540) 373–6500. Open daily for lunch and dinner and brunch on Sundays.*

Reservations recommended. The Riverview Room is a steak and seafood restaurant overlooking the Rappahannock River. Children's menu available.

The Savvy Gourmet, *600 William Street; (540) 370–0909.* This cafe offers sandwiches, subs, and hamburgers. Open Monday through Saturday. $$

Where to Stay

Best Western Johnny Appleseed Inn, *543 Warrenton Road; (540) 373–0000 or (800) 633–6443.* A traditional motel/hotel property.

Days Inn Fredericksburg North, *14 Simpson Road; (540) 373–5340 or (800) DAYSINN.* This lodging has an outdoor pool and includes the cost of a continental breakfast in the room rates.

Fredericksburg Colonial Inn, *1707 Princess Anne Street; (540) 371–5666.* This inn was built in 1928 and has twenty-nine rooms decorated with Victorian furniture.

The Kenmore Inn, *1200 Princess Anne Street; (540) 371–7622 or (800) 437–7622.* Four of the twelve guest rooms at this colonial-style inn feature working fireplaces. Dinner is served in either a casual or formal dining room. Children are welcome. Ask about the weekend package.

The Richard Johnston Inn, *711 Caroline Street; (540) 899–7606.* This antiques-filled inn offers rooms and suites and prefers children over 12.

Holiday Inn Select, *2801 Plank Road; (540) 786–8321.* This hotel has three tennis courts and a junior Olympic-size pool.

For More Information

Fredericksburg Visitors Center, *706 Caroline Street, Fredericksburg; (540) 373–1776. Web address: www. fredericksburgva.com.* The visitors center offers several walking tours. One leads through historic neighborhoods, one tours African-American sites, and

another "relives" the events of December 1862.

Spotsylvania County Visitor Center, *4704 Southpoint Parkway, Fredericksburg; (800) 654–4118. Open daily from 9:00 A.M. to 5:00 P.M.*

The Eastern Shore

riving through the small towns of Virginia's Eastern Shore takes you back centuries. Accomac, for example, has buildings that date to 1632. On Tangier Island, accessible only by boat, the residents can trace their ancestry back to Elizabethan times. Virginia's 70-mile portion of the Delmarva Peninsula (named for Delaware, Maryland, and Virginia) is dotted with small towns that received their names from Native American words such as Chincoteague, Wachapreague, and Onancock.

As much as possible, my family tries to get off U.S. Highway 13, a modern byway dotted with gas stations and strip malls. We prefer Seaside Road, sometimes called Route 600. This curvy country lane and its branches take us past roadside stands bursting with sweet corn and tomatoes and pick-up trucks whose beds are piled high with wobbly green pyramids of watermelons. In the morning seagulls flutter like angels above fields of soybeans, sorghum, and sweet potatoes. At dusk the setting sun falls gently on the frame farmhouses, turning the surrounding fields of cut corn stalks to spun gold.

In season at the dock in Oyster, a town just a few blocks long, you're likely to see fishermen unloading their crab pots. In Wachapreague fancy boats are moored at the Island House Marina where the shore's gentry lunch

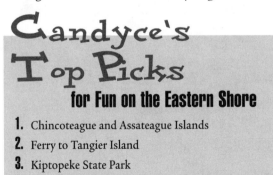

Candyce's Top Picks
for Fun on the Eastern Shore

1. Chincoteague and Assateague Islands
2. Ferry to Tangier Island
3. Kiptopeke State Park
4. Chesapeake Bay Bridge–Tunnel

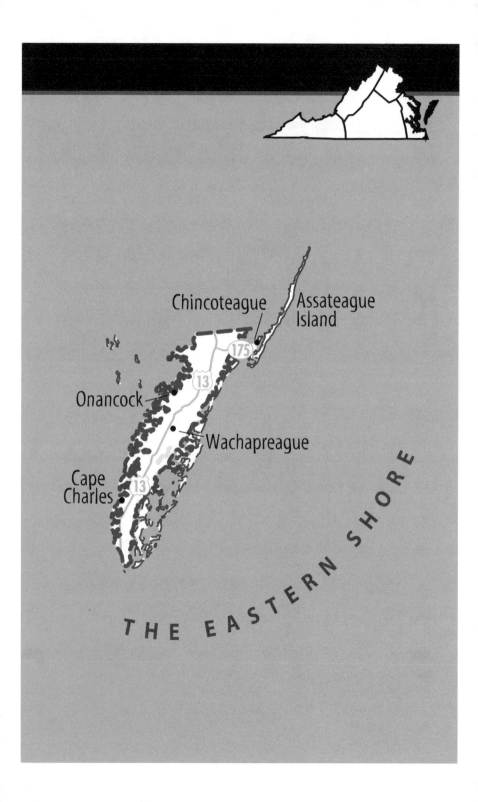

on succulent crabcakes. On Assateague Island the breezes may bring you the sounds of snow geese honking and the neighs of wild ponies. A walk here takes you along sunlit beaches and past wetlands where thousands of ducks roost and deer and otters dot the marsh.

Go slowly to explore Virginia's Eastern Shore. Drive the backroads and/or bicycle from place to place so that you may sample the charms of these shore towns.

Chincoteague and Assateague Island

Chincoteague is 83 miles north of Virginia Beach.

Although Misty, the pint-size pony from Marguerite Henry's book *Misty of Chincoteague*, may have made this area famous, there's a lot more than horses here. Chincoteague is for people. This town has shops, restaurants, camping areas, and hotels and also provides the only Virginia access to Assateague Island, home to Assateague Island National Seashore and Chincoteague National Wildlife Refuge. This barrier island has 37 miles of wild beach, and the only inhabitants include 260 different species of birds, the endangered Delmarva fox squirrel, white-tailed and Sika deer, and wild ponies. Grazing or galloping across a field, the ponies impart a sense of power and freedom to this landscape. Cars are allowed only in limited areas, so your best bet for enjoying the wildlife and undeveloped beaches is to hike or bike.

Both Chincoteague and Assateague also have museums where you can learn about the island's wildlife and the environment. Each year thousands of people visit the island to watch the famous pony penning held the last Thursday in July. The wild ponies are herded into the channel to swim to Chincoteague where they are auctioned off to benefit the volunteer fire department.

CHINCOTEAGUE NATIONAL WILDLIFE REFUGE AND ASSATEAGUE ISLAND NATIONAL SEASHORE (all ages)

Except for small parcels of land, the entire Virginia portion of Assateague Island comprises Chincoteague National Wildlife Refuge. When the entire island was designated Assateague Island National Seashore, the Virginia portion of the island remained Chincoteague National Wildlife Refuge. The National Park Service, Assateague Island National Seashore, helps to administer public uses on an assigned area of the beach that includes land from parking lot #1 south.

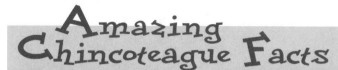

Amazing Chincoteague Facts

Chincoteague Ponies No one knows how the ponies arrived. Legends abound, including speculation that the first ponies swam ashore from wrecked Spanish galleons or were driven to the barrier island in the 1680s by colonists avoiding livestock taxes and the cost of fencing.

The refuge ends at the Virginia–Maryland border. The Virginia side and the Maryland side each contain about 9000 acres. The Maryland side offers more beach and primitive camping facilities, while the Virginia side has more winter waterfowl, denser pine forests, and a Victorian lighthouse.

Summer is certainly the prime time for families to visit here. The water's right for swimming and the shore can be crowded. The farther you walk away from the main beach access areas, though, the thinner the crowds. Take time in summer to drive or bicycle through the cool loblolly pine forests populated by white-tailed and Sika deer. With luck you'll encounter some of the island's famous wild ponies. Do not get too close and do not pet these animals; they are wild and may bite or kick. In summer, spring, and fall rangers lead guided walks (check at the visitors centers for details).

Some Interesting Pony Facts

- Just like us, if one pony in a group yawns, the others follow suit.

- The ponies may look fat to us; that's because the seaweed they eat is salty and they need to drink twice as much fresh water as do domestic horses.

- There's a pony hierarchy. The higher-ranking ponies get first access to water and seaweed.

- Some mares are continually pregnant, since gestation lasts for almost one full year.

- Ponies may look tame, but they are wild. Do not pet or feed the ponies.

Besides swimming, try such shore staples as surf fishing, clamming, and crabbing. The best place for surf fishing is at the southernmost tip of the island, just beyond the public beach. Crabbing is permitted along the banks of Swans Cove, and clams can be found in the saltwater marshes of Tom's Cove. Generally you don't need a permit for these activities, but you should obtain information at one of the visitors centers.

Fall and winter are special times to visit, too. There are 18,000 acres of natural landscape—no motels, condominiums, or fast-food restaurants to mar your communing with nature—and few crowds except during the peak of the fall migration. The island is located on the eastern flyway, so the sky is filled with thousands of migrating waterfowl in fall. Here the crisp, clear air vibrates with strange sounds, such as the high-pitched honk of snow geese and the throaty duck calls that carry from marsh to marsh. At this time of year there's enough space to walk hand-in-hand with your children along the shore, admiring how an arc of sunlight is caught in a wave.

In winter you can walk the miles of wild beaches bordered by dunes, bike through the acres of marshlands, and observe scores of black ducks, snowy egrets, and great blue herons. This is a special winter refuge, not just for the migratory waterfowl, but for beach lovers, bird-watchers, animal enthusiasts, and especially burned-out city dwellers. Both sides of the island offer unusually striking scenery: wind-blown dunes; gnarled pines; and storybook ponies. It's a world of subtle earth hues, from the wheat-colored reed grass caught in frozen freshwater ponds to the soft browns of tree bark and shrub thickets.

For More Information

Chincoteague National Wildlife Refuge, *8231 Beach Road, P.O. Box 62, Chincoteague, VA 23336; (757) 336–6122. Web address: http://Chinco.fws.gov.*

Tom's Cove Visitor Center, *Beach Road, P.O. Box 38, Chincoteague, VA*

23336; (757) 336–6577. Web address: www.nps.gov (National Park Service) and www.fws.gov (Fish and Wildlife Service).

Assateague Island National Seashore, *7206 National Seashore Lane, Berlin, MD 21811; (410) 641–1441.*

HIKES

The Virginia end of Assateague features more than 15 miles of winding trails through marshes and forests. Hikers can also explore the 10 miles of wild undeveloped beaches along the Atlantic. These are some suggested hikes:

■ **Woodland Trail:** A good path, especially for biking, is the beautiful 1.7-mile trip through a shaded loblolly pine forest. If your kids keep quiet, they might spot white-tailed deer, Sika deer, and Delmarva fox squirrels. If you're here in the spring or fall, listen for songbirds along the way. This trail also leads to an overlook where, with luck, you'll catch sight of the wild ponies and in fall and winter see waterfowl. Another good pony-spotting point is in Black Duck Marsh along Beach Road.

- **Wildlife Loop:** *Open to bikers and hikers daily during refuge hours, open to vehicles 3:00 P.M. to dusk.* After 3:00 P.M. you can drive the loop, but to get the best view of the shorebirds and the waterfowl, walk or ride the 3.2-mile trail.

- **Tom's Cove Beach:** Be sure to pause here. If you want to bicycle here, take the **Swans Cove Trail** from the Wildlife Loop. The 1.25-mile Swans Cove Trail ends at beach parking lot #1.

- **Swimming Beaches:** From Memorial Day to Labor Day, lifeguards patrol a section of the beach which is designated by flags. Swim here especially if you have young children. Certain areas of Tom's Cove on the bayside are open for swimming too. Please obey posted signs that indicate beach closings because of nesting birds.

- **Assateague Lighthouse:** An easy walk is the 0.5-mile loop to this historic lighthouse and back. Originally built in 1833, the current lighthouse was constructed in 1866–1867. It is one of many lights operated by the U.S. Coast Guard to warn ships as they approach the barrier islands of the East Coast.

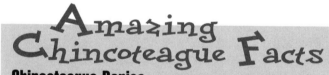

Amazing Chincoteague Facts

Chincoteague Ponies Six inches shorter than saddle horses, the brown, white, or dappled Chincoteague ponies are stockier than other breeds.

CAMPING

No camping is allowed on the Virginia side of Assateague, not even backcountry camping. It's an 11-mile hike from Virginia over to Maryland where backcountry camping is allowed, but this is too long a trek for most families. The Maryland side of the island offers some established camping areas. There are several campgrounds on Assateague Island; the Maryland State Park Service manages one campground, which is open April 1 through October 31; two others are run by the National Park Service and are open year-round. For more information about Maryland camping contact one of the Assateague offices: Campground/Ranger Office for Assateague Island National Seashore (410-641-3030); and Assateague State Park Campground Office (410-641-2918 in season or 410-641-2120 year-round).

OYSTER AND MARITIME MUSEUM (ages 5 and up)

7125 Maddox Boulevard; (757) 336–6117. Web address: www.chincoteague chamber.com/oyster/omm.html. Memorial Day through Labor Day and weekends from September through May. Admission.

Learn about the local oyster industry, from harvesting and shucking to shipping and eating. Other highlights include walrus jaws, Native American artifacts, shipwreck relics, and an exhibit showing the variety of places that oysters will colonize, such as bottles, pipes, and even inner-tubes.

REFUGE WATERFOWL MUSEUM (ages 7 and up)

7059 Maddox Boulevard; (757) 336–5800. Open daily Memorial Day through early October. Open weekends for most of the year; call ahead for specific hours. Admission.

Here your kids learn even more about Assateague Island as an established wintering site for migratory waterfowl. Along with rotating exhibits, the museum houses many works of art inspired by these winter birds, as well as weapons, boats, traps, and decoys.

NASA/WALLOPS VISITORS CENTER (ages 5 and up)

Located on State Highway 175, 5 miles from Chincoteague; (757) 824–1344. Web address: www.wff.nasa.gov. Open daily during July and August and Thursday through Monday March through November.

In 1945 NASA established a launch site on **Wallops Island,** then called the Langley Research Center. Research is still done at this facility. This visitors center is designed so that the public can learn about the NASA Goddard Space Flight Center, which is located on nearby Wallops Island. Exhibits include life-size models of planes, probes, and rockets. Special events are the model rocket demonstrations on the third Sunday during June, July, and August, and living in space demonstrations every Sunday, 1:00 P.M. The facility also offers puppet shows depicting life aboard the space shuttle every Saturday and Sunday at 11:00 A.M.

A **Side Trip to Accomac** Accomac is a quiet town. The Debtors Prison, Courthouse Row (757-787-3436), looks as it did in the early 1800s when jailer John Snead presided over imprisoned debtors. You can also check out Mary Scott Antiques, 23329 Back Street (757-787-2882), for glass, silver, furniture, and other collectibles.

Annual Events

APRIL

Easter Decoy and Art Festival, *Easter weekend.* Local and noted carvers and wildlife artists from around the country display their work. Local restaurants feature tastings as well.

Oyster and Maritime Museum Spring Craft Show, *Easter weekend; (757) 336–6117.* Raffles, silent auctions, door prizes, food, and fun.

MAY

International Migratory Bird Celebration, *Mother's Day weekend; (757) 336–6122.* Enjoy birdhouse building, guided walks, and other activities from 9 A.M. to 4 P.M.

National Fishing Week, *first week of June; (757) 336–6122.* Learn how to be a better fisherman, woman, or child.

JULY

Old Fashioned Fireworks Display, *July 4.* Chincoteague Volunteer Fire Company Carnival Grounds.

Chincoteague Volunteer Fireman's Carnival, *first and second weekends and the last two weeks of July, not including Sunday.* This is an old-fashioned carnival with rides, food, entertainment, prizes, and auctions.

Annual Pony Swim and Auction, *last consecutive Wednesday and Thursday of July.* Wild ponies from Assateague Island are rounded up for their swim to Chincoteague for a foal auction. This is reputed to be the oldest roundup in the United States and a memorable sight.

Blueberry Festival and Craft Show, *late July.* Goodies include homemade blueberry pies, cakes, muffins, ice cream, and jams as well as crafts.

OCTOBER

Oyster Festival, *Saturday of Columbus Day weekend.* The festival offers all-you-can-eat oysters, crabs, clam fritters, and hot dogs.

National Wildlife Refuge Week, *Columbus Day Weekend; (757) 336–6122.* More than 500 wildlife refuges celebrate the diversity of wild places. Sign-up for birding walks, workshops on wildlife, and other activities.

NOVEMBER

Waterfowl Week, *Saturday before Thanksgiving to the Sunday after Thanksgiving; (757) 336–6122.* Celebrate the marvel of migration by being able to drive the Wildlife Loop from 9 A.M. to dusk. Guided walks are held as well.

Chincoteague hosts many festivals. Check with the chamber of commerce for details. (757) 336–6161.

Where to Eat

Bill's Seafood Restaurant, *4040 Main Street; (757) 336–5831. Open daily year-round for breakfast, lunch, and dinner.* This restaurant offers a wide variety of seafood, plus homemade desserts. $-$$

Channel Side Restaurant, *7452 Eastside Drive; (757) 336–5644. Open daily April through late December.* This waterfront eatery, specializing in local seafood, steak, and crab cakes, overlooks the Assateague Lighthouse and the channel where the ponies swim. Children's and senior citizens' menus available. $-$$

Chincoteague Inn Restaurant, *6262 Marlin Street; (757) 336–6110.* Children's menu available. $$

Island Creamery, *6243 Maddox Boulevard; (757) 336–6236. Open daily from Easter to Thanksgiving.* Come here for a dessert of home-made ice cream and waffle cones, frozen yogurt, or slushies. $

Steamers Seafood Restaurant, *6251 Maddox Boulevard; (757) 336–5478. Dinner served daily from May through September.* A casual eatery, this restaurant serves all-you-can-eat shrimp and crabs on brown paper tablecloths. Children's menu available. $-$$

Where to Stay

Chincoteague offers motels, vacation homes, and cottages for weekly and extended stays as well as several inns and bed and breakfasts. Keep in mind that most lodgings close for the winter and not all inns and bed and breakfasts welcome children. Contact the chamber of commerce at (757) 336–6161 for more information.

Driftwood Motor Lodge, *7105 Maddox Boulevard; (757) 336–6557 or (800) 553–6117.* Open year-round, this lodge overlooks the wildlife refuge. Some rooms have a view of the Assateague Lighthouse.

Maddox Family Campground, *6742 Maddox Boulevard; (757) 336–3111.* Close to Assateague and also near the shops and restaurants of Chincoteague, this campground has a pool, playground, grocery store, laundry room, and modern bathhouse. Activities are shuffleboard, horseshoes, crabbing, and bird-watching. The campground is open March through November.

Tom's Cove Family Campground, *8128 Beebe Road; (757) 336–6498.* The campground offers waterfront camping plus a boat ramp and marina. Sites have hookups for water and electricity. Open March through November.

Refuge Motor Inn, *7058 Maddox Boulevard; (888) 831–0600. Web address: www.refugeinn.com.* Open year-round, this offers accommodations near the wildlife refuge and the beach, a refrigerator in every room, and a pool.

Waterside Motor Inn, *3761 South Main Street; (757) 336–3434.* This offers rooms on the waterfront and has a pool and tennis court. It is also open year-round.

Year of the Horse Inn, *3583 Main Street; (757) 336–3221 or (800) 680–0090. Web address: www.esva.net/ ~rhebert.* This sprawling white stucco house has three bed-and-breakfast rooms plus a two-bedroom apartment. Each guest room faces Chincoteague Bay and has a balcony. The apartment sleeps five. Continental breakfast is included in the B&B rates, and children are welcome. Open spring through fall.

For More Information

Chincoteague Chamber of Commerce, *6733 Maddox Boulevard, Chincoteague, VA 23336; (757) 336–6161. Web address: www.chincoteaguechamber. com. E-mail: pony@shore.intercom.net.*

Eastern Shore of Virginia Tourism Commission, *P.O. Box 460, Melfa, VA 23410; (757) 787–2460. Web address: www.esva.net. E-mail: esvatourism@esva.net.*

Onancock

One of the oldest towns in America, Onancock has buildings that date to the seventeenth century. Established on Chesapeake Bay in 1680 as Port Scarburgh, Onancock continues to be a fishing community. Onancock is popular, too, because it's one of the departure points for the ferry to Tangier Island, a classic Eastern Shore day trip. Staying overnight in Onancock makes it convenient to catch the morning ferry.

KERR PLACE (ages 7 and up)

69 Market Street; (757) 787–8012. Open Tuesday through Saturday, March through mid-December. Admission.

This is the headquarters of the Eastern Shore Historical Society. This museum was once the home of John Shepard, a wealthy merchant, who built his house in 1799. On the first floor you'll find the house as he lived in it, with furnishings and artifacts left from the early 1800s. On the second floor learn about local history through pieces such as the Custis trunk, brought by settlers in the 1620s, and artifacts from John Cropper, leader of the Accomack County Minutemen.

WALKING TOUR OF ONANCOCK (ages 12 and up)

Map available at the town office, 17 North Street; (757) 787–3363.

While walking along the shady lanes, you pass nineteenth-century homes with decorative trim and wrap-around porches, as well as older homes.

BLUE CRAB BAY COMPANY (all ages)

29368 Atlantic Drive, Accomack; (757) 787–3602 or (800) 221–2722. E-mail: bluecrabbayco@esva.net. Open year-round, Monday through Saturday from June to December and Monday through Friday during the rest of the year.

The small store offers seafood items and gifts such as seasonings, clam and crab dip, gift baskets, peanuts with seafood seasonings, and other delicacies for seafood lovers. You can also call for a catalog from this national wholesale and retail distributor of specialty foods from Chesapeake Bay.

CROCKET GALLERY

39 Market Street; (757) 787–2288. Web address: www.williecrockett.com.

Long-time Eastern shore residents, the Crocketts' art reflects the flavor of the area. Willie Crockett paints landscapes and his son Billy crafts award-winning carvings.

FISHING

Get a true flavor of the Eastern shore by getting out on the water and fishing. Contact:

- **Fish N'Finn Charters,** Onancock Wharf; (757) 787-3399.

- **James Gang Sportfishing and Cruising,** Onancock Wharf; (757) 787-1226.

TANGIER ISLAND (all ages)

P.O. Box 27, Tangier Island, VA 23340; (757) 891–2240 or (757) 787–8220. Cruises run daily Memorial Day through October 15. Closed during winter and early spring.

On Onancock's town dock you can purchase tickets for the one-and-a-half-hour tour-boat ride to Tangier Island. Situated in the middle of Chesapeake Bay 6 miles south of the Virginia/Maryland border, the 700-resident island is accessible only by boat or plane. Visitors stay on the island for two hours, enough time for lunch and a walk, before catching the ferry back.

Oystering and crabbing have been legacies on Tangier for generations, probably since its settlement in 1686. Still true to its watery traditions, Tangier sports work sheds along the wharf and narrow lanes of white-washed houses, many with centuries-old gravestones in their front yards, a sight my teenage daughter finds unnerving.

Day trippers come for the boat ride, the food, and a glimpse of a more traditional and quiet way of life. When we visit, we eschew the locals' offers of island tours in golf carts and instead rent bicycles or meander along the lanes and the wharf. On one outing, we watched a young mother bicycle home from the grocery store with her young child propped in the basket, a black Labrador retriever excitedly trotted into an inlet to accompany a fisherman, and children playing catch.

Like most of the ferry passengers, we lunch at the Chesapeake House, a simple, family-style restaurant reputed to serve the best crab cakes in Virginia (some say in Maryland, too). Unlike most, we stroll around the island first to avoid the midday dining crowd. My daughter Alissa, who doesn't even like seafood, relishes tasty crab cakes served at Hilda Crockett's with big portions of clam fritters, potato salad, corn pudding, and home-baked bread. Sated, tanned, and happily tired, we board the ferry back. As the waves break over the bow, splashing us into giggles, we can taste the salt spray and the Chesapeake Bay history, too.

Three places to stay on the island are Hilda Crockett's Chesapeake House (757–891–2331), Sunset Inn (757–891–2535), and Bay View Inn (757–891–2396).There's not much to do on Tangier and no beach, so your kids will probably like the island best as a day trip, and like it as much for the ride over and back as for the island. Another way to reach the island is via Tangier & Chesapeake Cruises, aboard the *Chesapeake Breeze*. The one-and-one-half-hour narrated cruise leaves from Buzzard's Point Marina in Reedville, Virginia, every day at 10:00 A.M. and returns at 3:30 P.M. (804) 453–2628. Web address: www.eaglesnest.net/tangier/tangier.htm.

Annual Events

JUNE AND JULY

Fireman's Carnival, *late June or early July.* A family festival filled with food and games.

SEPTEMBER

Onancock Regatta Weekend, *mid-September; (757) 787–3363.* Home tours, dinner dance, sailing, and kayaking.

Where to Eat

Armando's, *10 North Street; (757) 787–7574. Open year-round Tuesday through Saturday for dinner; closed Sunday and Monday.* This is a popular local eatery with a 1940s interior and an eclectic menu. Popular dinner creations include the margarita shrimp and mango chicken. Kid-size portions are available. $-$$

Hopkins & Brothers Waterfront Restaurant and 1842 General Store, *2 Market Street, Onancock; (757)* 787–3100. *Open daily Memorial Day through Labor Day; closed Monday and Tuesday the rest of the year.* Fresh, locally caught seafood for lunch or dinner. $$-$$$

Backfins, *47 Market Street; (757) 787–7626. Open year-round Monday through Saturday for breakfast, lunch, and dinner.* Sample some of the local seafood at this casual family restaurant. Children's menu available. $-$$

Where to Stay

Colonial Manor Inn, *84 Market Street (5 blocks from the harbor); (757) 787–3521.* This large Victorian home, on the town's main street, has served as an inn for more than sixty years. There are fourteen guest rooms (many are small but cozy), nine with private baths, including a two-room first-floor family suite. Guests are welcome to relax in the Victorian gazebo or curl up with a book on the quiet glassed-in sun porch. The inn welcomes families with well-behaved children. Rates include a full breakfast.

76 Market Street Bed and Breakfast, *76 Market Street; (757) 787–7600.* Closer to the shopping area is this one-hundred-year-old Victorian house with three bedrooms (all with private bath) furnished with period antiques. Call for reservations and to ask about the suitability for your family.

The Sleeping Swan, *(757) 789–3050. E-mail: 102140.1542@compuserv.com.* This fully furnished apartment sleeps six and is available year-round for overnight or a two-week rental. Rates include daily housekeeping.

Spinning Wheel Bed and Breakfast, *31 North Street; (757) 787–7311. Web address: www.esva.net/~evergreen/.*

Open from mid-April through early-October. Call for reservations. This 1890s home, furnished with period antiques, has ten spinning wheels. Guests are invited to sit and chat around the table while David and Karen Tweedie serve a three-course breakfast. There are five guest rooms, all with private baths. Children under 12 and pets are not allowed.

For More Information

Eastern Shore of Virginia Tourism Commission, *P.O. Box 460, Melfa 23410; (757) 787–2460. Web address: www.esva.net. E-mail: esvatourism@esva.net.*

Wachapreague

Many people think this little fishing village has the most scenic waterfront on the Eastern Shore. Known as the Flounder Fishing Capital of the World, Wachapreague is rich with other sorts of wildlife, too. More than 250 species of birds pass through the area as they travel along the Atlantic Flyway.

BOAT RENTALS

Charter a boat with a captain for offshore fishing or rent one for a day and captain it yourself (if you know how). Wachapreague is located between two favorite places for sport fishermen—Ocean City, Maryland and Virginia Beach. Charter boats are less expensive than in many beach areas.

For boat charters, May through October, contact Wachapreague Hotel Marina, (757-787-2105) and the Wachapreague Town Marina, 15 Atlantic Avenue; (757-787-1930). Ask about 16-foot-long fishing boats that handle up to four people as well as chartered boats for up to six people. Bait is also for sale.

Annual Events

APRIL

Wachapreague Spring Flounder Tournament, *mid-April.* Angling enthusiasts fish for trophy-size catches.

JULY AND AUGUST

The Fireman's Carnival, *late July to early August.* This small-town fête is always popular among families.

Annual Fish Fry, *late August.* Local fare is served.

SEPTEMBER

Wachapreague Fall Flounder Tournament, *mid-September.* Fishing enthusiasts angle for big flounder.

Custis Farms (all ages) *6118 Seaside Road in Nassawadox; (757) 442–9071 or (800) 428–6361. Open Monday through Saturday year-round. Admission.* This is a working farm operated by Phil and Barbara Custis. A four-hour walking tour and hayride describe farm life in detail; ask if tours can be shortened for your group. Your kids will enjoy the storytelling sessions at the house. Stay for lunch at the Victorian garden, where you'll dine on fried chicken, baked beans, rolls, and vegetables; make a reservation in advance.

Where to Eat

Island House Restaurant, *17 Atlantic Avenue; (757) 787–4242.* Located near the Hotel Wachapreague, the Island House is a popular eatery with locals. In summer you'll see fancy boats tied up at the dock so their skippers can lunch on the restaurant's crab cakes. $$

The Trawler Restaurant and Lounge, *Route 13 North, Exmor; (757) 442–2092.* Located beside the Best Western Eastern Shore Inn, the Trawler offers fresh seafood, including homemade chowder and crabcakes.

Where to Stay

The Burton House Bed and Breakfast and **Hart's Harbor House,** *9 and 11 Brooklyn Avenue; (757) 787–4560 or (757) 787–4848. Open year-round.* The Burton House is a Victorian home with period furnishings; Hart's Harbor House is a contemporary lodging. The Burton House has private and shared rooms, as does Harbor House, which also offers two cottages and houses for week-long stays. The properties have tennis courts and bicycles, and the host can set up guided birding tours or cruises to nearby Tangier Island. No children under age 12 are permitted in the bed and breakfast, but families with kids are welcome in the cottages.

Virginia Landing, *located at the end of Route 605 in Quinby; (757) 442–4853. Open April 15 through October 31. Call to make reservations.* Quinby is the closest town to Wachapreague with a campground. Amenities include a fishing pier, fish-cleaning station, restaurant, mini-golf, volleyball courts, and baseball fields.

Wachapreague Motel and Marina, (also called Hotel Wachapreague), *15 Atlantic Avenue; (757) 787–2105.* The motel has rental and charter boats as well as a bait-and-tackle shop. A two-double-bed apartment with a kitchen sleeps six or more. There is also a one-bed apartment with a kitchen and an efficiency available. Pets are allowed.

For More Information

Eastern Shore of Virginia Tourism Commission. *P.O. Box 460, Melfa 23410; (757) 787–2460. Web address: www.esvatourism.org*

Cape Charles

Cape Charles and its environs offer families the outdoors Eastern Shore–style.

KIPTOPEKE STATE PARK (all ages)

3450 Kiptopeke Drive; (757) 331–2267. Open year-round. Admission.

On 375 acres of beachfront, woods, and farmfields, Kiptopeke gives families a chance to unwind away from the crowds. My family fell in love with Kiptopeke for its simplicity. The 0.5-mile of Chesapeake Bay beach (lifeguards on duty between Memorial Day and Labor Day) is not particularly picturesque, but it's never crowded, and it's always calm due to the sunken World War II ship that serves as a breakwater for the waves. Young kids tumble in and out of tire tubes (bring your own), happily using the gradually sloping shoreline as a playground.

At the unlifeguarded north beach, a primitive swath of shore backed by wild grasses, locals angle for flounder or croakers from the fishing pier, a former ferry terminal. Scheduled activities include ranger-led fishing clinics, nighttime bonfires, lessons in becoming a "chicken-necker" (crabbing by using poultry necks as bait), as well as canoe treks through the salt marshes of nearby Racoon Creek.

Miles of hiking trails afford plenty of opportunities for sighting birds. Nature paths wind over sand dunes through groves of loblolly pines, sassafras, and wild cherry trees. The Baywoods Trail, a 1-mile loop, passes the gazebo that seems to flutter to life in September as a bird banding station for hundreds of migratory birds, songbirds, shorebirds, and hawks. In summer, though, the benches offer lazy hikers like us a pleasant place to picnic and pause to watch for rabbits and deer, and to listen for quail rustling in the red oak and bayberry trees.

Kiptopeke also has basic and full-service campsites. (Reservations are required, call 800–933–7275.)

THE EASTERN SHORE NATIONAL WILDLIFE REFUGE (all ages)

5003 Hallet Circle; (757) 331–2760. Open daily year-round; closed Thanksgiving, Christmas, and New Year's Day.

It's easy to drive right by the Eastern Shore of Virginia National Wildlife Refuge, because it's just before the northern terminus of the Chesapeake Bay Bridge–Tunnel. The wildlife refuge is a surprise with 651 acres of forests, myrtle thickets, grasslands, birds, and ponds. At this roadside oasis, the distant sounds of traffic are almost obliterated by the twittering of scores of birds and the swish of bushes and leaves in the breeze. The **Observation Trail** leads through an abandoned World War II bunker to an observation platform overlooking a view of grasslands and trees. If you visit in summer, remember that it's hot in these grasslands. Wear a hat, use sunscreen, and tote water. Stop at the visitors center for information.

The refuge is a must-visit during fall's migratory season. Species such as the bald eagle and peregrine falcon, along with many other birds, use the refuge's ponds and woods. Between late August and early November you can see hundreds of hawks, falcons, and songbirds in flight.

Annual Events

SEPTEMBER
Annual Cape Charles Day. Crafts and live music are part of this festival.

OCTOBER
Eastern Shore Birding Festival, *early October.* Located at various sites including Kiptopeke State Park and Sunset Beach. The two-day-long festival coincides with the peak of fall migration. Workshops, exhibits, children's activities, crafts, and bird art are held and shown.

Eastern Shore Harvest Fest. Held the first Wednesday in October, Harvest Fest celebrates the foods—such as seafood, sweet potatoes, crab, and chicken—that make Virginia's Eastern Shore famous. Craft vendors sell their wares.

Chesapeake Bay Bridge–Tunnel to Virginia Beach (all ages) *U.S. Highway 13 (757) 331–2960. Cars pay a $10, one-way toll.*
This is the world's longest bridge–tunnel complex stretching 17.6 miles from Virginia Beach/Norfolk to Virginia's Eastern Shore. As the structure loops over and under the bay, savor the sense of space and joy common to open roads, panoramic water views, and sea breezes. More than just a bridge, this structure has a seagull pier, a fishing pier, a souvenir shop, and several telescopes to give you a unique view of the bay and the Eastern Shore. Even at $10 one-way, it's worth the trip.

Where to Eat

Sting-Ray's Restaurant, *U.S. Highway 13 in Capeville, a 5-mile drive from Cape Charles; (757) 331–2505. Open daily for breakfast, lunch, and dinner.* From the outside, Sting-Ray's looks more like a convenience store attached to a gas station than a restaurant. Lunch is the stuff of unmemorable roadside fare such as fish sandwiches and fried food. In the evening, however, the locals swear by this restaurant's tasty seafood and spicy chili. $

Where to Stay

Best Western Sunset Beach Resort, *U.S. Highway 13; (757) 331–4786 or (800) 899–4–SUN.* This inn offers several rooms. Ask about its suitability for your children.

Chesapeake Charm, *202 Madison Avenue; (757) 331–2676 or (800) 546–9215.* This 1921 house is furnished in antiques and collectibles.

The three guest rooms all have private baths. A homemade breakfast featuring breads, muffins, fruits, and a daily entree is served. Children over the age of 2 are welcome.

Days Inn, *29106 Langford Highway, U.S. Highway 13; (757) 331–1000 or (800) 331–4000.* This is a traditional motel.

For More Information

Eastern Shore of Virginia Tourism Commission, *P.O. Box 460, Melfa 23410; (757) 787–2460. Web address: www.esvatourism.org.*

Central Virginia

entral Virginia offers families a wide variety of vacation possibilities including scenic rolling hills; lakes, rivers, and streams; a rich historical heritage; and cities that include the capital, Richmond, which was also the capital of the Confederacy during the Civil War. In Central Virginia visitors will find numerous historic sites, great museums, Southern charm, and good shopping.

The central section of the state, flanked by the Blue Ridge Mountains to the west and tidal rivers to the east, is particularly distinguished for being the home of notable patriots and presidents. Thomas Jefferson and Patrick Henry were born and lived here; James Madison and James Monroe made their homes in Central Virginia.

The area also has a rich Civil War history. Home to Appomattox, where Lee surrendered to Grant and ended the South's hopes for its own Confederate nation, Central Virginia offers children meaningful and memorable lessons about American history and the consequences of war. Be sure to prepare your children beforehand with books and videos, or, with younger kids, simple explanations about the Civil War.

With so much history, there's a lot to see. It's important to keep in mind that

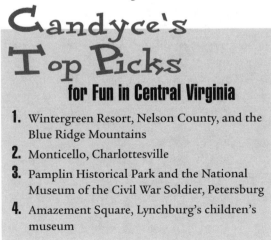

Candyce's Top Picks
for Fun in Central Virginia

1. Wintergreen Resort, Nelson County, and the Blue Ridge Mountains

2. Monticello, Charlottesville

3. Pamplin Historical Park and the National Museum of the Civil War Soldier, Petersburg

4. Amazement Square, Lynchburg's children's museum

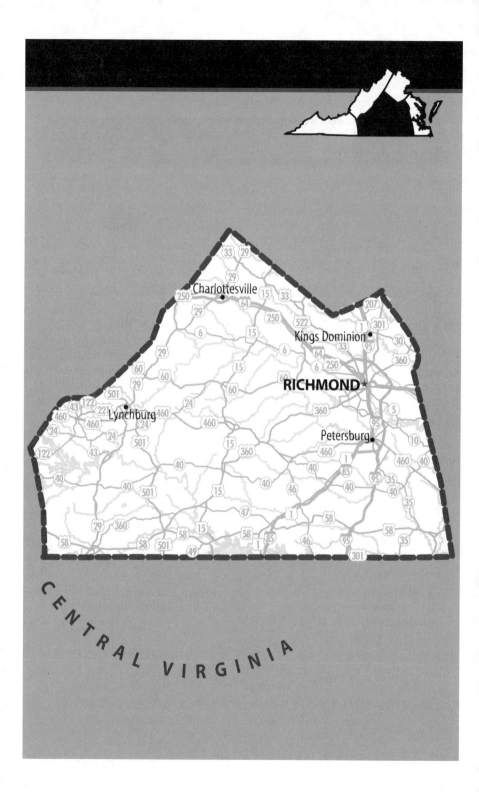

CENTRAL VIRGINIA

not every historic house, monument, and battlefield is going to fascinate a child, particularly younger ones. Try to offer a balance. Pick and choose your historic sites, and be sure to complement these with time out to enjoy the area's parks, forests, and theme parks.

Charlottesville and Albemarle County

Charlottesville, located in the foothills of the Blue Ridge Mountains along Interstate 64, is the home of the University of Virginia, which was founded and designed by Thomas Jefferson, third president of the United States. Indeed, Jefferson's influence is very strong in this city of some 40,000 and in the surrounding Albemarle County. If you have school-age or older kids, they may enjoy a visit to the home of a former president. Not far from Charlottesville is Monticello, the home of Thomas Jefferson; Ash Lawn–Highland, the home of James Monroe; and Montpelier, home of James Madison.

 VIRGINIA DISCOVERY MUSEUM (ages 2 to 8)

524 East Main Street, at the east end of the Downtown Mall (a 6-block-long pedestrian mall) near city hall; (434) 977–1025. Web address: www.vadm.org. Open Tuesday through Sunday, closed Monday. Admission.

The Virginia Discovery Museum offers toddlers through kids age 10 opportunities for interactive fun. Most of the activities, however, are geared for young kids.

Young children can step inside a reconstructed eighteenth-century pioneer log cabin filled with such period furnishings as a rope bed, cradle, and cooking hearth. In Jefferson's Corner, kids can use tools just like those used by Thomas Jefferson, including a polygraph to "write" Jefferson's signature. Kids enjoy the walk-in kaleidoscope, Virginia Faces, the dress-up area, and the Puppet Tree. Weekly self-directed art programs are offered in the Art Corner. At the computer lab kids can browse the Internet (under the supervision of a lab staffer), and in the magnet room kids craft mosaics with thousands of magnets. Near the changing exhibits area is a live beehive housed in a Plexiglass enclosure. Throughout the year there are **Free** drop-in programs, such as the Poetry Club on Tuesdays and Wednesdays' Toddler Time. During the school year (October to June), a Magic School Bus Science Club meets weekly staging hands-on activities for the family to do together.

UNIVERSITY OF VIRGINIA ROTUNDA (ages 9 and up)

On University Avenue, near what is known as "The Corner" (Main Street and University Avenue); (434) 924–7679. Web address: www.virginia.edu.

The University of Virginia sprawls along Old Main Street. Here you can see the original "Academical Village" designed by Jefferson, the university's founder, highlighted by the Rotunda modeled after Rome's Pantheon. The Rotunda now houses administration offices but was first used as a library in 1822. Step inside to see the bronze Liberty Bell Statue by Sir Moses Ezekiel; Jefferson's figure placed on a pedestal in the shape of the Liberty Bell has been standing here since 1907.

CABELL HALL

Follow the lawn extending from the south portico of the Rotunda.

Cabell Hall was designed by the noted architect Stanford White at the turn of the twentieth century. Along the walkway are pavilions built (and still used) for faculty housing, each influenced by a famous classical building. Behind each pavilion is a decorative garden, originally used by faculty members to grow vegetables and tend livestock. The original student dorms are located behind the gardens; although they now have central heating, they still have working fireplaces. Edgar Allan Poe was a student here, and his living quarters (Room 13, West Range) are open to the public.

Free walking tours of the Rotunda by University of Virginia Students are offered year-round (except during the winter break), although families with young kids might prefer a self-guided stroll around the campus.

MONTICELLO (ages 5 and up) (TT)

The Monticello Visitors Center is on State Highway 20 South (about a 0.5-mile from Interstate 64, exit 121, and about 2 miles from the estate; (434) 293–6789, TDD (434) 984–9822. Web address: www.monticello.org. About 150 yards from the Visitors Center, make a left onto Route 53 and follow the signs, about 2 miles. The house and Visitors Center are open daily year-round except Christmas, with reduced hours November through February.

Designed by Jefferson and built over the span of forty years, this mountaintop plantation is considered to be an architectural classic, not to mention a stunning, eye-catching beauty set in peaceful surroundings. Jefferson moved here in 1771, although construction continued until 1809.

To get the most out of your family's visit, start at the visitors center. Along with some 400 artifacts, many of which were found during archaeological excavations at Monticello, there are architectural models and drawings shown in a permanent exhibit, and a thirty-five-minute-long film, "Thomas Jefferson: The Pursuit of Liberty," is shown daily on the hour from 10:00 A.M. to 4:00 P.M. (June 15 to the end of August) and at 11:00 A.M. and 2:00 P.M. the rest of the year. You can buy a Presidents' Pass, a combination ticket for admission to Monticello, Ash Lawn–Highland, and the Historic Michie Tavern.

Guided tours are offered of the imposing main house, where many belongings of Jefferson and his wife, Martha, remain. Most of the furnishings are original. Jefferson's innovative thinking resulted in some unusual architectural touches throughout Monticello. For example, because he didn't like staircases (neither their appearance nor the amount of space they require), most are very narrow or not visible. Also take a peep into the concave mirror in the entryway, which shows your image upside down—a favorite with kids.

Monticello's Tour for Families Families with children ages 6 through 11 can smell vanilla beans, examine eighteenth-century nails, decipher secret codes, and learn about Jefferson's grandchildren on children-friendly house tours focusing on hands-on learning. These tours operate on the hour from mid-June to mid-August at no additional charge. Inquire at the ticket office.

Jefferson was a brilliant thinker and a number of his gadgets used to make life easier can be viewed throughout the house, such as a two-pen device that enabled him to make a copy of whatever he was writing. (All the more remarkable when you consider that Jefferson lived in a time when there were few gadgets.) The seven-day calendar clock, which he designed, is still in working order and is on display on a mantelpiece.

Visitors can also take tours through the restored orchard, vineyard, and vegetable gardens and view Jefferson's grave in the family burial grounds. From the house you can take a shuttle bus back to the parking lot or take a walk through the woods along a guided path. This huge property requires a fair amount of time to tour. Written guided tours of

Monticello are available in Braille, Chinese, French, German, Italian, Japanese, Korean, Spanish, and Russian.

Major activities in celebration of the two hundredth anniversary of the Lewis & Clark expedition will begin in January of 2003.

ASH LAWN–HIGHLAND (ages 5 and up) (TT)

1000 James Monroe Parkway, 4.5 miles southeast of Charlottesville on Route 795 and 3 miles southwest of Monticello; (434) 293–9539. Web address: www. avenue.org/ashlawn. Open daily year-round, except Thanksgiving, Christmas and New Year's Day, with reduced hours November through February. Admission.

This was the estate of James Monroe, fifth president of the United States. The 535-acre site is just a few miles from Monticello, and its proximity is no coincidence. Jefferson himself selected the site for Monroe, and even sent over his gardeners to plant orchards for his neighbor.

This small and cozy place is actually larger than it was when Monroe lived here; a later owner built additions on to what was a very simple farmhouse. Remember that Monroe was the first president to come from the middle class, which may explain the lack of grandeur.

There are picnicking spots that offer marvelous views of the Blue Ridge Mountains in the distance. Daily guided tours of the main house offer a glimpse into the past. Along with viewing many of Monroe's possessions, including gifts he received from prominent people and souvenirs from France, where he served as an envoy, you may be treated to a spinning or cooking demonstration. Check on the special events held throughout the year. Special celebrations are held on Monroe's birthday, April 28. On summer Saturdays, the plantation offers puppet shows, hands-on crafts, and storytelling. For Plantation Days in July, special tours show kids how a plantation operated. Check the schedule for summer's musical festivals (434-293-4500) and Christmas wreath trimming, caroling, and madrigals.

HISTORIC MICHIE TAVERN (TT)

State Highway 53, 683 Jefferson Davis Parkway; (434) 977–1234. Web address: www.michietavern.com. The restaurant serves lunch year-round. The museum is open year-round, with tours of the tavern given daily.

One of the oldest homesteads still standing in Virginia, this is now a restaurant with costumed hostesses who welcome you as "strangers," the eighteenth-century term for "traveler." The "ordinary" log cabin serves tasty fried chicken and other lunch fare at a bountiful buffet. Michie Tavern opened in 1784 as an "ordinary," a place along the stagecoach route to dine, rest, and socialize. While gentlemen passed time in the tap room, ladies enjoyed a decorated room in which they could sew or read while waiting for the next stagecoach to arrive. In 1927 the tavern was dismantled piece by piece and moved to its present location from Old Buck Mountain Road, in Northwest Albermarle, about 17 miles northwest of where it is now. Behind the building are re-created dependencies, including a log kitchen, a general store, a printer's market, smokehouse, dairy, and a "necessary" (outhouse). Kids age 5 and under eat **Free**.

MONTPELIER (TT)

11407 Constitution Highway, Northeast of Charlottesville on State Highway 20, 4 miles southwest of the town of Orange; (540) 672–2728. Web address: www.montpelier.org. Open daily year-round, except Thanksgiving, Christmas, and New Year's Day, with reduced hours December through March. Admission.

This home of James Madison, fourth president of the U. S.was spruced up considerable in 2001 in celebration of the 250th anniversary of Madison's birth. Furnishing were added and the Madison family cemetery was restored. The National Trust for Historic Preservation is in the process of restoring the house to reflect Madison's period. A cabin built in 1870 by George Gilmore, born a slave of Madison, is also being restored, with planned interpretive programs to give visitors a feel for the day-to-day life of the Gilmore family.

The acoustiguide relates the history of the family and buildings. The guided tour can last up to two hours, so younger children may get impatient. Check for special events to spark their interest, including Wednesday morning programs, July through mid-August, geared toward children ages 3 through 6 and 7 through 12.

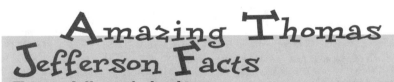

Amazing Thomas Jefferson Facts

Thomas Jefferson's daughter, who had spent some time in France, is said to have introduced the Round Dance to society at a party at Michie Tavern. She also reputedly danced the first waltz in America with a young French officer, who shocked the crowd when he put his arm around her waist. (Tell that to the MTV generation.)

Outdoor Fun in the Air, on Water, or on a Green

- **Bear Balloon Corporation** (434-971-1757 or 800-932-0152; www.tocomefly.com) and **Bonaire Charters** (434-589-5717; www.bonairecharters.com) offer scenic balloon flights over the Virginia countryside, morning and evening.

- **Highlands Golf Park** (434-985-2765; www.highlandsgolfpark.com) has an eighteen-hole putting course, professional instruction, and equipment. Open daily year-round.

- **James River Runners Inc.** (434-286-2338; www.jamesriver.com) will take your family bird- and wildlife-watching, fishing, canoeing, kayaking, and rafting on the beautiful James River, on half-day, all-day, or overnight excursions.

Annual Events

Dogwood Festival, *held every spring;* (434) 961-9824. Celebrates the state flower with entertainment, food, and crafts.

MARCH

Festival of the Book, *late March;* (434) 924-3296. Features readings by international authors, panels, book sales, and special programs for children.

OCTOBER

Virginia Film Festival, *last weekend in October;* (434) 982-5277. Features movies, film stars, and directors.

Where to Eat

Some of the town's most informal and inexpensive restaurants for families are located in and around University Corner.

Crozet Pizza, *12 miles west of town on State Highway 240 in Crozet; (434) 823-2132.* Crozet's known for having the best pizza in the state. $

Historic Michie Tavern, *683 Thomas Jefferson Parkway (State Highway 53); (434) 977-1234; the restaurant serves lunch from 11:30 A.M. to 3:00 P.M. daily.* The "ordinary" log cabin serves tasty fried chicken and other lunch fare at a bountiful buffet. Children age 5 and under dine **Free**. $-$$

Martha's Cafe, 11 Elliewood; (434) 971–7530. The restaurant has kid-pleasing homemade fare (try the enchiladas) and offers al fresco dining in the courtyard cafe when the weather is warm. Kids like the goldfish in the bathtub. $

The Old Mill Room, in the Boar's Head Inn, 1.5 miles west of Charlottesville on U.S. Highway 250; (434) 972–2230. Food such as prime rib and veal, with the tavern downstairs serving lighter fare. $$–$$$

Where to Stay

Best Western Mount Vernon, Junction of U.S. Highways 29 and 250 bypass; (434) 296–5501 or (800) 528–1234. This motel/hotel has 110 rooms, a full-service restaurant, and a large outdoor pool.

The Boar's Head Inn, U.S. Highway 250; (434) 296–2131 or (800) 476–1988. The inn was built in 1965 but has history surrounding it. An 1834 brick-and-wood waterwheel gristmill was used on the inn's property, with fieldstones from the mill's foundation used in the inn's fireplace and the mill's old pine planks used as flooring. Simple, but elegant, rooms and suites are furnished with antiques. Tennis and squash courts, three pools, a health club, spa, and sprawling grounds make this a nice—though fairly expensive—retreat, which may be better suited to families with older children.

Doubletree Hotel Charlottesville, 2350 Seminole Trail, (434) 973–2121 or (800) 494–7596. Really a hotel, this property is set on a twenty-acre wooded hillside location overlooking the Blue Ridge Mountains, 7 miles north of town. The hotel has 235 rooms, two restaurants, indoor and outdoor pools, and two tennis courts.

English Inn of Charlottesville, 200 Morton Drive; (434) 971–9900 or (800) 786–5400. This Tudor-style inn strives for an English club feel with its wood paneled lobby, wing chairs, and Oriental rugs. The eighty-eight-room inn welcomes children and has a large indoor pool.

Guesthouses Bed and Breakfast Reservation Service, P.O. Box 5737, Charlottesville 22905; (434) 979–7264 or (800) 934–9184. Web address: www. va-guesthouses.com. This service offers information on private houses, guest cottages, and traditional bed and breakfast accommodations in Charlottesville and the surrounding area.

Omni Charlottesville Hotel, 235 West Main Street; (434) 971–5500 or (800) THE–OMNI. This hotel is conveniently located to shopping, theaters, and sightseeing. Rooms have mini-refrigerators. There are indoor and outdoor pools. Kids get free milk and cookies at bedtime and a bag of goodies when they check in. There are also backpacks of activities families can check out at the front desk.

For More Information

Charlottesville/Albemarle Convention and Visitors Bureau, on State Highway 20 South off Interstate 64 at exit 121, P.O. Box 178, Charlottesville, VA 22902; (434) 977–1783 or (877) 386–1102. Web address: www.charlottesville tourism.org. Open daily except Thanksgiving, Christmas, and New Year's Day. Along with providing brochures and information, the convention and visitors bureau can make same-day lodging reservations. There's also a satellite visitors center in downtown Charlottesville at 108 Second Street, S.E.; (434) 977-6100.

Nelson County

History's great, but don't ignore the spectacular Blue Ridge countryside. Try to combine seeing some of Charlottesville's historic attractions with hiking, bicycling, and exploring the mountains, woods, and valleys of Nelson County, about 30 miles southwest of Charlottesville. In spring the foothills turn pink with apple blossoms; more than forty varieties of apples are grown in the county. Drive through this scenic countryside in spring when the trees blossom and come back in fall to buy apples by the bushel.

 HIKING OPPORTUNITIES

- Twenty-five miles of the **Appalachian Trail** cut through Nelson County. Maps are available at the visitor center in Lovingston on U.S. Highway 29, open daily year-round; (434) 263–5239 or (800) 282–8223.

- **Wintergreen Resort** maintains 30 miles of nature trails; maps are available at the Wintergreen Outdoor Center (434–325–8169), as are guided hikes. Maps are also available at the main check-in desk at the Mountain Inn, Wintergreen's main lodge (434–325–2200).

- Another great area hike for families is the **Crabtree Falls Trail,** which is accessible from State Highway 56. The moderately difficult hike, 3 miles one way, follows the Tye River before climbing through the mountains. (When my children were young we made the first overlook our goal and then headed back down.) Our family has always liked the hike for the reward: the waterfall, reputedly the highest waterfall east of the Mississippi River. Crabtree Falls descends 1,200 feet in a series of five cascades. The falls are most dramatic in spring and winter when the water is high. In summer the woods are cool and the waterfall pretty enough to be worth the hike.

BICYCLING

Nelson County is good biking country. Those people with mountain bikes can find challenging terrain in the Blue Ridge hills, and those who want paved, less challenging roads can follow routes mapped by the Nelson County Department of Tourism (434-263-5239 or 800-282-8223). Some routes include a:

- 22-mile ride along the Blue Ridge Parkway that begins at the Nelson County Visitor Center in Love and continues south to the Tye River;

- 31-mile loop from Walton's Mountain Museum that crosses rivers and picnicking spots and returns back to the museum;

- 24-mile loop that starts at Woodson's Mill convenience store on Route 778.

Wintergreen Resort has a mountain biking program, complete with guided tours, that includes 16 miles of single track on a mountain and 114 miles of terrain in adjacent George Washington National Forest.

Bicycling maps and suggestions are available from the Nelson County Visitors Center (see For More Information) and by calling (434) 263-5239 or (800) 282-8223.

Apple Picking Apple picking is a serious—but sweet— business in Nelson County, which grows acres upon acres of apples. The county visitors center has a scenic drive mapped out that winds past many of the orchards. This is an appealing drive in spring when the rolling hills seem painted with pink. In fall, the following farms offer apples and other produce for sale: Dickie Brothers Orchard, Route 666 off State Highway 56, Roseland (434-277-8609); Drumheller's Orchard, Route 741 off U.S. Highway 29, Lovingston (434-263-5036); Fitzgerald's Orchard, Route 682 off State Highway 56 West, Tyro (434-277-5798); Silver Creek–Seaman Orchards, Packing Shed, State Highway 56 West, Tyro (434-277-5824); and Saunders Orchard, State Highway 56 West, Piney River (434-277-5455).

For information on particular types of apples available at individual orchards, click on to the Nelson County web site, www.nelsoncounty va.org.

HORSEBACK RIDING

Rodes Farms at Wintergreen (434–325–8260; www.wintergreenresort. com) offers one-hour and sunset trail rides, riding lessons, and pony rides for kids. Mountain View Stable in Lyndhurst (540–949–5346) also offers riding lessons and trail rides.

WALTON'S MOUNTAIN MUSEUM (ages 5 and up)

6484 Rockfish River Road, between Charlottesville and Lynchburg on Route 617 in Nelson County; (434) 831–2000. Web address: www.waltonmuseum.org. Open daily, March through November, except Easter, Thanksgiving, Christmas, and New Year's Day. Admission.

The characters from *The Waltons* television show were based on real people in Nelson County, one of whom was the show's creator, Earl Hamner, Jr. The community has opened this museum, which features memorabilia from the television show as well as a recreation of John-Boy's bedroom, the family kitchen, and the Waltons' living room, complete with piano and Philco radio. There's also an exhibit from the Godsey's general store, from which postcards can be stamped "Walton's Mountain." If your kids remember the show or the movies, they may like this place; otherwise, it's too small to create a great deal of interest.

Wintergreen Resort, 43 miles southwest of Charlottesville, west on Route 250 to Route 1518; (434) 325–2200 or (800) 266–2444. Web address: www.WintergreenResort.com. This is a wonderful year-round resort for families. We've been here in all seasons. Although summer and fall are our favorite times to visit, spring brings wildflowers and winter brings skiing. At age 5, my daughter learned to ski in the resort's kids' program.

Wintergreen, an upscale resort sprawled on 10,800 acres in the valley and on a mountain, gives you Blue Ridge Mountains' magic from endless views to varied activities. The resort has 300 units (condos or homes with kitchens; most have fireplaces), a lake, six pools (one indoor), a wading pool, and a playground. You can also enjoy boating, golf, outdoor and indoor tennis, swimming, and horseback riding. Families here also learn about birds, fossils, wildflowers, and stream life on the frequent guided hikes through the resort's own nature preserve.

In summer, on holidays, and on selected weekends, the resort offers a Kids in Action program for ages 2½ to 5 and 6 to 12. With Kids Night Out (Friday and Saturday evenings July through Labor Day), ages 4 to 12 enjoy swimming and movies while parents savor moonlight and romantic dinners.

From December to late March, guests ski and snowboard. (Wintergreen has a sophisticated and powerful snowmaking system that is able to cover all twenty slopes and trails with 2 feet of snow in under three days.) There's also a U-shaped half-pipe for snowboarders and skiers. Various kids' ski programs are available for ages 5 to 12, as well as child care programs for nonskiing tots. There's also a mini-rider snowboarder program and a new 900-foot megatubing park. Wintergreen also has Virginia's only high-speed six-passenger lift. For après-ski, the Wintergarden Spa and Fitness Center offer indoor and outdoor pools, seven massage rooms, saunas and steam rooms, three hot tubs, and a Jacuzzi. Sometimes, because of the warm Virginia weather, the slopes can get fogged in. Nonresort guests are also welcome to ski on Wintergreen's nineteen slopes and trails.

Nonresort guests may also enroll their kids in the activity programs. These include a year-round Kids in Action, which introduces 2- to 12-year-olds to the wonders of nature in an action-packed day camp, and a summer Kids Campout, for ages 6 to 14. There is also a Family Outdoor Camp that includes the whole family in river rafting, spelunking, and camping.

In fall Wintergreen is glorious as the mountainsides are covered with brilliant red, orange, and yellow foliage. The chairlifts operate for easy and spectacular mountain views. The resort offers nature weekends and craft weekends.

One caution: we've always found the food at Wintergreen to be just average. Your family can bring provisions and cook simple meals in the condo, then dine out for variety in Nellysford. Wintergreen's restaurants are the Copper Mine, which serves breakfast and a more formal dinner (434–325–8090); Devils Grill Restaurant and Lounge at the Devils Knob Golf Course, with an informal atmosphere for lunch and dinner (434–325–2200); the Edge at Cooper's Vantage, an informal family restaurant (434–325–8090); and Stoney Creek Bar & Grill (434–325–8110), a casual family dining spot with a terrific view of the Blue Ridge Mountains. All of Wintergreen's restaurants have children's menus.

WOODSON'S MILL

Route 778, Lowesville; (804) 277–5604 or (800) 282–8223. Web address: jbwoodson.internations.net/woodsonsmill. Open Saturday only. **Free.**

If your kids have never seen a working mill, then visit Woodson's. The mill, originally built in 1794 and reconstructed in 1845, still uses water-driven millstones to grind wheat, corn, and other grains. An operating cider press is also on the property.

Where to Eat

Despite the fact that Nellysford is a small village, there are a number of dining options.

Basic Necessities, *State Highway 151; (434) 361–1766. Open for lunch Tuesday through Saturday and brunch on Sundays.* This cafe offers light lunches, salads, desserts, fresh homemade bread, and other "basic necessities." $

Jim & Stu's Bistro 151, *State Highway 151; (434) 361–1463. Lunch and dinner, Tuesday through Saturday.* This informal restaurant is known for its homemade pizza as well as seafood and steaks. Children's menu available. $–$$

Lovingston Cafe, *U.S. Business Highway 29 in Lovingston; (434) 263–8000. Break-* fast, lunch, and dinner, Tuesday through Sunday. Traditional American fare of steaks and seafood are the highlights here as well as vegetarian items and pizza. $–$$

Sunflower Natural Foods, *State Highway 151; (434) 361–1786. Lunch daily, dinner Thursday through Sunday.* Along with an assortment of natural cereals, juices, and other groceries, this natural-food store also sells frozen entrees (great for easy meals in your condo) and sandwiches.

Schuyler Family Restaurant, *next to Walton's Mountain Museum on Rockfish River Road on Route 617; (434) 831–3333.* Subs and sandwiches, homemade barbeque. $–$$

Where to Stay

The Acorn Inn Bed & Breakfast, *Route 634 in Nellysford; (434) 361–9357; www.acorninn.com.* The Acorn Inn is as laidback as a stroll on a backcountry road. This bed and breakfast eschews fancy antiques, spacious lodgings, and private baths for serviceable pieces in good enough rooms. Owners Kathy and Martin Versluys wanted to create a bed and breakfast in the European tradition: A clean space that is affordable.

The inn's style is a mixture of Dutch practicality, tasty health food, and lowcost touring. Ten rooms are in a renovated stable, and they are as big as—you guessed it—a horse stall. Though compact, the rooms are brightened with quilts. Showers, one for men and one for women, are down the hall.

In the evening gather around the Finnish soapstone stove in the skylit A-frame, an inviting room brightened with ceramic figures and quilts from Mexico. You're welcome to bring a pizza back for dinner, and afterwards sample the cookies that Martin bakes. The Acorn Inn welcomes children.

After a help-yourself-continental-plus breakfast of fresh fruit, homemade breads, and apple cobbler, try golf at the nearby Wintergreen Resort's courses, enjoy the pastoral stillness, or follow a bike route mapped out by Martin (bring your own cycles). Feel the wind at your back as you pedal past creek banks and meadows edged by the silhouette of the Blue Ridge Mountains.

There are two guest rooms in the main house plus a cottage with a kitchen, bedroom, and bath. Kids under 12 are **Free**.

Looking Glass House Bed & Breakfast, *State Highway 151 in Afton; (540) 456–6844 or (800) 769–6844. Web address: www.lookingglasshousebb.com.*This 1848 farmhouse is country comfortable; it's furnished with antiques and wicker. There is a swimming pool,

gazebo, and garden. A full breakfast is served in the dining room. Well-behaved children are welcome.

Meander Inn Bed & Breakfast, *Route 612 in Nellysford, 3100 Berry Hill Road; (434) 361–1121 or (800) 868–6116. Web address: www.meander inn.com.* This 80-year-old farmhouse sits on fifty acres overlooking the Rock-fish River. Sit on the front porch, bird-watch, or admire the Blue Ridge Mountain views. French Provençal dinners available. Well-behaved children 8 years old and older are welcome.

Resort Reservations; *(540) 456– 8300. Web address: www.rentalsatwinter green.com.* This company rents condo-miniums and homes at Wintergreen resort.

Royal Oaks Mountain Cabins, *Route 1, Love; (800) 410–0627. Web address: www.vacabins.com.* Royal Oaks rents one- and two-bedroom basic chalets that have kitchens and fire-places.

For More Information

Nelson County Tourist Information: *Visitors Center at 8519 Thomas Nelson Highway (Route 29), Lovingston, VA 22949; (434) 263–5239 or (800) 282–8223.*

Web address: www.nelsoncountyva.org or www.virginia.org. Visitors center open daily year-round.

Lynchburg

Sixty miles south from Charlottesville along U.S. Highway 29, Lynchburg nestles in the foothills of the Blue Ridge Mountains on the James River. The city, with a population of 67,000, is known as the City of Seven Hills and was a supply and communications base for the Confederate Army during the Civil War. Recognizing its importance, General Ulysses S. Grant issued orders to General Hunter to move on Lynchburg, leading to the Battle of Lynchburg, June 1864. Hunter's raid remained primarily on the outskirts of the city, and the Confederate forces prevailed, leaving the supply link to Lee's army intact. Two new attractions are now open for both older and younger generations: The National D-Day Memorial and Amazement Square and the Rightmire Children's Museum.

MONUMENT TERRACE (ages 9 and up)

In the center of downtown at Ninth and Church Streets.

This terraced monument honors soldiers from all of America's wars. If your family isn't up to climbing the 139 steps leading to the Old Court House and the memorial to Lynchburg's Confederate soldiers, take in the splendid view from the bottom of Court House Hill, at Church and Ninth Streets, where there is a statue honoring World War I doughboys.

POINT OF HONOR (ages 9 and up) (TT)

112 Cabell Street; (434) 847–1459. Web address: www.pointofhonor.org. Open to the public daily. Admission.

Once a 900-acre estate, the site was named for the duels fought on its lawns. Situated on Daniel's Hill, one of Lynchburg's seven original neighborhoods, the restored mansion overlooks the James River. Point of Honor was built by Dr. George Cabell, Sr., the personal physician of Patrick Henry. Christmas at Point of Honor, held the first Sunday in December, recreates a federal-style holiday with plantation party decorations (which remain throughout the month), as well as music and refreshments.

THOMAS JEFFERSON'S POPLAR FOREST (ages 9 and up) (TT)

West of Lynchburg 1 mile off U.S. Highway 221; (434) 525–1806. Web address: www.poplarforest.org. Open daily April through November, except Thanksgiving. Admission.

This home, designed by Thomas Jefferson and used as his personal retreat was where Jefferson found the "solitude of a hermit" away from the constant round of visitors at Monticello. In 1806, during his presidency, Jefferson actually helped the masons lay the foundation for this dwelling, which many consider one of his most original creations. A hands-on history tent, available Memorial Day through Labor Day weekends, offers kids a chance to experience activities from Jefferson's era, including brickmaking, building a bucket, and writing with a quill pen. Little ones play with puzzles and color at the toddler's corner. Check the schedule for special holiday events and celebrations on Jefferson's birthday (April 13). Near the museum shop, children can look through a viewing window at the Archaeology Lab to see work being done on discoveries from recent excavations. An annual Fourth of July celebration is held here.

AMAZEMENT SQUARE, THE RIGHTMIRE CHILDREN'S MUSEUM (all ages)

27 Ninth Street; (434) 845–1888. Open daily; reduced hours on Sunday and Monday. Admission.

With four floors of hands-on activities, plus an Amazement Tower with its tangle of pathways, tunnels, and stairs, kids keep busy at this inventive new children's museum. In Kaleidoscope, kids can paint a room from floor to ceiling, create and act out puppet shows, play musical instruments, and dance. In the Big Red Barn pre-schoolers can play in a hayloft, dress a scarecrow, and snuggle up with a book. Older children can explore electrical circuits, gravity, and velocity in the Science Gallery. In On The James! kids learn about the local area by creating rainstorms and flooding a mini-James River. Budding architects design and construct in Once Upon A Building while curious archeologists dig and listen to tales at Indian Island.

Check out Family Fun Night every fourth Wednesday of the month.

BLACKWATER CREEK NATURAL AREA (all ages)

Monticello Avenue, off Oakley Avenue; (434) 847–1640 (Parks and Recreation Division).

Take the kids for a stroll or bike ride through the 300 acres that make up the largest of the city's parks. There are 8 miles of trails, several picnic sites, and a number of scenic vistas. Near the center of the area is the Ruskin Freer Nature Preserve, a plant and animal sanctuary (434-847-1640).

LYNCHBURG'S HISTORIC DISTRICTS (ages 9 and up)

Brochures for self-guided tours are available from the Greater Lynchburg Historic Visitors Center.

If your kids won't be too bored, you might want to drive through these five historic districts to glimpse the elegant mansions built by tobacco tycoons.

COMMUNITY MARKET

Twelfth and Main; (434) 847–1499. Open Monday through Saturday.

The market, which has operated since 1783, is still selling fresh seasonal produce. It has, however, added ethnic foods and Virginia crafts and has special events, such as food festivals and music competitions, throughout the year.

THE OLD CITY CEMETERY

Fourth and Taylor Streets; (434) 847–1465. Open daily, dawn to dusk.

A registered historic landmark, this cemetery's oldest gravestone dates back to 1807. The Confederate Section contains over 2,000 graves of soldiers from fourteen states. The Pest House Medical Museum, the office of Dr. John Jay Terrell, contains items representative of the house's service as the quarantine hospital for Confederate soldiers during the war. Included here are an 1860s hypodermic needle, a chloroform mask (Dr. Terrell was the first in the area to use one), and a surgical amputation kit. On a more genteel note, the cemetery also has a garden of antique roses, a butterfly garden, and a lotus pond. Stop by the Cemetery Center (open daily) for copies of the brochures "A Kids Guide to the Old City Cemetery" and "A Quick Guide to Black History in the Old City Cemetery."

LEGACY MUSEUM OF AFRICAN AMERICAN HISTORY

403 Monroe Street; (434) 845–3455. Open Thursday through Sunday. Admission.

Situated in a one-hundred-year-old Victorian house, this museum has a fine collection of historical artifacts, documents, and memorabilia relating to Lynchburg's African-American community. Changing exhibiits deal with the lives of early town residents, professions and careers, and the churches.

Lynchburg Travel Tips
For additional information about African-American history in the Lynchburg area, ask at the visitors center for the free brochure "Explore Our Legacy: A Guide to African-American Heritage in Lynchburg and Central Virginia," which contains a brief history and more than twenty points of interest.

▤ APPOMATTOX COURT HOUSE NATIONAL HISTORIC SITE

Twenty miles east of Lynchburg and 2 miles northeast of Appomattox on State Highway 24; (434) 352–8987. Web address: www.nps.gov/apco. Visitor Center open year-round, with reduced hours in the winter. Closed on federal holidays, November through February. Admission.

This village has been restored to the way it looked on April 9, 1865, when General Robert E. Lee surrendered the Army of Northern Virginia to General Ulysses S. Grant, and the nation was officially reunited after a bitter civil war. Three days later the soldiers of the Army of Northern Virginia marched before the Union Army, stacked their weapons, laid down their flags, and headed home. The roads are closed to automobiles, so it's possible to stroll the quiet streets of the village memorialized forever in American history.

The reconstructed courthouse is the visitors center, where exhibits and slide shows can be viewed. Most of the twenty-seven structures on the site can be entered by the public. The parlor of the reconstructed McClean House is where the articles of surrender were signed. (Ironically, the McCleans had moved from their Masnassas, Virginia, home to get away from the war.) In the Plunket-Meeks store, visitors see the products a general store might sell during the Civil War.

Outside the village are several spots associated with the surrender, including the site of Lee's headquarters, which is northwest of the village and a five-minute walk from the parking lot on Highway 24. There's also a small cemetery just west of the village with the graves of one Northern and eighteen Southern soldiers killed on April 9. A hiking trail and highway connect the locations, and an official handbook for sale in the park describes the events and the village in detail. Park programs show how the war affected the village and the residents' day-to-day activities. Costumed interpreters answer questions in summer.

▤ THE NATIONAL D-DAY MEMORIAL

202 East Main Street, Bedford; (540) 586–DDAY or (800) 351–DDAY. Web address: www.dday.org. Open year-round, except Thanksgiving, Christmas, and New Year's Day. **Free**, *but parking fee.*

The Normandy Invasion of June 6, 1944 (also called D-Day) was the largest air, land, and sea landing ever undertaken, and included 5,333 ships, almost 11,000 airplanes, 50,000 military vehicles, and over 154,000 soldiers. Over 6,000 Americans died there. Bedford, Virginia, with a population of 3,200 in 1944, lost nineteen men in the first fifteen minutes of the invasion—the highest per capita loss of any single community in the U.S., which is why Bedford was chosen as the site of this memorial.

The memorial, dedicated on Memorial Day 2000, currently consists of a 44-foot-high granite arch opening onto Victory Plaza, with statuary and flags and a 16-foot story wall with a series of reflecting pools. Additional story walls and dioramas will be added eventually, and an education center, with hands-on, interactive activities, is scheduled to open in 2004.

Annual Events

JUNE

River of Time (Bateau) Festivals, *mid-June.* Replicas of the flat-bottomed merchant boats follow a 200-year-old trade route from the waterfront at Lynchburg, stopping at various communities along the way. Festivities include music, entertainment, and storytelling at several stops along the way, much of it about African-American, Native American, and Civil War history. (434) 528-3950.

OCTOBER

Railroad Festival, *mid-October. Appomattox Court House National Historic Site, 20 miles east of Lynchburg and 3 miles northeast of Appomattox on Highway 24; (434) 352–8987.* You'll be treated to a mix of history (Civil War memorabilia) and fun (miniature trains, carnival rides, and fireworks) at this annual festival.

Where to Eat

Bulls Steakhouse, *1887 Graves Mill Center in Forest;* (434) 385-7581. *Open Monday through Friday for lunch and dinner; Saturday for dinner only. Closed Sunday.* This restaurant features prime rib, steaks, and fajitas and also offers seafood, sandwiches, and soups. $-$$$

Shakers Good Food & Drink, *3401 Candlers Mountain Road (River Ridge Mall);* (434) 847–7425. *Lunch and dinner; closed Mondays.* Casual atmosphere with soups, sandwiches, prime rib, and fresh fish; children's menu. $-$$

China Royal Chinese Restaurant, *205 Gristmill Drive, Forest; (434) 385–0011. Open Sunday through Friday, lunch and dinner; Saturday, dinner only.* Restaurant has a sushi bar and a children's menu. $-$$

Piccadilly Cafeteria, *3405 Candlers Mountain Road in River Ridge Mall;* (434) 237-6549. *Open daily for lunch and dinner.* This restaurant offers simple country fare served in casual surroundings. $-$$

Where to Stay

Best Western of Lynchburg, *2815 Candlers Mountain Road; (434) 237–2986 or (877) 444–7088.* This hotel has a pool and includes continental breakfast in the room rate.

Comfort Inn, *U.S. Highway 29 at Odd Fellows Road; (434) 847–9041 or (800) 228–5150.* This lodging has an outdoor pool and includes continental breakfast, in-house exercise room, and popcorn in the lobby.

Hampton Inn, *5604 Seminole Avenue; (434) 237–2704.* A continental breakfast is included in the room rate of this moderately priced lodging. **ʄree** coffee and tea available all day long.

Once Upon A Time, *1102 Harrison Street; (434) 845–3561.* This B&B, located on historic Federal Hill, was built in 1874 and modeled after a French Second Empire mansion. Some rooms suggest fairy tales such as the *Frog Prince* or *Goldilocks and the Three Bears.* The friendly staff welcomes well-behaved children.

For More Information

Lynchburg Convention and Visitors Bureau, *Twelfth and Church Streets, Lynchburg, VA 24054; (434) 847–1811 or* *(800) 732–5821. Web address: www.lynchburgchamber.org. Open daily.*

Petersburg

At Petersburg, only 23 miles south of Richmond, the last decisive engagement of the Civil War occurred in 1864, when an important railway link fell to Union forces. Suffering from hunger and bombardments from cannons, the town was under siege for ten months before the campaign ended. Approximately 28,000 Confederate and 42,000 Union soldiers were killed, wounded, or captured during the Petersburg campaign.

PETERSBURG NATIONAL BATTLEFIELD VISITORS CENTER (ages 8 and up) (TT)

Visitor Center off State Highway 36; (804) 732–3531. Web address: www.nps. gov/pete. Open daily, except Thanksgiving, Christmas, and New Year's Day. Admission.

The Visitor Center offers an audiovisual presentation, maps, models, and artifacts from the long siege of Petersburg. It is also the starting point for the fifteen-stop, 26-mile-long self-guided driving tour of the 2,460-acre battlefield (a section of the road is reserved for hikers and cyclists). Walks lead to significant battle sites from four points on the road and there are audiovisual aids and wayside exhibits.

Probably the most fascinating—and sobering—site is the Crater, a deep depression caused by the explosion that occurred after Union volunteers dug a 500-foot-long mine shaft that ended under a Confederate fort and replaced the soil with black powder that they then ignited, killing 278 Confederate soldiers. At Grant's Headquarters at City Point (804-458-9504), a plantation house has rooms with period furnishings, an introductory video, a diorama, and a bookshop. During the summer, special tours give kids and adults a feel for the battle. At the one-day camp "Earthworks," held in July and August, kids dress in uniform, perform marching drills, and create a Civil War camp before turning scientist and performing water tests in a stream and taking part in a geographic scavenger hunt.

PAMPLIN HISTORICAL PARK AND THE NATIONAL MUSEUM OF THE CIVIL WAR SOLDIER (ages 8 and up)

6125 Boydton Plank Road; (804) 861–2408 or (877) PAMPLIN. Web address: www.pamplinpark.org. Open daily year round. Admission.

This $24 million, 363-acre historical campus just 30 miles south of downtown Richmond memorializes an important spot in Petersburg's history: where Union troops commanded by General Ulysses S. Grant broke through the defenses of General Robert E. Lee. The battle that took place on April 2, 1865, led to the evacuation of Petersburg and Richmond, and greatly contributed to Lee's surrender at Appomattox Court House one week later, ending the Civil War.

The story of Pamplin Historical Park is an interesting one of strife and Southern redemption. After the war the land passed out of the Boisseau family and was divided into small farms. Robert Pamplin, a Boisseau descendant, was eventually able to buy the land, restore Tudor Hall, and preserve it as a battlefield park.

The interpretive center has a video, battle map, and interactive computer exhibits that explain the battle and its significance. The 1.1-mile-long interpretive trail winds past well-preserved earthworks (the Fortifications Exhibit), some reaching 8 feet high, and picket posts. Tudor Hall, the Boisseau family plantation, small by manor house standards, has been restored to its mid-nineteenth-century use as a home and military headquarters for South Carolina General Samuel

McGowan. A new exhibit at the Tudor Hall complex: "The Field Quarter," a depiction of nineteenth-century slave life, includes two cabins and a collection of outbuildings such as a chicken coop, corn crib, and well house, plus plots where cotton, tobacco, corn, and wheat are grown. One cabin is outfitted as a typical spartan quarters of a field slave; in the other, a video featuring six characters from the late 1850s sharing their opinions on slavery is shown. Included is a planter-class slaveowning woman, a slave, a free Black man, a poor Southern farmer who doesn't own slaves, a Connecticut abolitionist, and a Midwestern farmer. This is a very powerful video (the "n" word is used, which may be offensive to some), and provides an excellent opportunity for families to discuss the issue of slavery and its ramifications in our modern society.

The focal point of the park is the National Museum of the Civil War Soldier. Three additions, including an outdoor pavilion and an indoor theater, are scheduled to open over the course of the next twelve years, with completion of the entire compound scheduled for 2011, coinciding with the 150th anniversary of the firing on Fort Sumter.

The museum has been designed to immerse the visitor in the life of an everyday soldier fighting in the Civil War. At the entrance each visitor is given a Soldier Comrade, whose experiences are intertwined with the exhibits. A child's Soldier Comrade is a 13-year-old drummer boy. Both children and adults are given a compact disc player with headphones to hear an audio tour of the seven galleries. (Audio tours geared to children ages 7 to 12 are part of the "Discovery Trail," an activities booklet that engages children in the whole park experience. The booklet can be purchased at the gift shop for less than a dollar.)

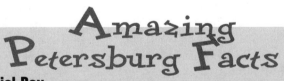

Amazing Petersburg Facts

Memorial Day Local lore credits Petersburg as being the place where Memorial Day got its start. Soon after the Civil War ended, a commander's wife observed schoolgirls placing flowers on graves of defenders of Petersburg at the Old Blanford Church. When she saw them repeat the procedure the following year, she told her husband, and he took measures that subsequently led to Decoration Day, later known as Memorial Day, being observed as a national holiday.

Special programs are available for children throughout the historical campus, both in the museum and at Tudor Hall. These include impromptu interplay with costumed interpreters, such as the soldiers in the encampment or doctors who practiced Civil War–era medicine (such as it was). There are also supervised day camps throughout the summer. (Call 877-PAMPLIN or 804-861-2408 for more information.)

OLD BLANFORD CHURCH AND RECEPTION CENTER (ages 7 and up)

319 South Crater Road; (804) 733–2396 or (800) 368–3595. Web address: www.rootsweb.com/~vacpeter/cemetery/blandfd1.htm. Open daily year-round. Admission.

An abandoned church (c. 1735) used as a hospital during the Civil War, its grounds contain the graves of 30,000 Confederate soldiers. The reception center has exhibits that include Civil War artifacts. The church's Tiffany windows, one of the largest collections in the world, were designed as a memorial to the Confederate dead. Louis Comfort Tiffany's stunning Cross of the Jewels, which he donated to the church (the other fourteen windows were sponsored by the former Confederate states and the local Ladies Memorial Association), is even more awesome when it's illuminated by the setting sun.

SIEGE MUSEUM (ages 5 and up)

15 West Bank Street; (804) 733–2400. Open daily year-round. Admission.

It's certainly worth a visit to see the exhibits and a twenty-minute film of how the citizens of Petersburg lived before and during the ten months they were under siege (the longest any city was under attack in the Civil War). This human side of the war is something that children can particularly understand. (Ask for the printed scavenger hunt for children.) Exhibits show how women hid food, ammunition, and supplies in their hoop skirts. You can also see one of only two revolving cannons ever built.

UNITED STATES SLOW–PITCH SOFTBALL ASSOCIATION HALL OF FAME (ages 5 and up)

3935 South Crater Road; (804) 732–4099. Web address: www.usssa.com. Open Monday through Friday year-round.

If there's a softball fan in the family, check out this place where you can watch a video presentation about the game and view related memorabilia, including information about the sixty-three inductees to the Hall of Fame.

Where to Eat

Alexander's, *101 West Bank Street; (804) 733–7134. Open for breakfast, lunch, and dinner.* Good Italian food. $–$$

Home Place Restaurant, *U.S. Highway Route 1 South in Dinwiddie; (804) 469–9596. Open 7:00 A.M. to 9:00 P.M.* Southern specialties—chicken, ham, pork—are served for dinner in this casual restaurant. Typical breakfast and lunch sandwiches, too. Children's menu available. $–$$

King's Barbeque, *3321 West Washington Street, U.S. Highway 1; (804) 732–5861 and 2910 South Crater Road; (804) 732–0975. Open 7:00 A.M. to 9:00 P.M. Closed Monday.* King's has been in business since 1949 offering Southern-style cooking. Locals swear by the barbecue and the fried chicken. $–$$

Leonardo's Deli and Cafe, *7 Bollingbrook Street; (804) 863–4830. Open for lunch and dinner.* $$–$$$

Pumpkins Family Restaurant & Gift Shop, *12204 South Crater Road; (804) 732–4444. Web address: www. pumpkinsrestaurant.com. Open daily for breakfast, lunch, and dinner.* Traditional American fare of burgers, chicken, steak, and pasta is served at this casual restaurant. Carry-out food is available, too. Children's menu offered. $–$$

Steven Kent Family Restaurant, *12205 South Crater Road (in the Quality Inn); (804) 733–0500. Open daily for lunch and dinner.* This casual restaurant serves traditional American fare of burgers, chicken, steak, and pasta. Carry-out food is available, too. Children's menu available. $–$$

Where to Stay

Best Inns & Suites, *405 East Washington Street and Interstate 95; (804) 733–1776 or (800) 796–8327.*

Econo Lodge, *25 South Crater Road; (804) 861–4680 or (800) 446–6900.*

Petersburg Radison, *East Washington Street and Interstate 95; (804) 733–0000.* A 192-room motel with all the amenities.

Picture Lake Campground, *7818 Boydton Plank Road in Dinwiddie; (804) 861–0174.* The campground features a thirty-five-acre lake and 200 campsites, half of which have full hookups.

Ramada, *501 East Washington Street; (804) 733–0730 or (800) 272–6232.* Refrigerators and microwaves in some of the rooms.

For More Information

Petersburg Visitors Center, *425 Cockade Alley, Petersburg, VA 23803; (804) 733–2400 or (800) 368–3595; TDD (804) 733–8003. Web address:* *www.petersburg-va.org. Open daily.* There is also a visitors center at the Carson Rest Area on I-95, open daily. (804) 246–2145.

Richmond

Did you know that George Washington posed for only one statue? You'll find it in Richmond, along with scores of other statues and monuments; The city is, after all, known as the City of Monuments. Once a victim of urban decline, the former Confederate capital, which has been the state capital since 1780, is now restored to its glory days and offers families a wide variety of entertaining and educational possibilities.

Richmond City Pass . . . gives you a 40 percent discount on five local attractions. Choose five attractions from among nineteen offered and pay $15 for a pass that will admit one person to all five and provide discounts at additional attractions. Contact the visitors center at (804) 358–5511.

COURT END (all ages)

Located between Leigh Street or State Highway 33 to the north, and Franklin Street to the south.

This is a sightseeing "must." Here you'll find seven national historic landmarks, three museums, and eleven state historic landmarks within an 8-block radius. Obviously, your family may not have the inclination or desire to "see it all." As is always important when traveling with kids, be selective, and allow plenty of time for dallying or unexpected adventures.

VIRGINIA STATE CAPITOL (ages 9 and up)

Ninth and Grace Streets, in the heart of the city of Richmond; (804) 698–1788. Open daily year-round.

The majestic Virginia State Capitol building was designed by Thomas Jefferson in 1785, and there's lots of history inside its halls. Jefferson was minister to France at the time, and the Capitol is patterned after an ancient Roman temple in Nimes that he admired. This is still the meeting place of the oldest law-making body in North America and the first in the world to function under a written constitution of a free and independent people. Jefferson was first to occupy the governor's office here, in 1788.

In the rotunda you'll find the famous life-size statue of Washington by Houdon, which was said to be a perfect likeness. There are also busts of seven other Virginia-born Presidents in the rotunda; strolling about and identifying them is a good activity for school-age kids. (The presidents are Jefferson, James Madison, James Monroe, William Henry Harrison, John Tyler, Zachary Taylor, and Woodrow Wilson.)

Ask at the legislative information desk on the first floor for a special packet of information for children.

GOVERNOR'S MANSION (ages 10 and up)
Capitol Square; (804) 371–2642.

After the Capitol, take a stroll of the capitol grounds. On the east, you'll see the oldest continuously occupied governor's mansion in the United States.

THE MUSEUM AND WHITE HOUSE OF THE CONFEDERACY (ages 7 and up) (TT)

1201 East Clay Street; (804) 649–1861. Web address: www.moc.org. Open daily, except Thanksgiving, Christmas, and New Year's Day. **Free** *visitor parking. Admission.*

This museum is great place for school-age kids who are sure to find something of interest. The complex includes a restored Confederate executive mansion and the adjacent modern museum, housing what is said to be the largest collection of Confederate artifacts in the world, including the sword Robert E. Lee wore when he surrendered at Appomattox and an assortment of Confederate flags.

A Walk Along Monument Avenue . . . is a walk into
Richmond past, with statues of Robert E. Lee (at Allen Avenue), J.E.B. Stuart (at Lombardy Street), and Jefferson Davis (at Davis Avenue). What began as an homage to the Confederacy was changed forever in 1995 with the addition of a statue honoring Richmond native Arthur Ashe (at Roseneath Street).

The adjacent White House of the Confederacy (though it's actually always been painted gray) was home to President Jefferson Davis and his family during the Civil War. After the war all the furnishings were removed and the house was saved from demolition in 1890 by the Confederate Memorial Library Society. Many of the original furnishings have been returned; the restored mansion is a wonderful example of Victorian style, and not just in decor. It's interesting to note just how close Davis's formal office was to the family's living quarters and how intertwined their political and personal lives were.

THE VALENTINE MUSEUM (ages 7 and up)

1015 East Clay Street; (804) 649–0711. Web address: www.valentinemuseum. com.Open Tuesday through Sunday year-round. Admission.

The Valentine Museum focuses on the life and history of Richmond from the nineteenth century to the present. It has exhibits on public events such as the 1824 U.S. tour of James Monroe, and the tobacco festival. It also has an exhibit on how history is created and how all of us influence community events. Changing exhibits at the History Center focus on American urban history, using collections of costumes and textiles, prints, and photographs.

VIRGINIA MUSEUM OF FINE ARTS (ages 7 and up)

2800 Grove Avenue; (804) 340–1401. Web address: www.vmfa.state.va.us. Open Tuesday through Sunday year-round. Closed New Year's Day, Fourth of July, Thanksgiving, and Christmas. Donations encouraged.

The largest art museum in the southeast, the Virginia Museum of Fine Art offers something that should pique the interest of even the fussiest museum-goer. All ages will be particularly entranced by the jewel-encrusted Fabergé eggs, which were created at the turn of the century for Russian tsars Alexander III and Nicholas II. Along with Egyptian statues and artifacts and a charming sculpture garden, there's a wide range of art, including colorful contemporary paintings that usually appeal to young children. The museum also has one of the country's best collections of art from India, Nepal, and Tibet, plus special programs for children on certain Saturdays.

SCIENCE MUSEUM OF VIRGINIA (ages 5 and up) (TT)

2500 West Broad Street; (804) 864–1400 or (800) 659–1727. Web address: www.smv.org. Open Tuesday through Sunday. Admission.

This is a must for kids. Children are intrigued by the hundreds of permanent and loaned interactive exhibits. A Foucault pendulum, demonstrating the earth's rotation, is located in the redesigned grand rotunda. More than 250 exhibits enable kids to practice take-offs and landings through computerized flight simulators, play laser pool, or challenge their sense of perception and reality in Alice's Parlor. In the Zoom Zone, kids solve problems with numbers and learn about sound, light, and motion. Throughout the year special events such as the Model Railroad Show take place here.

The Science Museum also houses the **Ethyl Universe Planetarium and Space Theater**. IMAX films and multimedia planetarium shows are presented in the five-story theater with a tilted-dome screen. The museum's web site has a terrific section just for kids.

CHILDREN'S MUSEUM OF RICHMOND (ages 12 and under)

2626 West Broad Street; (804) 474–CMoR or (877) 295–CMoR. Web address: www.c-mor.org. Open daily year-round. Admission.

Here kids can crawl under a turtle tank, sit in an eagle's nest, wiggle through the human digestive tract, build a dam, turn the gears of a clock tower, tinker in the inventor's lab, experiment with kitchen chemistry, and create a work of art. Focusing on children 2 months to 12 years old, this museum gives families a chance to experience things together. During July and August, try Saturday mornings' Musical Family Fun and Thursday nights' **Free** concerts on the Front Plaza. From July to September Little Wonders offers special activities for younger children on Friday mornings. During the first Mondays of each summer month, kids can try What's Cooking Kitchen, and Labor Day weekend has special family celebrations. Future plans include further development of the outdoor Learning Garden.

VIRGINIA AVIATION MUSEUM (ages 7 and up) (TT)

5701 Huntsman Road in Sandston (exit 47A off Interstate 64), at the Richmond International Airport; (804) 236–3622. Web address: www.smv.org/wvamhome. html. Open daily Tuesday through Sunday. Closed Thanksgiving and Christmas. Admission.

In 1990 the Science Museum of Virginia received this facility as a gift from the Virginia Aeronautical Historical Society. The museum houses vintage aircraft, dioramas on World War II, a special exhibit on Richard E. Byrd, early flight memorabilia, and the Virginia Aviation Hall of

Fame. The newest acquisition is an SR-71 Blackbird. Special events are held here, including Flight Day in June and a December celebration of the Wright Brothers' first flight.

EDGAR ALLAN POE MUSEUM (ages 9 and up) (TT)

1914 East Main Street; (804) 648–5523 or (888) 21E–APOE. Web address: www.poemuseum.org. Open daily Tuesday through Sunday. Admission.

Older school-age kids familiar with Edgar Allan Poe might enjoy a visit to this museum. Poe, a local boy orphaned at age 2, grew up in Richmond in the home of the Allans. Though he never lived in this 1737 Old Stone House, it is the oldest home in the city, and Poe was surely aware of its existence. The house has a shop and offers a short slide show on Poe's life; three buildings hold Poe's manuscripts and memorabilia, the largest such collection in the world. The Raven Room features illustrations by James Carling that were inspired by Poe's famous poem.

RICHMOND NATIONAL BATTLEFIELD PARK (ages 7 and up)

3215 East Broad Street; (804) 226–1981. Web address: www.nps.gov/rich. Open daily dawn to dusk year-round. Chimborazo Visitor Center, battlefield entrance on East Broad Street; (804) 226–1981. Visitor Center at Tredegar Iron Works, 470 Tredegar Street; (840) 771–2808. Admission.

This battlefield park commemorates the four-year struggle for the Confederate capital, the target of seven federal attacks during the Civil War. Richmond's position as a political, medical, and manufacturing hub made it ripe for military takeover; the war that raged here was devastating.

The visitor center rents three-hour-long auto tape tours with cassette players that detail the Seven Days Campaign of 1862. The tour covers all 80 miles of the battlefield. Don't, however, do all of this; a little bit goes a long way. Start at the Richmond Civil War Visitor Center at Tredegar Iron Works, which offers exhibits, audio visual programs, special walking tours, living history encampments, and other programs throughout the year. Smaller visitor centers are open at Chimborazo, where you see how the wounded and sick were cared for on and off the battlefield—at Cold Harbor, where 7,000 of Grant's men were killed or wounded in just thirty minutes, Fort Harrison, and the Glendale Cemetery Lodge. Chickahominy Bluff, Malvern Hill, Fort Harrison, and Drewry's Bluff have interpretive signs and audio stations.

MAYMONT HOUSE AND PARK (all ages)

*2201 Shields Lake Drive (in Byrd Park); (804) 358–7166. Web address: www.
maymont.org. House, Nature Center, Children's Farm Barn, Shop, and Cafe open
Tuesday through Sunday. Suggested donation. Grounds, gardens, and visitors center open daily. Tram rides, carriage rides, and hay rides through the park are
available.*

Although some historic houses leave most kids cold, this will be sure
to please because it comes with one hundred acres of grounds dotted
with gazebos and planted with a variety of gardens (especially nice are
the Japanese and Italian gardens), plus more than 300 animals. At the
Nature Center visitors see a 20-foot waterfall, an otter exhibit, and 125
feet of linked aquariums. The visitors center has an indoor cafe, an
expanded gift shop, and two Discovery Rooms with computers, microscopes, and wet lab habitats.

Maymont also has a Children's Farm Barn where kids can see (and
sometimes feed) piglets, chickens, sheep, donkeys, llamas, bison, and
black bears; and a Carriage House with displays of turn-of-the-century
horse-drawn vehicles.

This sprawling Victorian estate was purchased by Major James Henry
Dooley, a young, self-made millionaire, who built a mansion on the property. An ivory, art nouveau, swan-shaped bed and matching rocker, a
grand staircase, and stunning stained-glass windows are just a sampling
of the architectural and decorative surprises inside this opulent dwelling.

MEADOW FARM AND CRUMP PARK (all ages)

*At Mountain and Courtney Roads in Glen Allen, 12 miles north of downtown Rich-
mond; (804) 501–5520. Open Tuesday through Sunday.*

This 150-acre property, a great place to take a break from Civil War
history, was donated to the county as a public museum and park in
1975 by the family of the country doctor who practiced and lived here
after he inherited the farmhouse and grounds in 1840. Costumed interpreters answer questions, do chores, and cook on open hearths. The
house can be toured, too. Don't miss the "floating" balcony attached to
a wall on one side only; it's best viewed from the bottom of the stairs.
The grounds also include a smokehouse, farrier's shop, barn where
tobacco is dried, bird sanctuary, and goose pond.

POCAHONTAS STATE PARK (all ages)

Exit 61 off Interstate 95, then go west on State Highway 10 to Route 655, Beach Road; (804) 796–4255. Open daily.

This 7,604-acre park is only 20 miles south of Richmond, but it offers the serenity of Swift Creek and Beaver Lakes and their surrounding forests. Come here to stroll, fish, swim, or hike. The park also offers camping and cabins, along with interpretive programs in the summer, such as guided nature hikes, campfire programs, and children's activities.

RICHMOND RAFTING COMPANY (ages 7 and up)

4400 East Main Street; (804) 222–RAFT or (800) 540–7238. Web address: www.richmondraft.com. Generally offers trips from March to late fall November.

Richmond is Virginia's only major metropolitan area where there is white-water rafting right in the heart of town. A variety of trips are offered, (for those weighing at least fifty pounds), plus kayaking, snowskiing, and rivertubing.

ANNABEL LEE (ages 5 and up)

Cruises leave from 4400 East Main Street; (804) 377–2020 or (800) 752–7093. Web address: www.annabellee.com. Cruises run year-round. Reservations are required.

A pleasant way to spend a few hours is to take a two-hour-long lunch cruise up the James River aboard this reproduction of an 1850s riverboat. Lunch is served by costumed waiters and waitresses, who double as after-lunch entertainment, when they sing and dance accompanied by a three-piece band. There is also James River Plantation lunch, dinner, and Halloween Haunted cruises as well as Summer Kids' Cruises and Cruisin' with Santa.

RICHMOND BRAVES (ages 5 and up)

3001 North Boulevard; (804) 359–4444. Web address: www.rbraves.com. The baseball season runs from April to mid-September.

Sports fans can also find something to root for in Richmond. This Triple-A farm team for Atlanta plays at Diamond Stadium. The Richmond Braves have been the top minor-league club in the Atlanta Braves' organization since 1966. Call for schedule and ticket information.

WHERE TO SHOP

SHOPS AT CARYTOWN

A 9-block area along West Cary Street from Thompson Street to the Boulevard with over 200 restaurants, clothing boutiques, bakeries, antique dealers, bookstores, gift shop, and the historic Byrd Theater that still shows movies at nostalgic discount prices. Restaurants range from French-Vietnamese to New York deli, and there's an annual Watermelon Festival in mid-August.

SHOCKOE SLIP

East Carey Street from Twelfth to Fourteenth Streets.

Kids, especially teens, and adults like walking around the cobblestone streets of this trendy area. Former warehouses now house restaurants, boutiques, and clubs.

THEME PARK

KINGS DOMINION

Twenty minutes north of Richmond in Doswell (the Doswell/State Highway 30 exit from Interstate 95); (804) 876–5000. Web address: www.kingsdominion.com. Open from late March through early October.

For pure escapist pleasure, head to movie-themed fun at Paramount's Kings Dominion. Older kids get their kicks on one of eleven roller coasters. The newest coaster is the HyperSonic SLC, the world's first air-launched coaster, which goes 165 feet straight up—and straight down. For more thrills, there's Volcano: The Blast Coaster, reputedly the world's first linear induction suspended roller coaster. In other words, it blasts you out on your up-and-down journey with electromagnetic energy, propelling you at speeds of up to 70 m.p.h.

Younger tots have KidZville, where some of their favorite Hanna–Barbera characters such as Yogi Bear, Fred Flintstone, and Scooby-Doo can be found along with scaled-down rides perfect for the younger set. Pre-teens and teens like Wayne's World, complete with the Hurler giant wooden roller coaster, Wayne's basement, and some of Wayne and Garth's favorite hangouts.

Don't miss the Nickelodeon-theme area, Splat City. Get ready to be "GAKed" (playfully splattered with Nick's signature green slime) at the audience participation game show "Mega Mess-a-Mania" and sprayed by the erupting Slime Derrick. Kids will love climbing through a maze of the messy stuff at the Crystal Slime Aerobic Mining Maze, cooking up gooey creations at the GAK Kitchen, and getting shot (photographically, of course) awash in the gook at the Slime Shower. An ice show, stage entertainment, and summer fireworks round out the fun. A 332-foot replica of the Eiffel Tower provides a panorama of the piedmont.

In the warm weather months, enjoy Hurricane Reef Water Park, and its fifteen water slides, a kids' area, and the Lazy River, plus Water-Works, with its Big Wave Cay, a 650,000-gallon wave pool, and Surf City Splash House, a water-powered fun house.

NIGHTLIFE

DOGWOOD DELL (all ages)

Byrd Park, Boulevard and Idlewild Avenues (804) 358–5511.

In summer Richmond hosts its **Free** festival of concerts and plays here. Call Richmond's Visitors Center for performance information.

THEATRE IV (ages 3 and up)

114 West Broad Street; (804) 344–8040. Performances run from October through May. Reservations recommended.

Check out the Broadway and off-Broadway plays and musicals at the Empire Theatre, reputedly the second-largest children's theater in the nation.

THEATRE VIRGINIA (ages 9 and up)

2800 Grove Avenue in the Virginia Museum of Fine Arts; (804) 353–6161. Productions from October through June.

Broadway-style (and sometimes Shakespearean) productions are performed at this 500-seat theater. Call for performance schedule and ticket information.

Annual Events

APRIL

Annual Chesterfield Celtic Heritage Festival features bagpipes, living history displays, food, and crafts; (804) 748-1623.

JUNE

Scooper Bowl X celebrates the beginning of summer with music, food, children's activities, and entertainment—plus all the ice cream you can eat—at the Science Museum of Virginia; (804) 864-1400.

AUGUST

Riverfront Outdoor Movies, grab a blanket and relax every Thursday on Brown's Island; (804) 643-2826.

SEPTEMBER

Annual African-American History Festival at Pocahontas State Park; (804) 748-1623.

Annual Rainbow of Arts, arts and crafts, an Imagination Station for kids, Rockwood Park; (804) 748-1623.

Annual Hispanic Culture Day at Pocahontas State Park; (804) 748-1623.

Where to Eat

Joe's Inn, *205 North Shield Drive; (804) 355–2282. Open daily for breakfast, lunch, and dinner.* This casual place, in the Fan District, is known for its spaghetti (including a Greek variety, complete with feta cheese) and hearty soups and sandwiches. $

Peking Pavilion, *302 East Cary Street; (804) 649–8888. Lunch and dinner daily.* Try the Hunan chicken, Peking shrimp with scallops, beef and broccoli, sweet and sour chicken, fried rice, or other traditional dishes. $-$$

Strawberry Street Cafe, *421 North Strawberry Street, between Park and Stuart; (804) 353–6860. Open for lunch and dinner Monday through Saturday, brunch and dinner on Sunday.* The Victorian decor makes for a cheerful casual surrounding. Burgers, pasta, crab cakes, and quiche are served. It's tasty food at inexpensive prices. $-$$

Where to Stay

Bensonhouse of Richmond, *2036 Monument Avenue; (804) 353–6900 or (804) 355–4885. Web address: www. bensonhouse.com.* This bed-and-break-fast registry has listings for three inns, including administrator Lyn Benson's own B&B.

Crowne Plaza Hotel, *555 East Canal Street; (804) 788–0900.* A modern hotel overlooking the James River with an indoor pool.

Holiday Inn Koger Center South, *1021 Koger Center Boulevard; (804) 379–3800 or 800–HOLIDAY.* This property has comfortable rooms and an outdoor pool. It is located next to Huguenot Park's playground, jogging trails, and tennis courts.

Omni Richmond Hotel, *100 South Twelfth Street; (804) 344–7000 or (800) THE–OMNI.* The Omni is convenient to the Shockloe Slip attractions. Some rooms have great river views and there is an indoor-outdoor pool.

For lodging reservations through the area, call (888) RICHMOND.

For More Information

You can pick up helpful literature at one of Richmond's two visitor centers:

Greater Richmond Visitors Center, *405 North Third Street, Richmond, VA 23219; (804) 358–5511. Web address: richmondva.org. Open daily year-round.*

Richmond International Airport Visitors Center, *(804) 226–3000. Open daily.*

Southwest Blue Ridge Highlands

The southwest region of Virginia, from the southwestern tip of the state, stretches in a triangle-like formation from the Cumberland Gap National Historical Park through the George Washington and Jefferson National Forests to Blacksburg and then south to the Virginia–North Carolina border near Galax. This region encompasses some of the prettiest and least-spoiled territory in the state. Although the small towns feature some historical sites and small museums, the outdoors is the big draw for families. Plan to spend most of your time exploring the woods, trails, lakes, and paths of the state parks as well as the George Washington and Jefferson National Forests.

When Daniel Boone arrived here at the end of the eighteenth century to mark out the Wilderness Road westward to the Appalachian Mountains, the southwest Blue Ridge Highlands was the only frontier known to Americans. Today the Blue Ridge, Allegheny, and Cumberland Mountains still dominate this region. Along with the greenery and spectacular views, you and your family will find the mountain culture alive and well in crafts,

Candyce's Top Picks
for Fun in the Southwest Blue Ridge Highlands

1. Claytor Lake State Park
2. George Washington and Jefferson National Forests
3. Old Fiddler's Convention, Galax
4. Hungry Mother State Park
5. Cumberland Gap National Historical Park

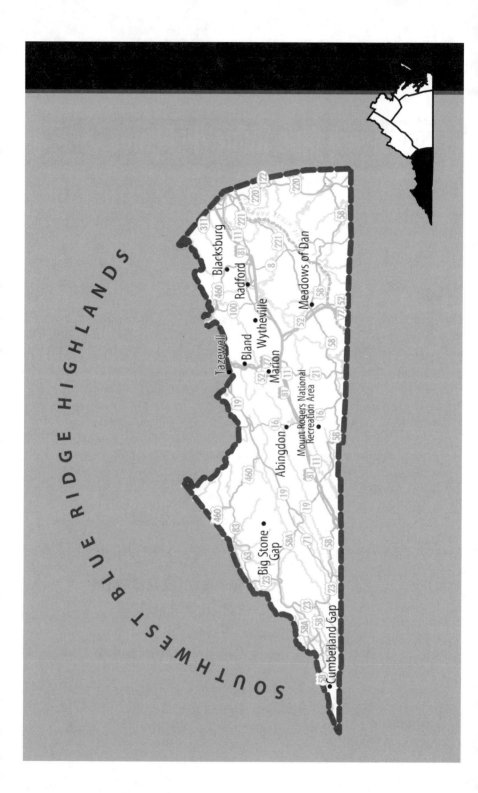

SOUTHWEST BLUE RIDGE HIGHLANDS

Blacksburg
Radford
Bland
Tazewell
Wytheville
Marion
Meadows of Dan
Abingdon
Mount Rogers National
Recreation Area
Big Stone Gap
Cumberland Gap

country songs, old-time fiddle music, and clog dancing. Summer's interesting festivals, such as the Old Fiddlers' Convention (276–236–5196 or 540–238–0376; www.bluegrassingalax.com) held in Galax and the Virginia Highlands Festival (800–435–3440; www.vahighlandsfestival.org) held each summer in Abingdon, provide a format for the culture.

If you're heading southwest or northeast in this region, Interstate 81 provides the shortest route; it's also possible to take the scenic Blue Ridge Parkway south or north to Interstate 77 and proceed until you reach its junction with Interstate 81. The route followed in this chapter is loosely circular, starting at Blacksburg and heading south near Galax and west to Cumberland Gap, then northeast to Breaks and then to Wytheville.

If you're heading south from the Charlottesville area along Interstate 81, you will come to the New River Valley between the towns of Blacksburg and Radford. Although the towns have some historic houses and museums, the real sites are just outside the towns in the scenic countryside. The abundance of state parks and vast expanse of the George Washington and Jefferson National Forests provide great recreational opportunities.

Sequoia and Browser The Blue Ridge Highlands Regional Information and Visitors Center distributes the *Sequoia and Browser,* a comic book which has maps of parks and trails as well as information about swimming pools, fishing spots, trout farms, and other places to have fun. Call (800) 446–9670 to request a copy before your trip.

Blacksburg

Located 9 miles off Interstate 81, Blacksburg is a city of 39,000.

VIRGINIA TECH MUSEUM OF NATURAL HISTORY (ages 7 and up) (TT)

428 North Main Street; (540) 231–3001. Open Wednesday through Friday 11:00 A.M. to 5:00 P.M., Saturday 11:00 A.M. to 3:00 P.M. during spring and fall semesters. **Free.**

The museum is near the campus of **Virginia Polytechnic Institute and State University,** the largest land-grant university in the state, with about 25,000 students and ninety buildings. Kids into creepy critters and woodland creatures enjoy the permanent research collections of insects, birds, and North American mammals. The Discovery Center has a dissection microscope for examining natural objects, from snake skins to feathers. Once a month on Science Saturday there are programs for families with pre-teens.

VIRGINIA TECH MUSEUM OF GEOLOGICAL SCIENCES (ages 7 and up) (TT)

2062 Derring Hall, Virginia Tech Campus; (540) 231–3001. Open Wednesday through Saturday 11:00 A.M. to 5:00 P.M. **Free.**

If your kids love looking at minerals, gemstones, or fossils, this museum will entertain them. A working seismograph measures earthquakes, and a life size skeleton of an Allosaur dinosaur towers over the paleontology section.

SMITHFIELD PLANTATION HOUSE (ages 7 and up) (TT)

Adjacent to the Virginia Polytechnic Institute, 1000 Smithfield Plantation Road; (540) 231–3947. Open Thursday through Sunday 1:00 to 5:00 P.M. from April 1 to December 1. Guided tours available. Admission.

This house built in 1773 by Colonel William Preston has a stockade. He named the estate for his wife, Susannah Smith. Three governors lived here in what was once one of the largest estates west of the Blue Ridge Mountains. The property also has pioneer artifacts in the Museum of Westward Expansion.

MUNICIPAL PARK (ages 2 to 10)

Located off Patrick Henry Drive; (540) 961–1135.

Highlights here are the Hand in Hand Playground, the Skate Board Park, the Aquatic Center, and an indoor pool.

Where to Eat

Bogen's, *622 North Main Street; (540) 953–2233.* A typical college town eatery, the cheap eats include salads, burgers, and roast beef sandwiches. Children's menu available. $

El Guadalupe's, *1410 South Main Street; (540) 953–0706. Open daily for lunch and dinner.* The moderately priced Mexican fare here is a favorite with local college students. Kids also like the tacos, enchiladas, burritos, quesadillas, and fajitas. Children's menu offered. $–$$

Sub Shack & Pizza, *2767 Market Street, Christiansburg; (540) 382–2082.* Good subs and pizza. $

Zeppoli's Inc., *810 University City Boulevard; (540) 953–2000.* Italian food. $–$$

Where to Stay

Amerisuites Blacksburg, *1007 Plantation Road; (540–552–5636).* All the accommodations are suites with a refrigerator, microwave, and coffeemaker. The property has an indoor pool and serves a complimentary continental breakfast.

Best Western Red Lion Inn, *900 Plantation Road, (540) 552–7770 or (800) 528–1234.* This property has 102 rooms, an outdoor pool, a tennis court, and a restaurant.

Comfort Inn, *3705 South Main Street; (540) 951–1500.* This motel offers moderately priced accommodations.

Mountain Lake Hotel, *Route 700 near Pembroke, off U.S. Highway 460 between Blacksburg and Pembroke; (800) 828–0490 or (540) 626–7121. Web address: www.mountainlakehotel.com. Open May through October and weekends in November.* Over the years we've brought children and dogs (check the current pet policy) and lots of novels to read while sitting in front-porch rockers. When my son was 8, he learned to fish from the resort's dock. This old-fashioned resort sits on 2,600 mountaintop acres (elevation 4,000 feet) near the Jefferson National Forest. The Mountain Lake Hotel has gained famed as the site where Patrick Swayze's movie *Dirty Dancing* was filmed. The 1936 stone lodge houses the main dining room and a row of rocking chairs. Activities center either on the 250-acre lake (swimming, fishing) and the woods (hiking and horseback riding). Guests also enjoy tennis and golf in summer and cross-country skiing in winter. Guests stay in hotel or lodge rooms, some spiffy and some a bit funky. Rooms in the lodge have Jacuzzis. Supervised children's activities are offered during summer and on some holidays. Rates include breakfast and dinner.

FOR MORE LODGING INFORMATION

B&B Reservation Service; *(800) 934–9184.* This ℱ𝓇𝓮𝓮 service can help you find a bed-and-breakfast inn that welcomes families.

For More Information

Blacksburg Regional Chamber of Commerce and Visitors Center, *1995 South Main Street, Suite 901, Blacksburg, VA 24060; (540) 552–4503. Web address: www.blacksburg-chamber.com.*

George Washington and Jefferson National Forests

The George Washington and Jefferson National Forests stretch across more than 1.8 million acres from Winchester to Abingdon and also from Breaks Interstate Park running southwest to Pennington. The George Washington National Forest occupies more than one million acres in the northern end, covering the Allegheny, Blue Ridge, and Massanutten mountain ranges. The Jefferson National Forest occupies the southern end of this scenic area.

Don't miss these national forests. The drives and hikes surrounded by thick woods and mountain peaks are good for the soul, especially for work-weary urban dwellers. Kids savor the feel of the woods and the views.

Remember that kids appreciate the unfolding scenic view from the car window; but you need to allow time to get out of the car, even for just a little bit.

Amazing Jefferson National Forest Facts

Mount Rogers' Peak At 5,729 feet **Mount Rogers'** peak is the highest point in Virginia.

SCENIC HIKES AND DRIVES IN THE GEORGE WASHINGTON NATIONAL FOREST

With more than 950 miles of trails, you can choose a path that leads to rivers, up mountains, and through dense woods.

- **Highlands Scenic Tour** is a 20-mile-drive on a twisting mountain road.

- **Augusta Springs Wetland Trail,** a 0.6-mile, fully accessible, easy loop with a boardwalk, through meadows, forest, and wetlands.

- **Appalachian Trail** cuts through the forest; a portion of the trail leads to Crabtree Falls, a cascading waterfall.

WHERE TO DRIVE AND HIKE IN THE JEFFERSON NATIONAL FOREST

This 690,000-acre forest has eleven wilderness areas and more than 1,100 miles of trails. Be sure to check out these favorites:

- **Pandapas Pond Trail,** located in Montgomery County (540–552–4641), is a 1-mile-long loop around an eight-acre pond. Enjoy fishing and canoeing.

- **Cascades Trail** is part of the Cascades Recreation area, located in Little Stony Creek Valley (540–552–4261). Four miles long round-trip, this moderate hike offers views of a 68-foot waterfall. This is one of the most popular trails in the forest and can be enjoyed by people of all ages.

- **John's Creek Mountain Trail,** a 3-mile-long scenic mountain route.

Two scenic drives are:

- **Big Walker Mountain Scenic Byway** leads 16 miles up the mountain past fishing ponds and old farmsteads to **Big Walker Lookout,** which has a swinging bridge and a lookout tower (open April through October). (See Wytheville section.)

- **Mount Rogers Scenic Byway** winds through valleys and across ridgetops (see Mount Rogers National Recreation Area).

Amazing Jefferson National Forest Facts

Miníe Ball Hill, near Mountain Lake, is a good place to find Civil War miníe balls (lead bullets). According to local lore, General George Cook, in his attempt to get by the Confederate troops, was forced to dump a significant amount of ammunition to lighten his load and hasten his flight.

For More Information

For additional information, call the Forest Supervisor, *5162 Valleypointe Parkway, Roanoke;* (888) 265–0019 or *(540) 265–5100. Web address: www.southernregion.fs.fed.us/gwj.*

Meadows of Dan

Located off the Blue Ridge Parkway at milepost 177 on U.S. Highway 58, Meadows of Dan is another good point from which to access the surrounding area. From this town it's also easy to reach Fairy Stone State Park.

MABRY MILL

266 Mabry Mill Road Southeast, at Milepost 176, where the Blue Ridge Parkway intersects with U.S. Highway 58; (276) 952–2947. Open from June through October.

A primary point of interest in the highlands section of the Blue Ridge Parkway is Mabry Mill, located north of the Meadows of Dan. A restored water-powered gristmill and sawmill that was in operation from 1910 to 1935, the mill now has demonstrations of blacksmithing and other trades.

FAIRY STONE STATE PARK

Twenty-three miles east of Meadows of Dan. Can be accessed from the Blue Ridge Parkway via U.S. Highway 58 and State Highways 8 and 57, 967 Fairy Stone Lake Drive, Stuart; (276) 930–2424. Web address: www.dcr.state.va.us/parks.

The main attraction here is the 168-acre swimming and fishing lake that adjoins Philpott Reservoir. Rowboats, canoes, and paddleboats are available to rent during the summer, and a fishing area is accessible to visitors with physical disabilities. Of course, there are the 25 miles of hiking and biking trails that are open year-round. Kids have fun searching for fairy stones, otherwise known as staurolite stones, a combination of silica, iron, and aluminum. When these minerals crystallize, they create a crosslike structure. Staurolite stones are also found in the mountains of North Carolina and Switzerland, but—supposedly—no place in the world has more staurolite stones shaped so nearly like crosses than Fairy Stone State Park and vicinity. The park has a fairy stone hunt site. Kids are allowed to keep the stones they find. In the summer, guides lead a park treasure hunt for these stones. Guided nature hikes, bluegrass music, and Junior Rangers programs are also available.

The Legend of the Fairy Stone

Long, long ago, fairies, naiads, and wood nymphs lived in this forest. One day an elf interrupted the dancing to tell them of Jesus Christ's crucifixion. The news so saddened these sprites that they wept, and when their tears touched the ground, they formed tiny crosses. For many years, these "fairy stones" were considered good luck and protection against witchcraft, sickness, and accidents.

THE BLUE RIDGE PARKWAY (all ages)

This scenic 469-mile parkway (see the chapter on the Shenandoah Valley; 800-228-PARK; www.blueridgeparkway.org) running through the Appalachian Mountains offers scenic views, mountain forests, and pioneer history. Area highlights.

Rocky Knob area, *near the intersection of the Blue Ridge Parkway and Virginia Route 8,* is a 4,000-acre recreation area with four marked trails. The Rocky Knob Visitor Center, *milepost 169,* offers information and maps.

The 10-mile Rock Castle Gorge Trail is a strenuous workout that starts out easy with the Hardwood Cove self-guided walking trail, a 0.8-mile easy loop, and with the Rocky Knob Picnic Loop, an easy 1-mile walk around the picnic grounds. From there the Gorge Trail goes over Rocky Knob and into the gorge, which is known for its glittering crystalline quartz formations. But be ready—it's an uphill walk back.

CHATEAU MORRISETTE WINERY (ages 7 and up)

P.O. Box 766, Meadows of Dan, VA 24120; (540–593–2865), www.chateau morrisette.com.

Located above the Rock Castle Gorge, Chateau Morrisette Winery is an interesting day trip for children who don't mind indulging their parents. Call ahead to see if winery tours are available or if the restaurant is open. On sale along with wines are Chateau Morrisette's Fire Dog Foods, tangy condiments that include roasted garlic grapeseed oil and spicy pecan vinegar.

OLD FIDDLER'S CONVENTION

Takes place the second weekend in August at Felts Park, Galax; (276) 238–8130 or (276) 236–8541. Arrive the weekend before the convention because the park fills up quickly, and book motel reservations many months or even a year in advance. Contact the Galax-Carroll-Grayson Chamber of Commerce or Galax Moose Lodge No. 733 for more information. Galax is located about 43 miles southeast of Meadows of Dan.

Try to attend the Old Fiddler's Convention at least once. This annual festival, billed as the oldest and largest fiddler's convention anywhere, gets you that old-time mountain music. Original tunes and folk songs ring out against the Blue Ridge background. Hear traditional and bluegrass rhythms played on mandolins, banjos, dulcimers, autoharps, and of course, fiddles. Watch flat-foot dancers (a mountain specialty) stomp in time to the ditties. Half the fun comes from watching the audience. They are down-home and dancing. Fans clog as performers play, and impromptu jam sessions break out in the parking lot and continue until the rooster crows. Musicians and bands compete from all over the world for the more than $15,000 in prize money. Since motels book up fast, many of the spectators simply camp in town or at Felts Park. People line up three or four days in advance for these campsites, and it's first come, first served.

Where to Eat

West Galax Diner, *1011 West Stuart Drive, Galax; (276) 236–0463.* Breakfast, lunch, and dinner family style. $

Where to Stay

Doe Run Lodge Resort and Conference Center, *Blue Ridge Parkway milepost 189, 10 miles north of Fancy Gap in Patrick County; (276) 398–2212 or (800) 325–6189; www.doerun.com.* South of Fairy Stone State Park, Doe Run Lodge offers chalets and two-bedroom villas equipped with kitchens. A restaurant serves breakfast, lunch, and dinner. There are tennis courts, volleyball, fishing, hiking, an outdoor heated pool, a fully stocked pond, a game room, and a golf course 5 miles away.

Fairy Stone State Park, *off State Highway 57; (276) 930–2424. Open March through December. For cabin or campsite reservations, call 800–933–PARK.* Along with a centrally located bathhouse, there are fifty-one campsites with electrical and water hookups. Eight rustic log cabins with electricity, appliances, basic furniture, kitchenware, and linens are for rent.

There are sixteen wood-sided concrete block cabins. All cabins are rented on a weekly basis.

Olde Mill Golf Resort, *Route 1, Box 84, Laurel Fork, VA 24352; (276) 398–2211.* The focus here is definitely golf. A more relaxed course than those at other more well-known resorts, this could be a good place to teach your kids the game. (Bring your own clubs and call ahead). Guests stay in two- or four-bedroom cottages equipped with kitchenettes. Kids can swim in the indoor pool. Niblicks Restaurant is on the property.

FOR MORE LODGING INFORMATION

B&B Reservation Service; *(800) 934–9184.* This service can help you find a bed-and-breakfast inn that welcomes families.

For More Information

Blue Ridge Highlands Regional Information and Visitors Center; 731 Factory Outlet Drive, Suite D8, Max Meadows, VA 24360; (800) 446–9670; Web address: www.virginiablueridge.org.

Radford

About 18 miles southwest of Blacksburg, Radford offers the outdoor activities of Claytor Lake State Park and Bisset Park, and the summer performances of *The Long Way Home*, a representation of the journey of Mary Draper Ingles.

 MARY DRAPER INGLES JOURNEY—*THE LONG WAY HOME* (ages 7 and up)

Located on Wilderness Road, 0.25 mile from exit 105 off Interstate 81; (540) 639–0679. Performances are held mid-June through August, Thursday through Sunday. Grounds open to visitors at 7:00 P.M. for a free walking tour of the original Ingle's property.

Radford is well-known for its summer outdoor amphitheater production of *The Long Way Home*. This tells the story of Mary Draper Ingle's capture by Shawnee Indians in 1755, the time she spent in captivity, her escape, and her subsequent 850-mile trip home from Big Bone Lick, Kentucky.

 **CLAYTOR LAKE STATE PARK (all ages)**

Take exit 101 from Interstate 81, 4400 State Park Road in Dublin; (540) 643–2500. Open daily year-round. Virginia state parks Web address: www. dcr.state.va.us.

The lake is the main attraction, and it's big: 4,500 acres 21 miles long, and 101 miles of shoreline. Boating, swimming, fishing camping, picnicking, pony rides for kids, and hiking are some of the activities here. With a valid Virginia fishing license, you can try your luck catching crappie and catfish, walleyes, and largemouth and smallmouth striped bass.

The park stretches over 472 acres and features 4 miles of hiking trails through an oak–hickory forest. The marina rents motor, sail, and rowboats. The historic **Howe House,** part of the visitors center, has interactive fish and lake ecology exhibits.

BISSET PARK

Off Norwood Street, Radford; (540) 731–3633.

This fifty-two-acre municipal park on the scenic New River sports jogging trails, tennis courts, a swimming pool, playgrounds, and picnic shelters. Available for rent are canoes, kayaks, and tubes.

Annual Events

JUNE

Family Fishing Tournament and Lake Clean-up Day at Claytor Lake. Kids and parents compete in fishing tournaments and help clean up the lake shore.

SEPTEMBER

Claytor Lake Arts and Crafts Festival, *Labor Day weekend*; *(540) 643–2500.* Local and regional craftspeople display jewelry, pottery, woodwork, and other crafts; also offers children's activities.

OCTOBER

Highlanders Festival, *mid-October.* This Scots and Applachian festival, sponsored by Radford University and the city of Radford, features sheepdog demonstrations, bagpipes, Celtic music, Irish folk tales, crafts, and foods.

For more information about these and other events, call the Radford Chamber of Commerce; *(540) 639–2202.*

Where to Eat

BT's, *218 Tyler Avenue; (540) 639– 2900. Open daily for lunch and dinner.* The eclectic menu features blackened catfish, lemon basil linguini, pork tenderloin, and rib-eye steak. Children's menu available. $–$$

Sal's Italian Restaurant and Pizza, *709 First Street; (540) 639–9669. Open daily for lunch and dinner.* Specialties are the home-made pasta, especially the spinach ravioli. Ask about half-portions for kids. $–$$

Spinnaker's, *1501 Tyler Avenue, in the Best Western Radford Inn; (540) 639– 3000. Open daily for breakfast, lunch, and dinner.* Soups, salads, pastas, sandwiches, steak, desserts. Kids' menu. $–$$

Where to Stay

The Best Western Radford Inn, *1501 Tyler Avenue; (540) 639–3000 or (800) 628–1955.* The property has seventy-two rooms, an indoor pool, and an on-site restaurant (see Spinnaker's).

Claytor Lake State Park, *4400 State Park Road in Dublin (540) 643–2500 or (800) 933–7275.* Twelve housekeeping cabins overlook the lake and there are 129 sites in four different campgrounds. Electrical and water hook-ups are available at forty-three sites.

Comfort Inn–Radford, *1501 Tyler Avenue, exit 109 off Interstate 81; (540)* 639–4800. This property has smoke-free rooms and includes a continental breakfast in the room rates.

Super 8 Motel, *1600 Tyler Avenue, Radford; (540) 731–9344.* Fifty-eight rooms, reasonably priced.

FOR MORE LODGING INFORMATION

B&B Reservation Service; *(800) 276–9184 .* This service can help you find a bed-and-breakfast inn that welcomes families.

For More Information

Blue Ridge Highlands Regional Information and Visitors Center; *731 Factory Outlet Drive, Suite D8, Max Meadows, VA 24360; (800) 446–9670; Web address: www.virginiablueridge.org.*

Radford Chamber of Commerce, *1126 Norwood Street, Radford, VA 24141; (540) 639–2202 or 633-0116. Web address: radfordchamber.i-plus.net*

Mount Rogers National Recreation Area

The Jefferson National Forest encompasses some 690,000 acres in western Virginia. Southeast of Abingdon, south of Interstate 81, and west of Interstate 77, the Mount Rogers National Recreation Area is a 114,000-acre section of the forest. The park includes Mount Rogers itself, the state's highest point at 5,729 feet.

Get your bearings as soon as possible because the area covers so much territory. A good start is the visitors center (there is only one in the area). The center dispenses helpful literature and information and the building also serves as a year-round forest ranger headquarters. The bookstore has a good range of nature and children's books.

The recreation area is particularly suitable for families who like to hike. A 60-mile segment of the **Appalachian Trail** runs through the park and is easily accessible from various points, including the visitors center. It's possible to do short segments with young children. Many other well-marked trails wind through the park; ask for literature at the visitors center. Volunteers and park rangers offer interpretive programs on summer weekends at the campsites. Activities might include short walks, slide shows, and environmental education talks.

FOR MORE PARK INFORMATION

The visitors center is at 3714 Highway 16, 7 miles southwest of Marion. Open daily from the end of May to the end of October (depending on the weather). Call for information about the recreation area; (276) 783–5196 or (800) 628–7202.

HIKES, SCENIC DRIVES, AND ACTIVITIES

With young children, try the **0.6-mile loop** outside the visitors center, a path that passes small ponds filled with bluegills.

You can't drive to the top of Mount Rogers, but you can hike to the top if your family is reasonably fit and ready for a lengthy outing of moderate difficulty. A 4-mile-long trail begins at **Grindstone Campground** (elevation 2,500 feet), *on State Highway 603, 6 miles west of Troutdale.*

Drive to the summit of **Whitetop Mountain** for panoramic views. On a clear day you can see Tennessee and Grandfather Mountain in North Carolina.

Virginia Fly Fishing, *17172 Jeb Stewart Highway in Abingdon; (276) 628–3826. Open daily except Sundays.* This outfitter has guided fly-fishing trips.

Llama treks, *Treasure Mountain Farm, Abingdon; (276) 944–4674.* These are great ways to hike into the heart of the woods without the burden of carrying gear because the llamas do it for you. Kids love learning to lead these animals.

GRAYSON HIGHLANDS STATE PARK (all ages) (TT)

On U.S. Highway 58, either 35 miles southeast of Abingdon, or 31 miles south of Marion via State Highway 16; 829 Grayson Highland Lane; (5276) 579–7092. The visitors center is 4.5 miles from the entrance off U.S. Highway 58. Open daily from Memorial to Labor Day and weekends only until mid-October. Reopens weekends May 1. Virginia State Parks Web address: www.dcr.state.va.us.

Adjacent to the Mount Rogers National Recreation Area, Grayson Highlands State Park's 4,935 acres in the Appalachian Mountains afford vistas of rugged alpine scenery.

Amazing Grayson Highlands State Park Facts

Massie Gap Many places in the park are named after pioneers in the region, including Massie Gap, named after Lee Massey, an early settler who lived in the gap in the late 1800s with his wife and five children.

Wilburn Ridge Wilburn Ridge is named after fearless bear hunter and wolf trapper Wilburn Waters, who triumphed over both creatures in these woods.

Along with helpful information, the visitors center (located near the summit of Haw Orchard Mountain) has a number of interesting mountain-life displays, such as arrowheads, farm tools, a weaving loom, and a fiddle belonging to a well-known local mountain musician. Crafts are available for sale at the Mountain Crafts Shop. On summer weekends the center might have a quilting demonstration, an autoharp player, or other mountain cultural activity.

The park appeals to families for a number of reasons, including its manageable size and interpretative programs. The park's nine hiking trails average 1 mile in length, just long enough for young kids to feel accomplished without feeling cranky. Some trails lead to waterfalls, some to vistas, and some to an old pioneer cabin. Follow the **Rhododendron Trail,** a 0.5-mile from the Masse Gap parking area, and you link up with the **Appalachian Trail,** which stretches from Maine to Georgia. The hearty can hike the Appalachian Trail across Mount Rogers, which at 5,729 feet is the highest point in Virginia.

Take time at the picnic grounds, about 2.5 miles from the visitors center, to view two log cabins, a spring house, and a cane mill. During the summer months check out the interpretive programs held Friday through Sunday in the amphitheater at the general campground. Themes might include music, edible plants, or wildflowers. A popular activity here from mid-July to about September 1 is picking blueberries and huckleberries (so bring along containers). Also take note that although there are no central swimming areas, there are numerous creeks where you can get wet. The park has excellent horse trails. Rent horses (if you are qualified) at Hope and Dreams Unlimited (800–899-6554).

Annual Events

For information on all of these events, call the Grayson County Tourist Information Center at (276) 773-3711.

MARCH

Whitetop Mountain Maple Festival, *held the last weekend in March in Whitetop,* features music, crafts, storytelling, and tours of the maple-tapping area and sugar house.

MAY

The highlight of the **Whitetop Mountain Ramp Festival,** *the third Sunday in May,* is a competition to see who can eat the most ramps, which are wild onions that grow in the surrounding mountains. Enjoy music, crafts, games, dancing, and lots of barbecue chicken.

JUNE

Wayne C. Henderson Music Festival, *third weekend in June.* A guitar competition and bluegrass mountain music concert. Admission.

SEPTEMBER

Grayson Highlands Fall Festival, *the last full weekend in September.* Features molasses and apple butter-making, cider-squeezing, live mountain music, dancing, a wild pony sale, crafts, and lots of food.

OCTOBER

Mountain Foliage Festival, *second Saturday in October,* is famous for its unique Grand Privy Race, where people race their specially designed outhouses for the coveted Chamber Pot Trophy, plus food, games, crafts.

Where to Eat

See restaurants listed for Marion.

Where to Stay

Grayson Highlands State Park, *(276) 579–7092.* The park has two campgrounds, one for horseback riders with their own horses (available on a first-come basis) and another for the general public. There are 165 campsites. Reserve online, www.dcr.state.va. us/parks, or call (800) 933-PARK. In Richmond call (276) 225-3867.

Grindstone (on State Highway 603, 6 miles west of Troutdale) and **Beartree campgrounds** (7 miles east of Damascus on Route 58), in Mount Rogers National Recreation Area, both offer a playground (swings and slides). Beartree has the only swimming facilities, on a fourteen-acre lake complete with a sandy beach (but no lifeguards). There are three campgrounds available for horseback riders. Open spring through December 1.

FOR MORE LODGING INFORMATION

B&B Reservation Service; *(800) 934–9184.* This service can help you find a bed-and-breakfast inn that welcomes families.

For More Information

Blue Ridge Highlands Regional Information and Visitors Center; *731 Factory Outlet Drive, Suite D8, Max Meadows, VA 24360; (800) 446–9670; Web address: www.virginiablueridge.org.*

Grayson County Tourist Information Center, *107 East Main Street in the Historic 1908 Courthouse, Grayson, VA 24348; (276) 773–3711.*

Marion

Marion, a town of some 7,000 people directly off Interstate 81, is a popular vacation base because of its proximity to Mount Rogers National Recreation Area, Grayson Highlands State Park, and Hungry Mother State Park.

HUNGRY MOTHER STATE PARK (TT)

Four miles north of Marion on State Highway 16, 2851 Park Boulevard; (276) 781–7400 or (800) 933–7275. Open year-round. Obtain information at the main office at the park entrance. Virginia State Parks Web address: www.dcr.state. va.us/parks.

Hungry Mother, a 2,215-acre state park, is a particular favorite with families, especially because of its 108-acre lake. In the heart of the mountains, the lake has a sandy beach, a bathhouse, paddleboat and rowboat rentals, and what many people consider to be the best northern pike fishing in the state.

The park offers more than 12 miles of trails—it would be a shame not to do at least one hike. For a fairly flat and easy walk try the **Lake Trail,** which runs for 3 miles along the lakeshore. The 1.1-mile-long **Middle Ridge Trail** and the 0.7-mile **Ridge Trail** are more challenging and afford some nice mountain views.

The park's interpretive programs, offered in spring, summer, and fall, are so good that they are one of the reasons this park is popular with families. The offerings might include an interpretive horseback ride; guided nature hikes; a "Critter Crawl," in which kids search for stream creatures such as salamanders and frogs (held on Thursday in the summer), music, crafts, and local history; and nocturnal programs such as night hikes and star gazing. In addition, Junior Naturalist programs are offered on Wednesday and Friday, and Wee Naturalist programs for ages 2 to 5 are offered on Wednesday. In summer there's a guided canoe program held twice weekly at the lake (children at least 6 years old can participate with a parent). The park hosts a three-day arts and crafts festival on the third weekend of July that features about 125 artisans with wares from toys to stained glass to paintings. The festival attracts about 15,000 people.

What's In A Name? How the park got its unusual name is a sad, but interesting, story. The most generally accepted legend is that a young boy named Adam and his mother, Molly, escaped from an Indian raid and wandered through the woods. When hunger set in, they searched for berries, but eventually Molly collapsed next to a small stream. Adam went for help. Hungry and exhausted upon reaching the next settlement, he could only get out the words "hungry mother." When a search party found Molly's body in the creek, they named it Hungry Mother Creek in her honor. Later, when the creek was dammed to make a lake, it was named Hungry Mother Lake. A trail that goes to the highest section in the developed area of the park is called **Molly's Knob.**

Horseback riding is also offered; the stables are located a 0.5-mile from the park entrance on State Highway 16. Call (276) 783-9700. Kids like the easy pace and scenic route of the thirty-minute guided horseback tours. Children must be 6 years old to ride on their own horse.

Where to Eat

The Apple Tree Restaurant and Gift Shop, *Highway 16 South; (276) 782–9977. Open for breakfast, lunch, and dinner.* Sandwiches, burgers, and pasta. $

Hayden's World Luncheonette, *137 East Main Street; (276) 783–7241. Open daily for breakfast and lunch. Dinner also available on Saturday.* Simple sandwiches and soup are the norm. $

Herb House, *107 Pendleton Street; (276) 783–4062. Open for lunch and dinner.* Located in an original drying room for herbs. Soups and sandwiches are served. $–$$

The Restaurant *at Hungry Mother State Park; (276) 781–7400. Open for lunch and dinner Wednesday through Sunday.* This facility has three dining rooms overlooking the lake and a gift shop. $$

Where to Stay

Best Western, *1424 North Main Street; (276) 783–3193 or (800) 528–1234.* More than one hundred rooms, an outdoor pool, and a restaurant.

Fox Hill, *8568 Troutdale Highway; 20 miles south of Marion via State Highway 16, Troutdale; (276) 677–3313. Web address: www.bbonline.com/va/foxhill.* Fox Hill sits on a mountaintop with panoramic views. Spread out on seventy acres of woods and pastureland, this lodging offers only six rooms and one suite, so be sure to reserve in advance. Kids enjoy the farm animals and the easy hiking trails on the property and in nearby Mount Rogers. There are no phones or television in

the rooms, but the sitting room has a television. A full breakfast is included in the rates, and a mom-and-pop diner is 2 miles away in Troutdale. Cribs are free.

Hungry Mother State Park, *State Highway 16; (800) 933–PARK for reservations.* Rental cabins are available from March 1 through November. During spring and fall, cabins may be rented for a two-night minimum; during summer they are available by the week only. There are three campgrounds within a few miles of the entrance; two have water and electric hookups, another is for tents only. All have bathhouses with hot showers.

For More Information

Blue Ridge Highlands Regional Information and Visitors Center; *731 Factory Outlet Drive, Suite D8, Max*

Meadows, VA 24360; (800) 446–9670; Web address: www.virginiablueridge.org.

Chamber of Commerce of Smyth County, *124 West Main Street, P.O. Box 924, Marion, VA 24354; (276) 783–3161.*

Abingdon

Abingdon, chartered in 1778, is the oldest town west of the Blue Ridge Mountains and has been designated a Virginia Historic Landmark. Located 133 miles southwest of Roanoke (from Interstate 81, take exit 17 into town), it is a cultural hub and home to some 10,000 residents. Abingdon is well known for its heritage crafts, and even kids who hate shopping might not mind browsing—or buying—here. The simple charm of the handcrafted dolls and toys especially appeals to the younger set.

BARTER THEATRE, STATE THEATRE OF VIRGINIA (all ages)
(276) 628–3991. Web address: www.BarterTheatre.com. Performances are from February through December.

One of Abingdon's premiere attractions is this theater. Founded in 1933 (when the admission price was "35 cents or the equivalent in produce") Barter claims fame as the oldest professional resident theater in the U. S. Noted for the caliber of both its productions and performers, Barter stars have included Gregory Peck, Hume Cronyn, Patricia Neal, Ernest Borgnine, Barry Corbin, Jerry Hardin, and others. During its season Barter performs on three stages: Barter Theatre Main Stage, Barter Stage II, and First Light Theatre for young people. Barter also offers workshops for kids.

PINNACLE NATURAL AREA PRESERVE

Northeast of Lebanon, near State Routes 640 and 721. For additional information, contact Hungry Mother State Park; (276) 781–7400.

Pinnacle takes its name from the dolomite rock formation that rises 600 feet in this sixty-eight-acre preserve. Trails lead you through fern grottoes and thickets of tall white-cedar trees along the Clinch River's rushing waters. In the clear water you might see the mussels that feed in the river.

If you and your kids are good swimmers, consider snorkeling the **Clinch River.** The river offers a variety of depths and lots to see, including seventy-one species of fish and nineteen species of mussels. The preserve may be closed on occasion for resource protection or management activities, so it's a good idea to call first.

VIRGINIA CREEPER NATIONAL RECREATION TRAIL

Trail begins near the corner of Glen Springs Road and A Street. Look for the locomotive that was the last steam engine on the Virginia Creeper Railroad. For more information call the Abingdon Convention and Visitors Bureau (276) 676–2282 or (800) 435–3440; Mount Rogers National Recreation Area (276) 783–5196 or (800) 628–7202.

Now a multipurpose recreational trail, the **Virginia Creeper Trail** starts in Abingdon and extends southeast for 34 miles to Whitetop Station at the Virginia–North Carolina border.

This scenic trail, a former Native Americans path, was used by pioneers and Daniel Boone. At the turn of the century, the trail was a mountain railroad that received its nickname, Virginia Creeper, from the early steam locomotives that struggled slowly up the railroad's steep grades. Now the railroad bed serves as a path for walkers, bikers, hikers, joggers, and equestrians and is off-limits to motorized vehicles. The trail eventually enters Mount Rogers National Recreation Area. You don't have to go too far to enjoy the trail's scenic splendor. Near the trail's beginning, you'll pass farmland and go over a small mountain range and creeks.

SHUTTLE SERVICE AND BIKE RENTAL

Blue Blaze Shuttle Service and Bike Rentals, *227 West Laurel Avenue; (276) 475–5095 or (800) 475–5095. Web address: blueblaze.naxs.com.* To fully explore the wilderness, you may want to take a transport service for bikers and hikers that gets you and your gear to high-country trailheads, including the Virginia Creeper. Bikes (including kid-size ones) can be rented by the hour (two-hour minimum) or day, helmets and water bottles included. And you can bring your dog—on a leash. Blue Blaze sponsors night rides to Whitetop Station on the Saturday closest to the full moon, May through September.

Adventure Damascus, *128 West Laurel Avenue; (888) 595–2453.* Shuttle service and bike rentals.

The Bike Station, *501 East Third Street; (276) 475–3629.* Shuttle service and bike rentals.

Mount Rogers Outfitters, *110 West Laurel Avenue; (540) 475–5416 or (800) 337–5416.* Bike rentals.

Highlands Bike Rental and Shuttle Service, *302 Green Spring Road; (540) 628–1329.* Bike rentals.

🛍 WHERE TO SHOP

The Cave House Craft Shop, *279 East Main Street; (540) 628–7721.* This non-profit 130-member cooperative is housed in a landmark Victorian home and features traditional and contemporary crafts.

Dixie Pottery, *located on U.S. Highway 11 (Lee Highway), between exits 10 and 13 on Interstate 81. Open daily until 6:00 P.M.* Dixie Pottery has been selling crafts since 1957. The 100,000-square-foot shop also has pottery, housewares, and decorative accessories, some of which catch kids' eyes, such as the brightly colored Mexican papiér-maché fruit.

153 West, 153 West Main Street; *(540) 628–1232.* This shop has a selection of the area's crafts.

Abingdon's downtown district, along West Main Street, also has a nice selection of collectibles and antique shops.

Annual Events

AUGUST

Virginia Highlands Festival, *from the end of July through the first two weeks of August; (540) 623–5266. Web address: www.va-highlands-festival.org.* One of the top twenty events in the Southeast, the Virginia Highlands Festival is a showcase of arts and crafts, antiques, music, photography, storytelling, and living-history re-enactments.

SEPTEMBER/OCTOBER

Washington County Fair and Burley Tobacco Festival. *Call Abingdon Visitors Bureau for information; (276) 676–2282 or (800) 435–3440.* You'll find a mix of country music, carnival rides, and displays of prize animals at this county fair/festival.

Where to Eat

Alison's, *1220 West Main Street; (276) 628–8002.* Famous for their baked potato soup and ribs. $–$$

Biscuit Connection, *789 West Main Street; (276) 676–2433.* Home of the world's biggest biscuit, they say. Good breakfasts and lunches, too. $

Hardware Company Restaurant, *260 West Main Street; (5276) 628–1111.* Originally a hardware store, this restaurant offers lunch and dinner at good prices. $

Starving Artist Cafe, *134 Wall Street;* *(276) 628–8445.* The cafe doubles as an art gallery. The gourmet sandwiches and tasty entrees make lunch and dinner enjoyable, as does the outdoor dining during nice weather. $

Stringer's Cafe, *909 West Main Street;* *(276) 676–2655. Open for lunch and dinner.* Family buffet. $

The Tavern, *222 East Main Street; (540) 628–1118.* Built in 1779, the Tavern is Abingdon's oldest building. German and American fare. $$–$$$

Where to Stay

Alpine Motel, *882 East Main Street;* *(276) 628–3178.* The motel is set back off the road and has views of the state's two highest mountain peaks, Mount Rogers and Whitetop.

Abingdon's Martha Washington Inn, *150 West Main Street; (276) 628– 3161 or (800) 555–8006. Web address: www.camberleyhotels.com.* An Historic Hotel of America, this inn creates a nineteenth-century élan with its antiques and period furnishings. Daily afternoon tea is served in the lobby or on the veranda; traditional and continental fare for breakfast, lunch, and dinner are available. There are sixty-one rooms and suites.

Four additional motels/hotels offering moderately priced accommodations are:

Comfort Inn *Interstate 81 at exit 14; (800) 221–2222 or (276) 676–2222.*

Empire Motel *Interstate 81 at exit 19; (276) 628–7131.*

Hampton Inn *340 Commerce Drive;* *(276) 619–4600.* The inn has an outdoor pool and gives a complimentary breakfast.

Holiday Inn Express *Interstate 81 at exit 19; (276) 676–2829.*

Summerfield Inn Bed and Breakfast, *101 West Valley Street; (276) 628– 5905 or (800) 668–5905. Web address: www.Summerfieldinn.com.* Located in Abingdon's historic district, Summerfield, a property built in 1921, features a library, wraparound porch, rockers, and private baths. A full breakfast is included in the room rate.

FOR MORE LODGING INFORMATION

The Blue Ridge Bed and Breakfast Reservation Service, *(540) 955–1246 or (800) 296–1246.* This service can help you find a bed-and-breakfast inn in the surrounding area that welcomes families.

For More Information

Abingdon Convention and Visitors Bureau, *335 Cummings Street, Abingdon, VA 24210; (276) 676–2282 or (800) 435–3440. Web address: www.abingdon.*

com/tourism. The visitors bureau has maps, information, and a brochure outlining a self-guided walking tour of Abingdon's 20-block historic district.

Blue Ridge Highlands Regional Information and Visitors Center; 731 Factory Outlet Drive, Suite D8, Max *Meadows, VA 24360; (800) 446–9670; Web address: www.virginiablueridge.org.*

Cumberland Gap

CUMBERLAND GAP NATIONAL HISTORICAL PARK

On U.S. Highway 25 East and U.S. Highway 58 South; (606) 248–2817. Web address: www.nps.gov. The visitors center, located at the U.S. Highway 25 East entrance, is open in winter from 8:00 A.M. to 5:00 P.M. and in summer from 8:00 A.M. to 6:00 P.M. Closed Christmas and New Year's Day.

An introductory film provides background on Daniel Boone and the pioneers who ventured over the gap. The exhibits, mostly from the pioneer era, include bearskin rugs and rifles. The museum displays a few war items as well.

The Cumberland Gap National Historical Park encompasses 20,305 heavily forested acres southeast of Middlesboro, Kentucky. The park, which includes parts of Virginia and Tennessee, traces Daniel Boone's pioneering trail. In 1750 Dr. Thomas Walker discovered an Indian footpath, and in 1769 Boone passed through the gap with a hunting party, eventually blazing what became the Wilderness Road in 1775. Despite the fact that the gap was a horse path until 1796, and no wagons passed, more than 200,000 people came through the gap, venturing into Kentucky and westward. A strategic point during the Civil War, this area changed hands four times, though no major battle was fought.

The park's approximately 70 miles of trails range from easy to strenuous. With younger kids, you needn't venture farther than the visitors center. Park officials call the nearby 2-mile Fitness Trail a "walk through the woods." If tired, you can cut back to the center after 0.75 mile.

One literal high point in the park is **Pinnacle Overlook,** elevation 2,440 feet. *Follow the park road for 4 miles (you must walk the last 100 yards).* The drive to reach the Pinnacle Overlook is a 4-mile mountain route of hairpin turns. Go slowly and be sure your kids can stomach the twists. Those who can are rewarded (on a clear day) with an impressive view of parts of three states: Kentucky, Tennessee, and Virginia. When park staff is available, shuttles to the overlook can be arranged for a nominal fee.

Another highlight, especially for young grade-school children, is the **Hensley Settlement.** This site is most easily reached by a shuttle service that requires reservations on the weekend. Otherwise this site is reached by Jeep or by a one-day hike.

The Hensley community existed on this site from 1904 to 1951. The original buildings include log houses, barns, and outbuildings. Although fairly contemporary, the settlement resembles one of the pioneer era. During the summer, park volunteers stay at the settlement to act as guides. Families can visit chestnut-hewn cabins and learn about the self-sufficient lifestyles of the original inhabitants.

Summer also brings some interesting interpretive programs given by a park ranger who dresses in period clothing. Learn about the Civil War and being a long hunter (the correct term for what Daniel Boone did for a living). Programs may include hiking a trail to a beaver dam and campfire activities. Some activities require reservations. Call (606) 248–2817.

Where to Eat

The Black Forest Steak House, *203 Harrel Street, Pennington Gap; (276) 546– 4754.* Steaks, burgers, and pasta are served. $-$$

Where to Stay

The Wilderness Road Camp-ground, *located off Highway 58 in Virginia; (606) 248–2817.* Available year-round. This facility has 160 campsites on a first-come basis and are available for tent, trailer, and RV campers. There are electrical hook-ups, as well as hot showers and potable water. Backcountry campsites are located throughout the park and require a backcountry use permit, which must be picked up at the visitors center.

For More Information

Blue Ridge Highlands Regional Information and Visitors Center; *731 Factory Outlet Drive, Suite D8, Max Meadows, VA 24360; (800) 446–9670; Web address: www.virginiablueridge.org.*

Big Stone Gap Area

BIG STONE GAP (all ages)

Located at the junction of three forks in the Powell River

Big Stone Gap, northeast of Cumberland Gap on U.S. Highway 23, forms a pass that goes through Stone Mountain. The setting inspired the novel of the early 1900s, *The Trail of the Lonesome Pine*, by John Fox, Jr. This tragic love story (based on a true event) details the changes in mountain life after the discovery of coal and is told through the eyes of the young June Tolliver.

Carter Family Fold Music Show and Museum *Take U.S. Highway 58 West to Hiltons, then turn right onto Route 614 East for 3 miles; (276) 386–9480; recorded information (276) 386–6054.* If you're driving to Big Stone Gap from Abingdon, consider timing your trip so you can partake of some down-home evening entertainment. In the town of **Maces Spring,** some 20 miles southwest of Abingdon, in a huge shed tucked away in the mountains, you can see some of the best country and bluegrass performers in the area every Saturday night at 7:30 P.M. The Carters claim to be country-music pioneers whose family recorded more than 300 songs from 1927 to 1942, one-third of them written by patriarch A.P. Carter. Whether or not Janette Carter and her brother Joseph Carter, the remaining performing Carters, are playing, your family will get into the toe-tapping rhythms of the bluegrass and country bands. Often locals head to the small dance floor to do popular mountain dances, such as clogging. Join in if you know how. Tickets are reasonably priced and kids under 6 are admitted free. There's also a museum of Carter family memorabilia that opens at 6:00 P.M. Come the first Saturday in August for an annual festival, which attracts music groups, artisans, and clog dancers.

JUNE TOLLIVER PLAYHOUSE (all ages) (TT)

Jerome and Clinton Streets; (276) 523–4707 or (800) 362–0149.

An outdoor musical drama by the same name as the novel, entertaining for families with school-age kids, is held in the summer at the playhouse. At the adjoining June Tolliver House, a crafts center, you can buy such items as coal carvings and hand-made dolls and quilts.

JOHN FOX, JR., MUSEUM (ages 9 and up)

117 Shawnee Avenue; (276) 523–2747 or (800) 362–0149. Open Memorial Day through Labor Day, Wednesday through Sunday 2:00 to 5:00 P.M.

If you see the play about June Tolliver, it may pique your family's interest into visiting the author's rambling, two-story home which now houses this museum. The property is furnished as it was during the time of the Fox family.

HARRY W. MEADOR, JR., COAL MUSEUM (ages 9 and up) (TT)

505 East Fifth Street; (276) 523–9209. Open year-round Wednesday through Saturday 10:00 A.M. to 5:00 P.M. and Sunday 1:00 to 5:00 P.M.

Located in an historic building, this museum details the history of the region's coal mining—past and present—using artifacts such as a shuttle car, crank calculator, and hundreds of old photos.

SOUTHWEST VIRGINIA MUSEUM (ages 7 and up) (TT)

Downtown on West First Street and Wood Avenue; (276) 523–1322. Open from March through December. Memorial Day through Labor Day open Monday through Thursday 10:00 A.M. to 4:00 P.M., Friday 9:00 A.M. to 4:00 P.M., Saturday 10:00 A.M. to 5:00 P.M., Sunday 1:00 to 5:00 P.M. Before Memorial Day and after Labor Day, closed on Monday.

The museum, located in the former home of a state attorney general, was built during the 1880s. The museum is dedicated to the area's early settlers and the coal boom period of the 1890s. The exhibits, which rotate twice a year, include Indian artifacts and hand-made quilts, a century-old gun collection, and mining memorabilia. The museum staff also conducts a variety of programs to educate the public about the area's heritage. In October there's Appalachian Ghost Storytelling. A Festival of Trees, with seventy-five decorated Christmas trees, is featured mid-November through late December.

NATURAL TUNNEL STATE PARK (TT)

18 miles southeast of Big Stone Gap on U.S. Highway 23. At Duffield travel 4 miles west on Route 871; (276) 940–2674; www.dcr.state.va.us/parks. The chair lift is open daily Memorial Day through Labor Day; in May, September, and October on weekends only; closed November through April. Picnic facilities and the swimming pool are open from Memorial Day through Labor Day. Tunnel tours start from the visitors center and lead to the mouth of the tunnel.

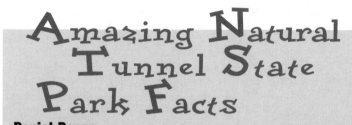

Amazing Natural Tunnel State Park Facts

Daniel Boone was probably the first white man to see the tunnel.

Lt. Col. Stephen H. Long The first written account of the tunnel was by Lt. Col. Stephen H. Long in a geology journal in 1832.

As the name suggests, this state park is centered around an enormous natural tunnel. The tunnel's formation began more than a million years ago in the early glacial period, when groundwater containing carbonic acid crept through crevices, gradually dissolving the surrounding bedrock of limestone. Then, geologists believe, what's now Stock Creek was diverted underground to continue the carving process over many centuries. In 1890 the South Atlantic and Ohio Railroad arrived and laid tracks through the tunnel. The railroad still passes through today. Later acquired by the Commonwealth of Virginia, the tunnel, which is about 850 feet long and 100 feet in diameter, along with 850 acres now make up the focal point of this popular park.

Take a chair lift (located right next to the visitors center) to see the sights or opt for one of the many hiking trails. Within a mile or two of the visitors center, there are picnic facilities (shelters can be reserved in advance), an Olympic-size swimming pool, a large bathhouse, and a concession building. Seven walking trails—the longest is only 1.1 miles—allow for short strolls. The most popular trail follows the rim of the cliff from the visitors center to **Lover's Leap,** 0.3 mile away.

Interpretative programs, generally held at the campground on summer weekends, emphasize local culture, with presentations on basketweaving and blacksmithing and environmental science. Evening campfire talks feature local folklore and, sometimes, night hikes. The new "Cove" has an educational center with eight dormitory rooms, an auditorium, and a library with computers designed to accommodate groups and classes. Ask about the park's cave tours and geology workshops.

BREAKS INTERSTATE PARK

Located on State Highway 80 off Interstate 460; (276) 865–4413 or (800) 982–5122. Web address: www.breakspark.com. Open April 1 to December 21.

Pick up brochures as well as information on special events at the entrance gate. Less than a 0.5-mile away are the park headquarters, where trail maps are available. The park is jointly administered by Kentucky and Virginia.

This park occupies 4,600 acres on the Kentucky–Virginia border at the eastern edge of the Cumberland Mountain Plateau. Visitors come here to see what some have dubbed the "Grand Canyon of the South." At this site the Russell Fork of the Big Sandy River has cut a 1,600-foot-deep gorge through Pine Mountain.

Breaks Canyon is the park's highlight. A paved road leads through a forest of evergreens to the rim of this beautiful canyon. Here, from four different overlooks, you'll be treated to superb views of the gorge, springs, caves, and rock formations—such as the **Towers Overlook,** a 0.5-mile pyramid of rocks—as well as a blossoming array of colorful rhododendron. A recreational area just a short distance from the entrance sports a swimming pool and a playground.

Laurel Lake is not suitable for swimming. But there are paddle-boats, and fishing is allowed. Bluegills and bass are what anglers hope to catch. Obtain a fishing license at park headquarters. Horseback trail rides are available. Among the annual special events that stand out are a summer arts and crafts fair and the Autumn Gospel Song Festival on Labor Day weekend, which is the region's biggest song festival.

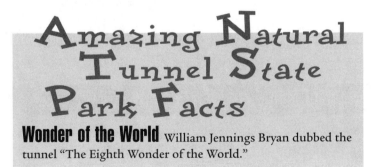

Amazing Natural Tunnel State Park Facts

Wonder of the World William Jennings Bryan dubbed the tunnel "The Eighth Wonder of the World."

Where to Eat

Rhododendron Restaurant, *Breaks Interstate Park, State Route 80; (276) 865–4413 or (800) 982–5122. Open from April 1 through December 21, serving breakfast, lunch, and dinner.* The restaurant serves basic fare such as steak, pasta, salads, and hamburgers. Children's menu available. $–$$

Where to Stay

Breaks Interstate Park Campground, *Open daily April through October.* Tent, camper, and RV sites. Electrical hook-ups, water, and sewer. No reservations taken.

The Country Inn Motel, *627 Giles Avenue, Big Stone Gap;* (540) 523–0374. This moderately priced lodging has forty-two rooms.

Natural Tunnel State Park, (800) 933–PARK. Twenty-two campsites are available on a drop-in or reservation basis. Electric and water hook-ups are available.

Rhododendron Lodge, *Breaks Interstate Park, State Route 80; (540) 865–4413 or (800) 982–5122. Web address: www.breakspark.com. Open from April 1 to the Sunday before Christmas.* This thirty-four-room lodge overlooks Breaks Canyon. Four housekeeping cottages are also available and can be rented by the week or month.

For More Information

Heart of Appalachia Tourism Authority, *P.O. Box 207, Cloverleaf Square, Suite G3, Big Stone Gap 24219; (888) SWVA–FUN, (276) 523–2005; www.heartofappalachia.com.*

Blue Ridge Highlands Regional Information and Visitors Center; *731 Factory Outlet Drive, Suite D8, Max Meadows, VA 24360; (800) 446–9670; Web address: www.virginiablueridge.org.*

Tazewell County and Bland County

POCAHONTAS EXHIBITION MINE AND MUSEUM (ages 5 and up) (TT)

At the junction of routes 644 and 759 in Pocahontas; (276) 945–2134. Web address: wvweb.com/pocahontas_mine. Open daily from April through October.

Admission. Joint tickets for the mine and the museum available at a discount at either entrance.

The area's coal-mining history is brought to life through exhibits of mining equipment and demonstrations of coal cutting, blasting, and loading. It's cool inside—a constant 52 degrees—so bring a jacket.

WOLF CREEK INDIAN VILLAGE & MUSEUM (ages 3 to 9)

U.S. Highway 52, off Interstate 77, exit 58, Bastian; (276) 688–3438. Open daily 9:00 A.M. to 5:00 P.M., but hours vary in the winter, depending on the weather. Admission.

This one-hundred–acre site, part of an archeological dig, was once a Shawnee and Cherokee hunting ground. The re-created Native American village is based on the excavations of the 600-year-old site. Some of the recovered tools and arrowheads are on display. The life of European settlers is portrayed through nineteenth-century weapons, horse-drawn equipment, tools, furniture, and the eight log and two stone buildings on the premises. Although Wolf Creek is not as large as some of the better-known living history museums, younger children may find the size just right for them. Kids will enjoy the opportunity to interact with the museum interpreters to learn about how to tan hides, make pottery, and work with flint.

LLAMA TREKKING: VIRGINIA HIGHLAND LLAMAS

Route 1, Bland; (276) 688–4464. The treks operate from April through November; stop during deer-hunting seasons.

In Bland families can find a way to hike the southwest Virginia mountains with ease. You do the walking while a beast of burden (not your spouse) carries your gear. Llama trekking with Virginia Highland Llamas takes the work out of walking. On these scenic day trips guided by Bob and Carolyn Bane, you lead your llama for 3 miles to the top of Big Walker Mountain. Both of you take a break for lunch and enjoy the expansive views. The llama grazes while you munch a Southern picnic of fried chicken, potato salad, lemonade, and homemade pecan tarts. For those who prefer, there's also a shorter, less strenuous trek to a beautiful spring called Walker Creek.

The mountain is sweetest in spring when wildflowers dot your path, and in fall, when the hills turn russet and yellow. To complete your outdoor fantasy, the Banes, if you ask ahead, permit camping on their 900-acre farm.

HISTORIC CRAB ORCHARD MUSEUM AND PIONEER PARK (ages 5 and up) (TT)

Crab Orchard Road at U.S. Highways 19 and 460, Tazewell; (276) 988–6755. Web address: histcrab.netscope.net. Open Memorial Day through Labor Day, Monday through Saturday 9:00 A.M. to 5:00 P.M., Sunday 1:00 to 5:00 P.M. Family rates.

This historical museum and five-acre pioneer settlement is the region's cultural museum; it tells the story of the area's earliest Native American inhabitants and those who came after them, through the periods of the Revolutionary and Civil Wars. Costumed interpreters interact with visitors and provide information about the pioneer lifestyle.

BICYCLING

The Heart of Appalachia Bike Route and Scenic Drive winds for 128 miles through Tazewell, Russell, and Wise Counties in southwest Virginia. Pedal past creeks, along river beds, and in mountain foothills.

Annual Events

MAY

Bland County 4-H Horse Show, *at the Bland County Fairgrounds; (276) 688–3542.*

JULY

Annual Main Street Festivall, *in Tazewell.* Food, crafts, and entertainment.

Where to Eat / Where to Stay

Cuz's Restaurant and Cabins, *U.S. Highway 460, 30 miles south of Bluefield; (276) 964–9336. The restaurant is open March through December, Wednesday through Saturday from 3:00 to 9:00 P.M.* Cuz's is a country combination of restaurant and lodge. Cuz's Uptown Barbeque, the restaurant, serves ample portions of steak and fish. On weekends bluegrass bands and country singers entertain. The cabins are simple; kids like the teepees in which they

can camp. The property has an outdoor pool and tennis courts.

The Laurel Inn Bed and Breakfast, *386–7 West Water Street in Pocahontas, located within walking distance of the coal mine; (276) 945–2787.* The Laurel Inn Bed and Breakfast consists of two adjacent brick colonial buildings. Guests have the use of a communal living room and kitchen as well as a pool. A continental breakfast is served.

For More Information

Blue Ridge Highlands Regional Information and Visitors Center; *731 Factory Outlet Drive, Suite D8, Max Meadows, VA 24360; (800) 446–9670; Web address: www.virginiablueridge.org.*

Wytheville-Wythe-Bland Chamber of Commerce, *150 East Monroe Street, Wytheville, VA 24382; (276) 223–3365. Web address: chamber.wytheville.com.*

Wytheville

As you drive south on Interstate 77, the next major stop is Wytheville, a town of 8,000 and a popular vacation hub nestled between the Blue Ridge and Allegheny Mountains. Wytheville was a prime Union target during the Civil War because it possessed both valuable lead mines and the only salt mine in the South. Here's an interesting tale to tell your kids, one especially appreciated by daughters. A Union attempt to take the town was thwarted by Molly Tynes, who rode 40 miles over the mountains to inform the home guard to come to the town's defense. If you've been in the woods for any extended time, you may appreciate Wytheville's shopping, which includes outlet and antique malls.

NEW RIVER TRAIL STATE PARK AND SHOT TOWER HISTORICAL PARK

At Jackson's Ferry, 6 miles east of Wytheville on Interstate 81, then 7 miles south on U.S. Highway 52; or take the Poplar Camp exit off Interstate 77 South; (276) 236–8889. Foster Falls Visitors Center (off Interstate 77) serves these parks. Virginia State Parks Web address: www.dcr.state.va.us/parks. Admission to Shot Tower.

New River Trail State Park is a 57-mile greenway that follows an abandoned rail bed. Paralleling the New River for 39 miles, the trail slopes gently, making it ideal for young children. There are bicycle paths (bikes can be rented), trails for horseback riding, and canoes for rent. Tubing this stretch of the river is also popular.

Shot Tower Historical Park serves as one of the entrances to New River Trail Park. This is something different. Built in 1807, the tower, which looks like a fortress, sits on a bluff over the New River, 75 feet above the ground, with a water tank sitting 75 feet below ground. The tower was used to make ammunition. First the lead was brought to the top room where it was melted, then poured through sieves with various size openings. The lead became round during its 15-foot descent (it was thought necessary to drop it this far to change shape) before hitting the water. The pellets were then sorted by rolling them down an incline, with faulty ones sorted out and remelted. There's an historian on site to answer questions.

Other entrances to New River Trail are at Galax, Cliffview, Gambetta and Chestnut Yard, Byllesby Dam, Draper, Foster Falls (where the visitors center is located), Pulaski/Xaloy, Fries, and Ivanhoe. The park can also be accessed at Hiwasee, Allisonia, Austinville, and Lone Ash, but there are no developed parking areas at these entrances.

BIG WALKER LOOKOUT

Twelve miles north of Wytheville on U.S. Route 52, on the Big Walker Scenic Byway; (276) 228–4401. Open April 1 through October 31.

Don't miss a visit to this great view of the heart of the Appalachians. On a clear day you can see five states from the 100-foot observation tower at an elevation of 3,405 feet; there's also an observation deck across the street. The kids will like the walk over an old-fashioned wood-and-steel-wire swinging bridge that leads from the souvenir shop and cafe to the observation tower.

Where to Eat

Log House 1776, *520 East Main Street; (276) 228–4139.* Kids like the log house's pioneer-like exteriors, interior with fireplaces, and backyard with rabbits to pet. The menu features chicken, ham, and other country staples. $-$$

Scrooge's Restaurant, *315 Holston Road, next to the Comfort Inn; (276) 228–6622.* The entrees of steak, seafood, and sandwiches take their names from Charles Dickens's *A Christmas Carol.* $-$$

Skeeter's World Famous Hot Dogs, *165 Main Street; (276) 228–2611.* Part of the E.N. Umberger Store, this old-fashioned eatery offers counter food complete with red swivel stools and old signs. The locals swear by the cheese hot dogs and chili. $

Where to Stay

Best Western Wytheville Inn, *355 Nye Road, Interstate 77 North, exit 41; (276) 228–7300.* This lodging has a pool, ninety-nine rooms, and a restaurant.

Comfort Inn, *Holsten Road; (276) 228–4488.*

Days Inn, *adjacent to the Shoney's Restaurant, 150 Malin Drive; (276) 228–5500 or (800) DAYSINN.*

Hampton Inn, *1090 Pepper's Ferry Road; (276) 228–6090 or (800) 426–7866.*

Holiday Inn, *U.S. 11, Interstates 77 and 81, exit 73. (276) 228–5843 or (800) HOLIDAY.*

The KOA Kampground, *Interstates 77 and 81 at exit 77.* Along with cabins, campsites, and full hook-ups for recreational vehicles, this KOA brings in locals who come to swing at the

camp's batting cages and use the mini-golf course.

Ramada Inn, *955 Peppers Ferry Road; (276) 228–6000 or (800) 2–RAMADA. Web address: www.wytheville.com/ ramada.* This hotel has 154 rooms, an outdoor pool, and a restaurant.

For More Information

Blue Ridge Highlands Regional Information and Visitors Center; *731 Factory Outlet Drive, Suite D8, Max Meadows, VA 24360; (800) 446–9670; Web address: www.virginiablueridge.org.*

Wytheville-Wythe-Bland Chamber of Commerce, *150 East Monroe Street, Wytheville; (276) 223–3365. Web address: chamber.wytheville.com.*

Annual Events

JUNE

Chautauqua Festival, *third week in June. For more information contact the chamber of commerce; (276) 228–8212.* A nine-day music festival, the Chautauqua also includes performing arts, a hot-air balloon rally, chili cook-off, children's activities, and art shows.

JULY

Fourth of July Celebration, *the Rural Retreat Lake Campground; (276) 223–6022.*

Index